# Creating a Better World

# Creating a Better World

## Interpreting Global Civil Society

edited by
## Rupert Taylor

Kumarian
Press, Inc.

*Creating a Better World: Interpreting Global Civil Society*
Published in 2004 in the United States of America by Kumarian Press, Inc.,
1294 Blue Hills Avenue, Bloomfield, CT 06002 USA

Index by Robert Swanson
Proofread by Jody El-Assadi

The text of this book is set in 10/12 Janson Text.

Production and design by Joan Weber Laflamme, jml ediset

Printed in the United States of America by Thomson-Shore, Inc.
Text printed with vegetable oil-based ink.

∞The paper used in this publication meets the minimum requirements of the
American National Standard for Information Sciences—Permanence of Paper for Printed Library Materials, ANSI Z39.48–1984.

---

**Library of Congress Cataloging-in-Publication Data**

Creating a better world : interpreting global civil society / edited by Rupert
Taylor.
    p. cm.
  Includes bibliographical references and index.
    ISBN 1–56549–188–2 (pbk. : alk. paper) — ISBN 1–56549–189–0 (cloth :
alk. paper)
  1. Social movements. 2. Civil society. 3. International organization. 4.
Non-governmental organizations. 5. Globalization—Social aspects. I.
Taylor, Rupert, 1958–
HM881.C74 2004
303.48'4—dc22
                                2004009896

---

13 12 11 10 09 08 07 06 05 04   10 9 8 7 6 5 4 3 2 1   First Printing 2004

# Contents

# Figures and Tables

# Acknowledgments

This book is very much the product of global nongovernmental organizational networks, and in this respect is rooted in "global civil society." The initiative for *Creating a Better World: Interpreting Global Civil Society* came from a joint decision between the board of the International Society for Third Sector Research (ISTR), under the presidential lead of Virginia Hodgkinson, and myself, as editor of *Voluntas: International Journal of Voluntary and Nonprofit Organizations*, to hold an ISTR workshop and *Voluntas* symposium entitled "Transnational Third Sector: Reviewing the Present and Charting the Future" with forty invited participants from around the world. This event was held in Bergen, Norway, May 2–4, 2002, in conjunction with the Centre for Development Studies at the University of Bergen. Selected papers from the meeting were subsequently published in a thematic issue of *Voluntas* (vol. 13, no. 4, December 2002). These papers, in revised form, constitute about half this book (Chapters 1, 2, 5, 7, 8, and 9). Drawing on global academic networks, and with the encouragement of Guy Bentham and Jim Lance at Kumarian Press, I sought a further set of papers to take this forward in book form (Chapters 3, 4, 6, 10, and 11).

At the Bergen meeting, academics and practitioners agreed that serious research was required into the meaning and significance of global civil society—particularly with regard to its transformative potential. Thus, from the outset, the central aim of *Creating a Better World: Interpreting Global Civil Society* has been to present analyses that advance a sociological understanding of global civil society—assessing its deeper meaning and significance. As most contributors to this book creatively straddle the disciplines of political science and sociology, and as eight of the chapters are grounded in primary research, a number of new and important social-scientific insights are offered in the pages that follow. The various interpretations presented, it is envisaged, will encourage further debate, research, and theorizing on what is undoubtedly a momentous—but as yet insufficiently understood—political and social force.

As well as acknowledging the support of colleagues and students in the School of Social Sciences at the University of the Witwatersrand, Johannesburg, I especially want to thank the following people for their important advice and valuable comments relating to various aspects of compiling and editing this book: Helmut Anheier, Erin Brown, L. David Brown, John Clark, Carol Coary Taylor, Donatella della Porta, Marc Edelman, Anthony Egan, Alan Fowler, Adam Habib, Finn Heinrich, Virginia Hodgkinson, Joan Laflamme, Kerstin Martens, Mammo Muchie, Paul Opoku-Mensah, Jenny Pearce, Mario Pianta, Yolanda Radebe, Alison van Rooy, Greg Ruiters, Jackie Smith, Neil Stammers, Peter Waterman, and Elke Zuern.

Key involvement with this book project has also come from a number of university-based research centers concerned with the study of global civil society, including the Centre for Civil Society at the University of KwaZulu-Natal, Durban, South Africa; the Centre for the Study of Civil Society at the London School of Economics and Political Science, United Kingdom; and The Hauser Center for Nonprofit Organizations at Harvard University, United States. Finally, the book has benefited from association with CIVICUS: World Alliance for Citizen Participation.

RUPERT TAYLOR
June 2004

# Abbreviations/Acronyms

| | |
|---|---|
| ACTU | Australian Council of Trade Unions |
| AFL-CIO | American Federation of Labor–Congress of Industrial Organizations |
| ATTAC | Association for a Tobin Tax to Assist the Citizen |
| CITU | Centre of Indian Trade Unions |
| COSATU | Congress of South African Trade Unions |
| CSO | Civil society organization |
| CTC | Citizens Trade Campaign |
| CUT | Central Única dos Trabalhadores (Brazilian Union Federation) |
| DAN | Direct Action Network |
| DOSTANGO | Donor-state-NGO |
| EC | European Commission |
| ECOSOC | UN Economic and Social Council |
| EEB | European Environmental Bureau |
| EMO | Environmental movement organization |
| EZLN | Ejército Zapatista de Liberación Nacional (Zapatista National Liberation Army) |
| EU | European Union |
| FARC | Fuerzas Armadas Revolucionarios de Colombia (Revolutionary Armed Forces of Colombia) |
| FoE | Friends of the Earth |
| G8 | Group of Eight nations |
| GATT | General Agreement on Tariffs and Trade |
| GCS | Global civil society |

| GROOTS | Grassroots Organizations Operating Together in Sisterhood |
| GSF | Genoa Social Forum |
| ICEM | International Chemical and Engineering Workers Union |
| IFG | International Forum on Globalization |
| IGO | International governmental organization |
| ILO | International Labor Organization |
| IMC | Independent Media Center |
| IMF | International Monetary Fund |
| INGO | International nongovernmental organization |
| ISTR | International Society for Third Sector Research |
| KCLC | King County Labor Council |
| KCTU | Korean Confederation of Trade Unions |
| KMU | Kilusang Mayo Uno (May First Movement) |
| LSE | London School of Economics |
| MST | Movimento dos Trabalhadores Rurais Sem Terra (Brazilian landless-rural-workers movement) |
| NAFTA | North American Free Trade Agreement |
| NGO | Nongovernmental organization |
| NGR | Network for Global Rights |
| NLI | New labor internationalism |
| NSDF | National Slum Dwellers Federation |
| OAS | Organization of American States |
| OECD | Organization for Economic Cooperation and Development |
| PFT/NO!WTO | People for Fair Trade/Network Opposed to the WTO |
| SDI | Slum/Shack Dwellers International |
| SEWA | Self Employed Women's Association (India) |
| SIGTUR | Southern Initiative on Globalization and Trade Union Rights |

| | |
|---|---|
| SMO | Social movement organization |
| SPARC | Society for Promotion of Area Resource Centres |
| UN | United Nations |
| UNICEF | United Nations Children's Fund |
| USAID | United States Agency for International Development |
| WEF | World Economic Forum |
| WIEGO | Women in the Informal Economy Globalizing and Organizing |
| WOs | White Overalls |
| WSF | World Social Forum |
| WTO | World Trade Organization |
| WWF | World Wide Fund for Nature |

# 1.
# Interpreting Global Civil Society

*Rupert Taylor*

## Introduction

The phrase *global civil society* is now fairly commonplace—within academia, in the mass media, and among a broader public. This has been a recent development, within the last decade or so. That said, the topic of global civil society is one of much confusion and contestation; among commentators there is a sense that this is a phenomenon which is less than fully understood and which defies conventional means of analysis. For example, Henry Milner has made the point that "though much is written about GCS [global civil society] both in academe and in the mainstream and alternative media, it remains very much under-researched, and, indeed, under-defined" (Milner 2003, 190); and Peter Waterman has remarked that the provenance of the term is not well grounded and that global civil society has not yet passed "through the forge of theoretical clarification or the sieve of public debate" (Waterman 1996, 170). Similarly, writing in the journal *Contemporary Sociology*, Peter Evans has argued that "analysis and theory have not caught up to practice when it comes to progressive action at the global level" (Evans 2000, 231); and Paul Kingsnorth has observed that "often the language and the methods are not yet available to describe what is happening" (Kingsnorth 2003, 233–34).

Indeed, *global civil society* has been taken to refer to many different organizational forms and types of global action. When employed, the term has served as a kind of catchall term for nongovernmental organizations (NGOs) and social movements of all shapes and sizes operating in the international realm. Typical is the view of *The Economist* (1999), which refers to a diverse and diffuse range of actors, campaigns, and events as falling within the ambit of global civil society: NGOs and citizens' groups; 50 Years Is Enough and Jubilee 2000; the Rio Earth Summit and the battle of Seattle. In general, the ever-increasing number of

1

international nongovernmental organizations (INGOs) and global social movements—spurred by increased scope for involvement, participation, and networking in and through international governmental organizations (IGOs)—is emphasized to signify the advent of a global civil society (e.g., O'Brien et al. 2000), but just *what* this means is subject to considerable debate.

To date, existing social-scientific work has tended to interpret global civil society in negative terms: as being ideologically too contested, or as facing too many limitations to exert any effective presence. Such readings, the contributors to this volume argue, fall short in understanding the significance of global civil society. Accordingly, this book endeavors to advance a more sociologically informed interpretation of global civil society and its transformative potential, a task best achieved, it is argued, by fully connecting the study of global civil society with a central concern of social theory—the need to grasp both objective *and* subjective dimensions of social reality.

## Contested Meaning

The normative content of global civil society *is* highly contested—so much so, as Ronaldo Munck argues in the next chapter, that its meaning remains indeterminable. Global civil society is often read to be far from constituting a unified field. At issue is whether global civil society is reactionary or progressive. Is it to be interpreted as part of hegemonic global governance or is it better seen as contesting and resisting such a world order?

On the one hand, analysts point to an emerging global civil society comprising nongovernmental networks and social movements that—in the context of neoliberal globalization and a power shift to multilateral organizations and multinational corporations—is seen to assist, influence, and broaden hegemonic power (e.g., Pasha and Blaney 1998). In this regard increased ties between NGOs and IGOs, promoted through international summits, have resulted in the growing formation of coalitions and networks to lobby and prompt nation-states to modify rules and laws. Tellingly, international relief-and-development NGOs—which, as Terje Tvedt maintains in Chapter 8, are embedded in the international state system—are now responsible for delivering more aid than is the United Nations.

On the other hand, global civil society can be positioned to represent those organizations and actors who are concerned to directly challenge the undemocratic and debilitating practices of neoliberal globalization (e.g., Brecher, Costello, and Smith 2000). From this perspective global civil society is a relatively autonomous space in which people organize and resist both the IGOs that embody the interests of hegemonic states and the multinational corporations that pursue global commodification practices (Klein 2001). Most notable here is a series of mass demonstrations around the world directed at challenging the major institutions supporting neoliberal globalization: the World Trade Organization (WTO), the International Monetary Fund (IMF), and the World Bank— as well as the G8. In particular, huge protests in Seattle (United States) against the Millennium Round meetings of the WTO in late 1999 (see Chapter 3), and Genoa (Italy) against a G8 summit in the city in mid-2001 (see Chapter 4) are read as portentous.

One way around this contested meaning of global civil society has been for social scientists to adopt a non-normative approach—to argue that global civil society has to be defined in terms of structural organizational forms, not its ideological characteristics. As the editors of the first *Global Civil Society Yearbook*—Helmut Anheier, Marlies Glasius, and Mary Kaldor—openly state: "We believe that the normative content is too contested to be able to form the basis for an operationalisation of the concept" (Anheier, Glasius, and Kaldor 2001, 17). Hence, a dominant tendency in approaching global civil society, especially in third-sector scholarship, has been to pursue empirical data collection in which both "good" and "bad" elements are included. From such a value-free basis, wide-ranging typologies of global civil society can be developed. For example, Mary Kaldor's typology in *Global Civil Society: An Answer to War* includes "the allies of transnational business who promote a market framework at a global level"; fundamentalist movements; and "neo-Nazi hate groups that exchange repugnant rhetoric over the Internet" (Kaldor 2003, 80–81, 107, 231).

How far, however, is analysis going to proceed within a normative vacuum? The answer, it would seem, is descriptively—too far, theoretically—not far enough. For, with global civil society defined as "the sphere of ideas, values, institutions, organizations, networks, and individuals located *between* the family, the state, and the market and operating *beyond* the confines of national societies, polities, and economies" (Anheier, Glasius, and Kaldor 2001, 17), we confront a universe that would include the 25,540 INGOs cited in the *Yearbook of International Organizations* (2002), and more besides. The scope of analysis has to be defined with more sociological specification than this: For what, then? What would be the meaning of this universe? Theoretical advance requires that empirical social research must be combined with moral and political understanding (Bernstein 1978; Horkheimer 1972); questions of organizational structure cannot be separated from questions of ideology and practice, especially if any transformative purpose is to be comprehended.

That global civil society, according to Munck (Chapter 2), is perceived to be a "contested political terrain where different social and political forces vie for hegemony" should not rule out the taking of a more sociologically critical position. Indeed, if any social theoretical advance is to be made, such a position must of necessity be taken.

As is argued and made evident in the pages that follow, at a subjective level the intent of global civil society activism is to confront neoliberal globalization and create a better world through advocating a fairer, freer, and more just global order, whether with regard to advancing, for example, concern over international trade (Chapter 3), workers' rights (Chapter 6), or the environment (Chapter 9). Accepting this, at an objective level, global civil society structurally relates to a multi-organizational field that encompasses both those organizations that tend to work within the INGO and nation-state system, follow professionalized advocacy styles and agendas, and are involved in complex multilateralism *and* those movements—anti-neoliberal and anti-corporate alike—committed to street protest and other forms of direct action. The former do not stand in marked opposition to the latter; many INGOs—Amnesty International, ATTAC, Friends of the Earth, Greenpeace, Human Rights Watch, Jubilee 2000, Médicins Sans Frontiers, Oxfam, and Plan International— promote progressive global campaigns (Clark 2003), and, as revealed in Chapters 3 and 4, Seattle and Genoa would not have been possible without broad collective action. Global civil society, then, should be taken to be a complex multi-organizational field that explicitly excludes reactionary—racist, fascist, or fundamentalist—organizations and movements.

## Limitations and *Their* Limits

An alternative interpretative position has been to short-circuit the issue of contested meaning by questioning the very existence of a global civil society. From influential social scientists schooled in mainstream political sociology (Nash 2000), with its state-centric view of politics and corresponding social movement theory on political opportunity structures and resource mobilization (e.g., McAdam, McCarthy, and Zald 1996), has come the argument that the structural preconditions for the genesis of a global civil society are lacking—primarily because there is no "global state" and the power and influence of the nation-state remains dominant. Thus, Sidney Tarrow (1998, 2001), for one, has maintained that in the absence of a global state there are serious collective action problems for global mobilization and identity formation. It is asserted that with a limited resource infrastructure and lack of close-knit social networks to promote face-to-face interaction, the prospects for global civil society are dim. The dictates of nation-state sovereignty—supported by the persistence of national, linguistic, and cultural differences—are seen to trump any form of global power.

The best-known and most widely read studies relating to the study of organizations and campaigns operating beyond the nation-state—namely, Margaret Keck and Kathryn Sikkink's *Activists Beyond Borders* (1998); Ann Florini's (ed.) *The Third Force* (2000); Michael Edwards's and John Gaventa's (eds.) *Global Citizen Action* (2001); and Gordon Laxer's and Sandra Halperin's (eds.) *Global Civil Society and Its Limits* (2003)—are all to some extent theoretically located in the above context. Moreover, and not without analytical significance, these works are all methodologically tied to the case-study approach.

Again and again, reflecting mainstream focus, individual case studies of particular organizations or campaigns are interpreted as deeply embedded in, and constrained by, national-level civil society and politics. To take, for example, the case of the International Campaign to Ban Landmines, studied in both *The Third Force* and *Global Citizen Action*, it is concluded that "although the cause was global, the focus of the work was mostly domestic," and that "the initiative and readiness to start projects had to come from the national civil society" (Mekata 2000, 148, 153; see also Scott 2001). The overriding position of *Global Civil Society and Its Limits* is that, "the state remains the central locus of power and potential control . . . [and] national politics remains the most effective vehicle for anti-globalism resistance" (Halperin and Laxer 2003, 13, 16). Reflecting this, case-study chapters on the Zapatistas (Johnston 2003) and the defeat of the Multilateral Agreement on Investment (Laxer 2003) are strongly framed to challenge the very notion of global civil society.

Such skepticism toward global civil society is also expressed in the conscious choice of many authors—in *Activists Beyond Borders*, *The Third Force*, and *Global Citizen Action*—to use the far more restrictive term *transnational*, as opposed to *global*. To maintain, however, that no organization is "truly global, in the sense of involving groups and individuals from every part of the world" (Florini and Simmons 2000, 7) is theoretically weak. It is to overlook, as Jan Aart Scholte has argued, that the term *global civil society* "is not meant to imply that the associations in question span every location on earth, but to indicate that they operate in the world as a single social space" (Scholte 2001, 3).

To be fair, in *The Third Force* and *Global Citizen Action* there is only limited concern with theory verification—and even less with theory generation. Rather, following practitioner concerns, focus is directed to evaluating the impact of organizations or campaigns on IGOs and state policymaking, and more especially to advancing specific policy prescriptions ("lessons") with respect to advancing transparency, democracy, and representativeness. Hence, Florini, in the context of the six case studies that make up *The Third Force*, asserts, "Those involved in transnational civil society networks must become far more transparent about who they are, what they are doing, why they are doing it, and who is paying for it"

(Florini 2000, vi). Likewise, from a number of mainly descriptive case studies, Edwards and Gaventa present "Lessons for Good Practice," instructing that as "transnational civil society is far from democratic," it should "be subject to guidelines that governs its conduct and behavior" (Edwards and Gaventa 2001, 7, 11). Such lessons are all well and good, but if case studies are not collectively assessed with respect to social theoretical concerns (either to refine existing theory or arrive at new theory), it can surely be argued that the interpretative limitations of these works outweigh the very limitations they impute to global civil society.

In *Activists Beyond Borders* Keck and Sikkink do go further than the single-case-study approach and direct attention to covering multiple cases—relating to human rights, environmentalism, and women's freedom from violence—so as to advance comparative analysis. Keck and Sikkink engage in inductive reasoning to show how the success of international advocacy NGOs derives from the "boomerang effect" of issue networking, whereby international norms are advanced through national NGOs networking with INGOs who exercise more effective suasion within the former's host country. Limiting here, however, as Paul Nelson persuasively argues in Chapter 7, is that this approach only covers specific issue areas and forms of INGO political action; it does not, for example, apply to financial policy and trade issues. Moreover, Keck and Sikkink do not positively link their work to global civil society and do not probe how NGOs are connected to broader social movements and global campaigns, preferring instead to interpret global civil society as "a fragmented and contested area" (Keck and Sikkink 1998, 200).

Altogether then, the insights offered through the best-known studies, with their methodological adherence to a case-study approach and theoretical deference to pre-given theory, are too limited. Case-study research has done little to advance theory and does not address, let alone reveal, the complexity of the broader multi-organizational context within which cases fall. The theoretically informed arguments derived from mainstream political sociology are not without value, but they by no means fully accord with social reality.

As indicated, in certain cases—and as shown by Christopher Rootes in his analysis of European environmentalism in Chapter 9—the difficulties confronting the advance of global civil society may be severely constrained by national politics and culture, but this is not the whole picture. Many of the actions that typify global civil society defy the self-interested rationality that informs much social movement theory; collective action *is* primarily driven by substantive moral purpose and, moreover, *does* eclipse nationally framed repertoires of protest. If the collective-action problems are so severe, how *do* we account for the Seattle and Genoa protests? To tie global civil society to the existence of a global state is not especially compelling; what drives global activism is that "we have a system that might be called *global governance without global government*, one in which a few institutions—the World Bank, the IMF, the WTO—and a few players—the finance, commerce, and trade ministers, closely linked to certain financial and commercial interests—dominate the scene" (Stiglitz 2002, 21–22). Also, contrary to expectations—as Kumi Naidoo and I indicate in Chapter 11—within global civil society many movement organizations eschew formal and professionalized hierarchical structures, and primary interaction and embedded ties are not of such central import.

On reflection, given that mainstream social movement theory itself rests on state-centric presuppositions drawn from a specific national and historical context—namely, twentieth-century America (Mayer 1995)—perhaps it should not be surprising to find that the structural form and social activism of global civil society does not readily conform to existing theoretical expectations.

## Theoretical Re-articulation

Clearly, the dominant approaches adopted with respect to interpreting global civil society have restricted purchase; they suffer from weak description and inadequate theorization. The way forward rests on acknowledging that the study of global civil society requires theoretical re-articulation. Specifically, what has to be recognized is that any general interpretation must delineate both the objective structural and subjective ideological dimensions of global civil society and analyze their dialectical relation—as Anthony Giddens emphasizes in *Central Problems in Social Theory*, the notions of structure and action *"presuppose one another"* (Giddens 1979, 53).

To this end, the present volume adopts a more global approach to studying a global phenomenon and makes it evident that global civil society is marked by—at a structural level—an emerging complex multi-organizational field with innovative network forms and—at an ideological level—transformative purpose. Furthermore, several contributors to this book reveal how new dynamic forms of networking have transformed the very nature of collective action, and they show how the relationship between new structural forms and changed consciousness are mutually dependent.

Integral to advancing such understanding is a turn to more comprehensive social research methods—especially contextual and interpretative methods that enable the subjective meaning of what is experienced by actors within global civil society to form a central part of analysis. Contributors to this book do move beyond the limitations of the case-study approach and seek to probe thoroughly people's experiences, perceptions, and feelings. Gillian Murphy's chapter about the battle of Seattle is grounded in the extensive set of primary research data found in the World Trade Organization History Project at the University of Washington, Seattle. Massimiliano Andretta and Lorenzo Mosca's analysis of the Genoa protest relies upon various forms of field research—including a questionnaire administered to demonstrators. In examining grassroots movements in the South, Srilatha Batliwala is very much concerned to put the actor's standpoint at the forefront of analysis; and Robert Lambert and Edward Webster, in researching new labor internationalism, endeavor to study human action in terms of Alain Touraine's approach of social interventionism (Touraine 1983).

In structural terms the key networked organizational forms that have arisen and that are highlighted in this book include the Seattle coalition (Chapter 3), Genoa Social Forum (Chapter 4), and World Social Forum (Chapter 10). With respect to events in Seattle, Murphy shows how strategic coordination of movement organizations—centered on People for Fair Trade/Network Opposed to the WTO, the American Federation of Labor-Congress of Industrial Organizations, and the Direct Action Network—provided a network for action that helped link the diverse interests of local activists to global concerns. Crucial to this was coordinated, multi-focus, and inclusive issue framing that "minimized conflict" and "maximized participation," allowing for multiple strategies of protest. As Murphy asserts, the Seattle coalition created a template for future protests. In like manner, Andretta and Mosca, in analyzing the Genoa protest, emphasize the centrality of the Genoa Social Forum—a highly participative and flexible network of organizations that linked ATTAC, Network for Global Rights, Rete Lilliput, and the White Overalls. In addition, Andretta and Mosca, through their questionnaire findings, reveal how overlapping network membership is a key feature of collective identity formation.

In the analyses of both the Seattle and Genoa protests it is apparent that differences are affirmed within inclusive organizational structures that allow for coordinated action, such that as Jonathan Neale has also observed, "Different campaigns don't compete: they reinforce each other" (Neale 2002, 105). It also emerges that new technological advances have changed the nature of social ties with respect to the meaning of co-presence (Cerulo 1997); virtual interaction through the Internet does not seem significantly less important in promoting mobilization than face-to-face contact.

The role of network structures in advancing new forms of social activism and solidarity are further revealed in Chapters 5 and 6, where particular focus falls on linkages that have been forged between the local and the global. In Chapter 5 Batliwala shows how grassroots movements relating to women in informal employment (Women in the Informal Economy Globalizing and Organizing) and slum and shack dwellers

(Slum/Shack Dwellers International) are emerging as global movements that reconfigure the relationship between the local and the global by creating international advocacy bodies and devising concrete strategies. Similarly, in Chapter 6 Lambert and Webster discuss how the Southern Initiative on Globalization and Trade Union Rights (SIGTUR), as a new formation grounded in democratic trade unions in the South, has adopted a social movement unionism that endeavors—with the use of new technology—to build progressive global networks promoting new forms of global action. Both chapters point to how organizational structures are decentralized and participative, and how local issues are globalized and global issues localized.

In transformative terms, global civil society seeks to reclaim democracy and reconfigure power by generating a sense of global citizenship within which there is increasing awareness of how social issues—near or far—that were once differentially focused and geographically bounded are actually interpenetrated and interdependent. What is apparent in many of the following chapters is how, following R. B. J. Walker, "the interests of human beings begin to take priority over the interests of human beings as citizens of states" (Walker 1988, 106). Nowhere is this more evident than with regard to the World Social Forum (WSF), and associated continental social forums. The WSF, an annual initiative located in the South—the first being held January 25–30, 2001, in Porto Alegre, Brazil, with some twenty thousand people attending—assertively promotes an alternative world to that underwritten by neoliberal globalization. Reflecting the increasing popularity of the WSF, the fourth, held January 16–21, 2004, in Mumbai, India, drew well over 100,000 people.

In Chapter 10 Jacklyn Cock shows—through participant observation of the third WSF—that the WSF is not just an event but also a point of convergence for an ongoing process of forming, consolidating, and strengthening global networks, networks that involve many of those organizations and movements that participated in the Seattle and Genoa protests. Importantly, as elsewhere in global civil society, the organizational form of the WSF—which is characterized by autonomous, decentralized, and non-hierarchical structures—must be seen to be prefigurative, as being both outcome *and* medium of human action.

Cumulatively, the contributors to this volume reveal a converging multi-organizational field comprised of innovative organizational and network structures and new forms of social activism. Contrary to the assumption that global civil society is undercut by a lack of unity, its very diversity and fragmentation makes it energizing; and as against prevailing orthodoxy, global civil society does not exhibit a weak presence but is in a strong state of becoming. In sum, as Naidoo and I reiterate in the final chapter, global civil society is best interpreted as a transformative project concerned to create a better world, a project that is globally evolving in the context of the new organizational structures and new forms of activism.

## Future Direction

Global civil society has considerable potential to contribute to emancipatory change, but much social research remains to be done to develop an empirical and theoretical understanding of its multidimensional breadth and depth. The issues of transparency, democracy, and representativeness, as raised in some of the best-known studies (Florini 2000; Edwards and Gaventa 2001) cannot be ignored, and certainly the question of how global civil society has been affected by the resurgence of a state-centric view of the world in the wake of September 11, 2001, discussed in Chapter 11, is apposite; but what is most important to better interpret global civil society is further theoretical articulation of its objective and subjective dimensions, and how these co-evolve.

A number of specific issues merit detailed investigation: mapping the connections and relations within the multi-organizational field; assessing the scope for autonomous action; and measuring the impact of global civil society. In particular, future research needs to focus on how the work of those organizations lobbying and agitating for change within the WTO, IMF, and World Bank are linked to grassroots movements and the campaigns on the street (e.g., Fox and Brown 1998; Scholte and Schnabel 2002). What distinctions can be drawn between NGOs and social movements in terms of their degree and type of involvement inside or outside of established economic and political institutions? How are different forms of collective action interrelated? How symmetrical are power relations? And to what extent are antagonistic relationships present?

*Creating a Better World: Interpreting Global Civil Society* also indicates that the study of global civil society needs to be more global in approach. Further collaborative multi-institutional and interdisciplinary research programs—such as that represented by this book and by initiatives to promote critical engagement between researchers and practitioners (Brown 2002)—are required. Here, as James Riker has suggested, a significant step forward would be "to create a global civil society research network comprised of academic centers and practitioner organizations in both the North and South" (Riker 2003, 16). Future research on global civil society *itself* needs to be global.

### References

Anheier, Helmut, Marlies Glasius, and Mary Kaldor. 2001. Introducing global civil society. In *Global Civil Society 2001*, ed. Helmut Anheier, Marlies Glasius, and Mary Kaldor, 3–22. Oxford: Oxford University Press.

Bernstein, Richard J. 1978. *The Restructuring of Social and Political Theory*. Philadelphia: University of Pennsylvania Press.

Brecher, Jeremy, Tim Costello, and Brendan Smith. 2000. *Globalization from Below: The Power of Solidarity*, Cambridge, Mass.: South End Press.

Brown, L. David, ed. 2002. *Practice Research Engagement for Civil Society in a Globalizing World*. Cambridge, Mass.: Hauser Centre for Nonprofit Organizations, Harvard University; Washington, D.C.: CIVICUS.

Cerulo, Karen A. 1997. Reframing sociological conceptions for a Brave New (virtual?) World. *Sociological Inquiry* 67, no. 1: 48–58.

Clark, John, ed. 2003. *Globalizing Civic Engagement: Civil Society and Transnational Action*. London: Earthscan.

*The Economist.* 1999. The non-governmental order: Will NGOs democratize, or merely disrupt, global governance? December 11–17.

Edwards, Michael, and John Gaventa, eds. 2001. *Global Citizen Action*. London: Earthscan.

Evans, Peter. 2000. Fighting marginalization with transnational networks: Counter-hegemonic globalization. *Contemporary Sociology* 29, no. 1: 230–41.

Florini, Ann, ed. 2000. *The Third Force: The Rise of Transnational Civil Society*. Washington, D.C.: Carnegie Endowment for International Peace; Tokyo: Japan Center for International Exchange.

Florini, Ann, and P. J. Simmons. 2000. What the world needs now? In Florini 2000, 1-15.

Fox, Jonathan A., and L. David Brown, eds. 1998. *The Struggle for Accountability: The World Bank, NGOs and Grassroots Movements*. Cambridge, Mass.: MIT Press.

Giddens, Anthony. 1979. *Central Problems in Social Theory: Action, Structure and Contradiction in Social Analysis*. London: Macmillan.

Halperin, Sandra, and Gordon Laxer. 2003. Effective resistance to corporate globalization. In Laxer and Halperin, *Global Civil Society and Its Limits*, 1–21.

Horkheimer, Max. 1972. Traditional and critical theory. In *Critical Sociology: Selected Readings*, ed. Paul Connerton, 206–224. Harmondsworth: Penguin.

Johnston, Josée. 2003. We are all Marcos? *Zapatismo*, solidarity, and the politics of scale. In Laxer and Halperin, *Global Civil Society and Its Limits*, 85–104.

Kaldor, Mary. 2003. *Global Civil Society: An Answer to War*. Cambridge: Polity Press.

Keck, Margaret E., and Kathryn Sikkink. 1998. *Activists Beyond Borders: Advocacy Networks in International Politics*. Ithaca, N.Y.: Cornell University Press.

Kingsnorth, Paul. 2003. *One No, Many Yeses: A Journey to the Heart of the Global Resistance Movement*. London: The Free Press.

Klein, Naomi. 2001. *No Logo*. London: Flamingo.

Laxer, Gordon. 2003. The defeat of the Multilateral Agreement on Investment: National movements confront globalism. In Laxer and Halperin, *Global Civil Society and Its Limits*, 169–88.

Laxer, Gordon, and Sandra Halperin, eds. 2003. *Global Civil Society and Its Limits*. Basingstoke: Palgrave Macmillan.

McAdam, Doug, John D. McCarthy, and Mayer N. Zald, eds. 1996. *Comparative Perspectives on Social Movements: Political Opportunities, Mobilizing Structures, and Cultural Framings*. Cambridge: Cambridge University Press.

Mayer, Margit. 1995. Social movement research in the United States: A European perspective. In *Social Movements: Critiques and Concepts*, ed. Stanford M. Lyman, 168–95. London: Macmillan.

Mekata, Motoko. 2000. Building partnerships toward a common goal: Experiences of the International Campaign to Ban Landmines. In Florini 2000, 143–76.

Milner, Henry. 2003. Civic literacy in global civil society: Excluding the majority from democratic participation. In Laxer and Halperin, *Global Civil Society and Its Limits*, 189–209.

Nash, Kate. 2000. *Contemporary Political Sociology: Globalization, Politics, and Power*. Oxford: Blackwell.

Neale, Jonathan. 2002. *You are G8, We are 6 Billion: The Truth Behind the Genoa Protests*. London: Vision Paperbacks.

O'Brien, Robert, Anne Marie Goetz, Jan Aart Scholte, and Marc Williams. 2000. *Contesting Global Governance: Multilateral Economic Institutions and Global Social Movements*. Cambridge: Cambridge University Press.

Pasha, Mustapha Kamal, and David L. Blaney, 1998. Elusive paradise: The promise and peril of global civil society. *Alternatives* 23, no. 4: 417–51.

Riker, James V. 2003. Advancing theory and informing practice in transnational civil society: Toward meaningful North-South research collaborations. Paper. The Democracy Collaborative, University of Maryland.

Scholte, Jan Aart. 2001. Building transnational civil society. Memorandum. Centre for the Study of Globalisation and Regionalisation, University of Warwick, UK.

Scholte, Jan Aart, and Albrecht Schnabel, eds. 2002. *Civil Society and Global Finance*. London: Routledge.

Scott, Matthew J. O. 2001. Danger—Landmines! NGO-Government collaboration in the Ottawa Process. In Edwards and Gaventa, *Global Citizen Action*, 121–33.

Stiglitz, Joseph. 2002. *Globalization and Its Discontents*. London: Penguin.

Tarrow, Sidney. 1998. Fishnets, Internets, and catnets: Globalization and transnational collective action. In *Challenging Authority: The Historical Study of Contentious Politics*, ed. Michael P. Hanagan, Leslie Page Moch, and Wayne te Brake, 228–44. Minneapolis: University of Minnesota Press.

———. 2001. Beyond globalization: Why creating transnational social movements is so hard and when is it most likely to happen. Online.

Touraine, Alain. 1983. *Solidarity: The Analysis of a Social Movement, 1980–1981*. Cambridge: Cambridge University Press.

Walker, R. B. J. 1988. *One World, Many Worlds: Struggles for a Just World Peace*. Boulder, Colo.: Lynne Rienner.

Waterman, Peter. 1996. Beyond globalism and developmentalism: Other voices in world politics. *Development and Change* 27, no. 1: 165–80.

*Yearbook of International Organizations*. 2002. Munich: Union of International Associations and K. G. Saur Verlag.

# 2.
# Global Civil Society: Myths and Prospects

## Ronaldo Munck

### Introduction

The way Georges Sorel referred to the "myth" of the general strike could be an interesting new way to approach the increasingly influential notion of a global civil society (GCS). For Sorel:

> the general strike is . . . the *myth* in which socialism is wholly comprised, i.e., a body of images capable of evoking instinctively all the sentiments which correspond to the different manifestations of the war undertaken by socialism against modern society. (Sorel 1961, 127)

As with the myth of the general strike, that of GCS allows us to provide, in Sorel's terminology, a "co-ordinated picture" bringing together a series of images and sentiments with great intensity, thus providing us with an instant perception: "that intuition of socialism which language cannot give us with perfect clearness" (ibid.). This approach captures something of the powerful imagery conveyed by the GCS notion but also the inevitable illusions and even mystifications associated with even a positive Sorelian understanding of myth. To provide some clarity on the pitfalls and prospects for GCS, we must start by deconstructing the myth so as to better understand the parameters of its possible future transformations.

The birth of the GCS myth can be conveniently (if somewhat mythically) dated at the Rio Earth Summit of 1992. The parallel NGO Forum or alternative summit at Rio was certainly unparalleled in terms of its media impact. For many, it represented the genuine emergence of a GCS that could network, develop strategies, and even have an impact on global governance. The 1995 Beijing Conference on Women and the Copenhagen Social Development Conference that same year were, as Mario Pianta puts it, "points of no return for the visibility, relevance, and mobilisation of civil society" (Pianta 2001, 174). It is significant that the International Confederation of Free Trade Unions had demanded a place at the "top table" at Copenhagen in keeping with traditional International Labor Organization tripartism. It was only after the Copenhagen event, in which it eventually participated as part of the NGO Forum, that the international trade union movement began to conceive of itself as, effectively, an NGO and hence, by implication, part of GCS.

The GCS myth takes on its more robust adult shape in the 1995 report of the Commission on Global Governance. This influential group of the "good and the mighty" argued that "to be an effective instrument of global governance in the modern world, the United Nations (UN) must . . . take greater account of the emergence of global civil society" (Commission on Global Governance 1995, 253). These "new actors," in essence the NGOs, are seen to play a crucial and increasing role in the "management of global affairs." Essentially, the commission was seeking to coopt GCS, as expressed through the NGO movement, into the sphere of influence of the United Nations in the interest of better governance. The key word in this discourse is "consultation," with the traditional actors of state and capital being urged to listen more carefully to the representatives of "the people" in the shape of the NGOs. Much of what was proposed by the Commission on Global Governance is now common currency, but it still serves as a founding statement of the benign view of economic neoliberal globalization as being matched in some way by an emerging transnational civil society.

In the academic terrain there have been a number of authors, broadly in the Gramscian tradition, advocating GCS as a means of building a "globalization from below" to counter the dominant "globalization from above." This tradition can be seen as the "radical" counterpart to the commission "line" in many ways. For Richard Falk (1999) and Ronnie Lipschutz (1992), for example, GCS is a realm distinct from both the state system and the capitalist economy where the oppressed may organize and resist. The aim should be the expansion of GCS and not the overthrow of state power. The expansion of GCS is seen, at least in part, to result from the adverse social effects of economic neoliberalism. Accepting some of the above analysis, but closer to the liberal politics of the Commission on Global Governance, are authors such as Daniel Archibugi and David Held (see Archibugi and Held 1995), for whom democracy in a rapidly globalizing world needs to be fundamentally rethought. Welcoming the decline of the traditional nation-state, they advocate a new "cosmopolitan democracy" based on transnational civil society and, essentially, a revitalized United Nations.

Most recently and most ambitiously, the London School of Economics' (LSE) *Global Civil Society Yearbook* (Anheier et al. 2001) has sought to codify and consolidate the GCS concept. The LSE "school" is broad and its definitions sufficiently fluid and multifaceted to appeal to many. To move beyond the "methodological nationalism" of most contemporary social science would seem overdue, as would be "operationalization" of the GCS concept. However, it seems unclear, for example, why the definition of GCS (a sphere outside of family, state, and market and beyond the confines of the nation-state) should "serve operational purposes only" (Anheier 2001, 225), particularly if, as the same author suggests, "global civil society is essentially a normative concept" (224). If we are to view GCS as part of a civilizing process, then our definitions must necessarily be normative too, one would assume. Another aspect that should be developed is the LSE group's notion that GCS is "a shared discursive framework" (Anheier et al. 2001, 12) where opponents and proponents of global capitalism find a common language. Does everyone really share this common discursive terrain?

Even this extremely cursory overview of how GCS came to prominence indicates some of the tensions present. The concept seems to slide among the descriptive, analytical, and normative terrains much the same as it might be said that the big battalions of the NGOs that make it up, such as Oxfam or Greenpeace, slide between the grassroots and the powerful players in the new global governance game. Yet this is precisely how Sorel conceived of his mythically constituted subjects in an indeterminate, "*non-apriori*" way (Laclau and Mouffe 1985, 41). Given this indeterminacy in the construction of a myth and its development through a social movement, we can understand why GCS can never be conceived of as a unitary terrain. This means that from the start we need to reject a teleological conception of GCS akin to the traditional socialist view of the proletariat, heading toward a predefined end. Conversely, a perspective of radical indeterminacy may be a useful lead in to the discussion around the current prospects of GCS, stressing the very real role of struggle in shaping the political impact of various elements within what is currently viewed as GCS.

## Problems

That the concept of GCS has acquired such prominence in both academic and policy circles in so short a period of time indicates that it has some theoretical or political purchase in our changing times. The danger remains that although a new concept may capture some novel social or political transformation under way, its momentum may lead us to minimize problems and inconsistencies in its formulation. There is an undoubted problem of conceptual inflation at play here, whereby GCS is made to explain too much on too weak a foundation. This is not unusual in the social sciences, and we need only think of the concepts of democracy or community to see the point. Nor is it at all clear from much social-scientific literature when we are dealing with a theoretical concept or when with a normative choice—with considerable slippage between the two in much work. So before we can even begin to speculate on the prospects for GCS in the decade to come, we need to explore some more of the problems associated with the concept so as to have a slightly clearer idea of what it is we are talking about and, indeed, what we are not talking about.

A key problem to focus on has been dubbed the issue of presentism that seems to bedevil much of the GCS literature. This is an assumption that present-day observable phenomena are essentially novel in some way. It is a perspective that lacks historical perspective and is thus, at the very best, partial. In the broader globalization literature, of which GCS is a subset, the phenomenon of presentism is very marked indeed. For example, we can take the influential recent studies by Noreena Hertz (2001) and Naomi Klein (2001) on the "new" global capitalism. With breathless audacity they recycle 1960s (even 1950s) radical ideas on the corporation, consumerism, and the "death" of democracy. It is, to some extent, understandable that each radical generation needs to find out things for itself. However, it is disabling to present as new an analysis of, for example, the multinational corporation that has been around for at least a quarter of a century. On the other hand, much that is genuinely new in the globalization debates, such as cultural hybridity, interpenetration of the local and the global, and so on, is simply missed out in this posturing presentism.

In terms of the GCS debate more specifically, Fred Halliday has questioned the assumed novelty of the non-state actors that supposedly animate it. For Halliday, "the erosion of the Westphalian system rests upon a contemporary optic, and illusion" (Halliday 2000, 27). The "new" non-state actors can, in fact, trace their heritage back to long before the nation-state "Westphalian" system became dominant. This means that, while not wishing to deny what is new about the present, we should not ignore the degree of continuity with the past. Whether it is the history of nationalism or religion, socialism or banking, we can take a non-state perspective at least as plausibly as a statist one. From this perspective the current interest in GCS can be seen as simply part of a parochial shift in international-relations theory from the realist or statist perspective toward a concern with non-state or civil society actors and issues. Certainly, a long-term historical perspective on GCS would add depth and nuance to some of the current presentist perspectives.

We can also see how abruptly the GCS approach and its emphasis on the global tends to obliterate an older history of transnationalism, not to mention internationalism. One cannot understand the events in Seattle in 1999 without going back at the very least to 1919. The ups and downs of labor internationalism (see Munck 2002) are not just an interesting historical backdrop on the present but an essential explanatory element. Yet labor internationalism—in the present, never mind the past—seems strangely absent from the GCS discourse. If we take up a transnational movement that GCS theory is often concerned with—namely, the international women's movement—we see again the partial view it tends to have of transnational politics. Thus Alejandro Colás correctly notes:

> Put bluntly, no amount of dedicated websites, conference network-ing or INGO umbrella groups can replace the legacy of "classical" feminist internationalism as the major factor in explaining the ex-istence of global women's movements today. (Colás 2001, 15)

In other words, a Beijing conference cannot be understood properly with-out going back to the socialist feminism of the 1970s and, probably, Clara Zetkin and the 1920s as well.

A further problem that needs to be addressed is the irredeemably Eurocentric bias in much of the GCS literature in spite of its importance in Latin America, for example (see Friedman et al. 2001). For John Keane, GCS names an "old tendency of local and regional civil societies to link up and to penetrate regions of the earth that had previously not known the ethics and structures of civil society in the modern European sense" (Keane 2001, 28). It seems that a very clearly European Enlightenment version of democracy, civility, and ethics underpins the notion of GCS—whatever lip service is paid to selected other parts of the world. The cultural universalism of this model does not really allow for diversity or the distinctive paths to modernity that different parts of the globe have taken. In the "cosmopolitan" global democracy project this Eurocentrism presented as universalism becomes most explicit, and "Enlightenment man" is seen as the privileged actor in the GCS play we are asked to support.

If we examine the NGOs, the main actors in the structure of GCS according to this paradigm, we also find the North-South question com-ing to the fore. For critics like James Petras and Henry Veltmeyer, the INGOs are quite simply "in the service of imperialism," given that "NGOs foster a new type of cultural and economic colonialism—under the guise of a new internationalism" (Petras and Veltmeyer 2001, 132). This perspective may be somewhat Manichean, and it certainly assumes a pristine revolutionary consciousness diverted by the NGOs, but there is certainly a critique here that needs to be addressed by the more starry-eyed NGO and GCS enthusiasts. The NGOs are hardly nongovernmental any more in any real sense of the word. They are not uniformly virtuous entities, and they are certainly not immune to Northern biases, subtle and not so subtle. The point, however, is not to argue that NGOs are "bad" against those who think they are "good." We simply need to take a more critical and robust political view of the world of NGOs as part of civil society and as key players in the new field of GCS.

To point to the clear Eurocentric bias of the whole GCS problematic is not, on the other hand, to argue for an outdated "thirdworldism." Indeed, the anti- or counter-globalization movements are well able to coopt a "developing countries" perspective, through, for example, the Third World Network. Although this perspective may offer a useful corrective to the Northern environmentalist or caring consumer, it is hardly a *global* alternative. This is virtually the same problematic as that of the Brandt Report and the New International Economic Order of the 1970s. Not only did this project fail, but the game has changed since then. Within the international workers' and women's movements, on the other hand, we find a new transnationalism that transcends these old debates. As argued below, if we accept that globalization is complex and not reducible, for example, to corporations taking over the world, then we can assume that transnational social resistance to it will also be complex, multifaceted, and innovative.

A further general issue to confront here is the neglect or downplaying, at least in the GCS literature, of conflict. If we go back to the civil society debates, on which the GCS concept must inevitably rest, we can see why this might be the case. Ellen Meiksins Wood mounted an early but still influential critique of civil society from an orthodox Marxist perspective, arguing that the concept "which indiscriminately lumps together everything from households and voluntary associations to the economic system of capitalism, confuses and disguises as much as it reveals" (Wood 1990, 65). What it disguises for Wood and fellow critics is, of course, capitalism, which is slipped in along with other more desirable democratic characteristics of civil society. Some authors (e.g., Cohen and Arato 1992) have redefined civil society to exclude business organizations in order to "cleanse" the concept. However, we cannot by definitional fiat, as it were, rid the concept of civil society of all its ambiguities and simply banish all its "uncivil" elements or those the writer is simply uncomfortable with. Conflict is, in fact, central to an understanding of civil society.

For Lipschutz, "the growth of global civil society represents an ongoing project of civil society to reconstruct, re-imagine or re-map world politics" (Lipschutz 1992, 391). GCS in this discursive construction seems to be conceived as a unified field, as an actor with a "project," and as an unambiguous human good. The nation-state is being challenged "from below" (on which more below), and the result can only be more and better democracy according to this "radical" perspective. However, in practice it is more or less impossible to separate social movements from the socioeconomic relations they are part of, or, for that matter, from the states that they contest but also seek to influence. What is most striking, though, in relation to the theme of conflict, is that this benign view of GCS completely ignores the hierarchical and conflictual relations that prevail within civil society. Even a cursory familiarity with the world of civil society would alert the observer to the divisions of gender, ethnicity, culture, and region, among others, not to mention of political orientation, which makes the notion of a unified GCS look distinctly utopian and unrealistic as a guide to practice.

In terms of the current debates on global governance, the arena defined as GCS is also highly contested. We have now clearly moved into a post–Washington consensus era in which the likes of the WTO, the IMF, and the World Bank would have to invent the concept of a GCS counterpart if it did not already exist. As André Drainville puts it,

> As the *plan directeur* of a new order, global governance is . . . politically dependent on finding social interlocutors with both a comprehensive—that is to say transnational—vision of the world economy, and the means to realise the necessary *grands travaux*. (Drainville 1998, 53)

The INGOs certainly have the cosmopolitan grand vision to build GCS, but this project will not, in all likelihood, generate consensus and support from those excluded from the globalization process. The growing process of social exclusion within and between nations will not be overcome by the warm glow of GCS. Nor will the sometimes-complacent advocates of humanitarian intervention have much purchase on those in revolt against the unjust and oppressive new world order.

To conclude this section, we can usefully return to the concept of civil society without the "global" epithet to understand some of the problems GCS must necessarily clarify if it is to have theoretical and political coherence and purchase. Wood was wrong to argue that "Gramsci's conception of 'civil society' was *unambiguously* intended as a weapon against capitalism, not an accommodation to it" (Wood 1990, 63, emphasis added), but she did have a point. When the World Bank becomes a fervent supporter of civil society (and social capital as well), we can safely assume it is not because of its radical anti-capitalist potential. Yet Gramsci did not invest the concept with unequivocal anti-capitalist content, and the ambiguity in the concept was there from the start. In fact, a contextual and historically grounded reading of Gramsci would show that he conceived of civil society as simultaneously the arena in which capitalist hegemony was exercised and the terrain on which the subaltern classes in modern societies could forge alliances and contest that hegemony.

In terms of GCS it seems clear that the concept derives from a particular Central European conception that prevailed in the 1980s revolt against state socialism. The primacy granted to civil society was almost absolute, and its contradictions were buried in rhetoric. Civil society was associated with liberty and then became a cornerstone of the "Third Way." In Latin America in the 1980s democratic struggles against the military dictatorships then prevailing granted a considerably more ambiguous meaning to civil society. It was more of a refuge for those who had contested state power, and it was not invested with any undue effectiveness on the whole. More than twenty years later we are less prone to see civil society as a politics quite distinct from capitalism and socialism. GCS may have some radical or at least reformist potential, but it would be naive to ignore the very large extent to which it has been coopted as the "social" wing of neoliberal global capitalism. Although the Gramscian spirit is usually claimed by those who see GCS as part of a globalization "from below," contesting the hegemony of the nation-state, another reading of Gramsci is possible. Following Gramsci's complex (even contradictory) reading of civil society, we could conceive of GCS as at one and the same time the terrain where global governance builds its hegemony and also where the subaltern may organize transnationally to contest the impact of globalization.

## Prospects

As to the future, we could do worse than start by adopting a realist epistemology. What we observe in the world around us is taken to be real even if the complex causal mechanisms at play may not be obvious. Thus, GCS may indeed refer to incipient tendencies within the international domain. Now, realism in international-relations theory may verge on an amoral and cynical view of the world, but there is much to Halliday's "cold shower" treatment regarding what he calls the "romance of non-state actors" and his conclusion that GCS "is a society that is in many ways violent, contested and with an uncertain future" (Halliday 2000, 23). Most concepts in the social sciences are, of course, contested, so that verdict should not dismay us. Most societies suffer from conflict and violence, so that should not shock us either. That the future is uncertain would only worry those who make a career out of futurology.

A complexity approach to GCS would stress the way in which multiple and contingent causation mechanisms are combined. Complexity explanations are meant to be foundationalist but never reductionist. They recognize that general metanarratives have generally failed to capture the complexity of social (as other) processes. Complexity theory rejects teleological explanations and accepts that processes could always turn out otherwise (for a fuller explanation, see Byrne 1998). So we need to go beyond theories of GCS based on simple unilinear projections—confronting the nation-state, for example—to embrace contingency and complexity in terms of causation and future projects. So, for example, to posit GCS as a globalization "from below" contesting a globalization "from above," as the so-called radical approach to GCS does, simply misses the point. Not only is this an impoverished binary opposition, but in ignoring the critical transformations of global state power (see Shaw 2000) it totally disempowers the radical movement it is seeking to enlighten.

Another general meta-theoretical problem for GCS is its reliance on the traditional language of boundaries or domains within society. The vocabulary is simplistic and naturalistic in the extreme: *civil society, the state, the economy, the global,* and so on. It is a terminology reminiscent of the architectural analogies of traditional Marxism with a "base" and a "superstructure" in society. Separating these spheres of social life may be analytically necessary up to a point, but the rigid boundaries set up between them are certainly not. Societies are constructed and reproduced in complex ways that cannot be reduced to children's building blocks. The local-global divide, for example, has long been superseded in the critical globalization literature (see, e.g., Featherstone et al. 1995; Smith 2001). Finally, to construct a radical politics of transformation on this basis is impossible when global social movements can be seen in practice to disrupt the neat social and spatial categories they are placed in theoretically but which cannot contain them in practice.

Thus, contrary to the claims of the LSE yearbook, GCS is not in fact "a shared discursive framework" (Anheier et al. 2001, 12). The architects of globalization and the anti-globalization protestors may talk about some of the same issues, but is this really communication and dialogue in any meaningful sense? What we can say safely is that GCS is a contested political terrain where different social and political forces vie for hegemony, and this includes, of course, a definition of what GCS is or should be. We could say further that GCS can be conceived of as a "floating signifier" by which Ernesto Laclau refers to a contested political category "whose emptiness results from the unfixity introduced by a plurality of discourses interrupting each other" (Butler et al. 2000, 305). Thus, GCS must be taken not as a given, a shared or common ground, but rather as a site where there is a struggle over/for meaning. A radical democratic GCS would be one way of filling the empty signifier of GCS, but we should always remember that it is not the only option.

In practice we can see many of these rather theoretical ideas coming into play. In Central America the demilitarization and democratization

processes of the 1990s saw a significant role for GCS. Building and supporting local civil society was the way through which GCS sought to
encourage these processes. Yet very different agendas were at play here
to the extent that GCS can hardly be presented as a unified field. On the
one hand, many European NGOs channeled aid indirectly to the local
guerrilla movements struggling for power. On the other hand, US donors such as USAID began in the early 1990s to place a huge emphasis
on civil society building of a very different nature. According to one
exhaustive study of the GCS role in Central America,

> support for civil society building in this, essentially neo-liberal,
> approach thus appears to be synonymous with guaranteeing free
> markets, privatising public services and meeting immediate needs
> of the poor to prevent social unrest. (Biekart 1999, 94–95)

Democratization and economic liberalization went hand in hand in this
discourse, with civil society providing the common denominator.

In terms of its specifically global interventions there can only be, to
date, a mixed verdict on the effectiveness of GCS actions. For every reading of Seattle 1999 as a milestone in the battle to civilize globalization
(e.g., Kaldor 2000), there are many other scathing debunkings of the
radical NGO role. Michel Chossudovsky, for example, writes:

> In Seattle the big divide will be between those who are genuinely
> opposed to the New World Order and those "partner" civil society
> organizations which have all the appearance of being "progressive"
> but which are in fact creatures of the system. (Chossudovsky 1999,
> 3)

Often funded by government (indirectly if not directly), the NGO
can pose as spokesperson of civil society but work in fact as Her Majesty's
Loyal Opposition, according to the critics. The reality of civil society (or
NGO) participation in the global summits is probably more prosaic.
According to a recent careful survey of the issue, "the voice of GCS may
be heard in official summits charged with framing issues but when it
comes to summits with enforcing power these tend to be closed to that
voice" (Pianta 2001, 190–92).

Does the realist version of events presented above invalidate GCS as a
terrain for progressive politics? For Jan Aart Scholte, very much an opti-
mistic reformer,

> Global civil society certainly offers much potential for enhancing
> security, equity and democracy in the world political economy;

however, a long haul of committed endeavour is required in order
to fully realise those benefits. (Scholte 2000, 173)

Scholte recognizes that currently GCS lacks the diversity and
representativity that would be healthy for its development. Less clear is
whether a globalized version of what is essentially a Scandinavian (or
Dutch) version of the traditional social democratic project would be either viable or able to deal with current global contradictions. We need to
be skeptical, for example, of the ability of the recently announced International Criminal Court (The Hague) to be operational without the support of the United States, Russia, and China, not to mention Israel or
Indonesia. However, on balance the concern with the transformation of
democracy in the era of globalization (see McGrew 1997) can only be
positive in terms of renewing and revitalizing the radical democratic
project.

The proponents of GCS tend to adopt a universalist vision. For Peter
Waterman, GCS "means a non-capitalist/non-state, or anti-competitive/
anti-hierarchical, sphere for democratic efforts, within and without the
multiple existing global terrains" (Waterman 1998, 227). This may sound
very much like something we once called socialism and the analogy is
extended to the universalism so dear to European Enlightenment thinking. For Waterman, "cultural universalism has been essential to the development of liberal democracy, its place of residence being civil society" (ibid., 232). In this vision particularism is broken down and the
common values of "humanity" come to prevail. Rational Western man
will help inculcate a global ethic of responsibility on the recalcitrant and
rebellious mob across the world. Even in its more democratic version
this is a problematic vision because of its elitism and its ignorance of
diversity.

Universalism cannot just be proclaimed; it must be constructed politically. For Slavoj Zizek (based on Laclau), "The Universal is empty . . .
hegemonised by some contingent, particular content that acts as its stand
in . . . each Universal battleground on which the multitude of particular
contents fight for hegemony" (Butler et al. 2000, 59). So, GCS can be
seen as an empty signifier currently hegemonized by Western liberal
notions of civility and citizenship. It thus excludes other voices, the proliferation of particularisms that have emerged with and against globalization. It legislates that Blair is good and Saddam is bad; the Contras are
good and the FARC are bad. This universalism of the cosmopolitan has
occluded the mechanisms of global capital and its rampant attacks on
subaltern peoples. A broader, more democratic conception of universality is needed, following Laclau, "so that we can have a full social imagi-
nary capable of competing with the neo-liberal consensus which has been

the hegemonic horizon for world politics for the last 30 years" (ibid., 306).

In more practical terms we can follow Drainville's reconstruction of the Québec 2001 protests and the making of transnational political subjects in that process (Drainville 2001). When the NGOs and other representatives of GCS got together at Québec to protest the Summit of the Americas, they assumed there was a transnational subject to act on behalf of. But, as Drainville puts it, "puffed up and ensconced in reverent absolutes, the peoples . . . of the world will not struggle for themselves or establish and sustain positions against transnational power" (ibid., 15). We cannot simply assume that the workers, the women, the peasants, or the poor of the world will make their voices heard at these global forums. They are nested in particular communities of struggle and their transnational voices are not heard without a complex process of mediation and "translation" into the common language of the counter-globalization forums. This is neither a simple nor an innocent process.

In the influential LSE *Global Civil Society Yearbook* there is a section buried toward the end called "The question of politics" (Pianta 2001, 191). We learn here that when GCS confronts the neoliberal strategy of globalization "it has inevitably to engage the political sphere." This is, of course, correct, but it is also a bit of an understatement. GCS is hardly politically innocent, the product of an immaculate conception in an ethical vacuum. If the Commission on Global Governance can be seen as "the right" in GCS discourse, and globalization from below "the left," it would seem that the LSE study is taking the politics of "beyond left and right" (see Giddens 1995). That politics of non-politics is actually part of the general liberal ethos of our time and not a transformative project. Contrary to the liberal progressive telos of *Our Global Neighbourhood* (Commission on Global Governance 1995), for example, GCS is not heading toward a predefined end. The notion of GCS has suffered from conceptual inflation but has also created exaggerated expectations in regards to its potential. We need to move beyond vague and ultimately meaningless liberal notions that GCS mobilizes the citizens of the world and examine the real global social movements that are currently within and against the complex processes of globalization.

We cannot just say that *only* GCS can contest globalization, because reality is much more "messy" than that. Nor should we argue that *only* the local level can represent an alternative to globalization. Most social movements now strategize and operate simultaneously on the local and global levels and in between, refusing any debilitating binary oppositions. The Polanyi problem (see Evans 2000) of the era of globalization is about how the operation of free markets can be regulated by society. This is a problem for the managers of globalization as well as for those who suffer its effects. That is why global governance strategists require a structured GCS as a valid interlocutor. Within that GCS terrain there will, of course, be different projects contesting for meaning and for political direction. It is not a terrain that can be avoided by any movement for social transformation, whatever problems we may still face in clarifying the nature of this emerging discursive field.

## References

Anheier, Helmut. 2001. Measuring global civil society. In Anheier, Glasius, and Kaldor 2001, 221–30.

Anheier, Helmut, Marlies Glasius, and Mary Kaldor, eds. 2001. *Global Civil Society 2001*. Oxford: Oxford University Press.

Archibugi, Daniel, and David Held, eds. 1995. *Cosmopolitan Democracy: An Agenda for a New World Order*. Cambridge: Polity Press.

Biekart, Kees. 1999. *The Politics of Civil Society Building: European Private Aid Agencies and Democratic Transitions in Central America*. Utrecht, The Netherlands: International Books.

Butler, Judith, Ernesto Laclau, and Slavoj Zizek. 2000. *Contingency, Hegemony, Universality: Contemporary Dialogues on the Left*. London: Verso.

Byrne, David. 1998. *Complexity Theory and the Social Sciences*. London: Routledge.

Chossudovsky, Michel. 1999. Seattle and beyond: Disarming the New World Order. Online.

Cohen, Jean L., and Andrew Arato. 1992. *Civil Society and Political Theory*. Cambridge, Mass.: MIT Press.

Colás, Alejandro. 2001. The promise of international civil society: Global governance, cosmopolitan democracy, and the end of sovereignty. Online.

Commission on Global Governance. 1995. *Our Global Neighbourhood*. Oxford: Oxford University Press.

Drainville, André. 1998. The fetishism of global civil society: Global governance, transnational urbanism, and sustainable capitalism in the world economy. In *Transnationalism from Below*, ed. Michael Peter Smith and Luis Eduardo Guarmizo, 35–63. London: Transaction Books.

———. 2001. Québec City 2001 and the making of transnational subjects. In *The Socialist Register 2002: A World of Contradictions*, ed. Leo Panitch and Colin Leys, 15–42. London: Merlin Press.

Evans, Peter. 2000. Fighting marginalization with transnational networks: Counter-hegemonic globalization. *Contemporary Sociology* 29, no. 1: 230–41.

Falk, Richard. 1999. Global civil society: Perspectives, initiatives, movements. In *Predatory Globalisation: A Critique*, ed. Richard Falk, 137–53. Cambridge: Polity Press.

Featherstone, Mike, Scott M. Lash, and Roland Robertson, eds. 1995. *Global Modernities*. London: Sage.

Friedman, Elisabeth J., Kathryn Hochstetler, and Ann Marie Clark. 2001. Sovereign limits and regional opportunities for global civil society in Latin America. *Latin American Research Review* 36, no. 3: 7–35.

Giddens, Anthony. 1995. *Beyond Left and Right*. Cambridge: Polity Press.

Halliday, Fred. 2000. The romance of non-state actors. In *Non-State Actors in World Politics*, ed. Daphné Josselin and William Wallace, 21–37. London: Palgrave.

Hertz, Noreena. 2001. *The Silent Takeover: Global Capitalism and the Death of Democracy*. London: Heinemann.

Kaldor, Mary. 2000. "Civilising" globalisation? The implications of the "Battle in Seattle." *Millennium* 29, no. 1: 105–14.

Keane, John. 2001. Global civil society? In Anheier, Glasius, and Kaldor 2001, 23–47.

Klein, Naomi. 2001. *No Logo*. London: Flamingo.

Laclau, Ernesto, and Chantal Mouffe. 1985. *Hegemony and Socialist Strategy: Towards a Radical Democratic Politics*. London: Verso.

Lipschutz, Ronnie. 1992. Reconstructing world politics: The emergence of civil society. *Millennium* 21, no. 3: 389–420.

McGrew, Anthony G. ed. 1997. *The Transformation of Democracy*. Cambridge: Polity Press.

Munck, Ronaldo. 2002. *Globalisation and Labour: The New Great Transformation?* London: Zed Books.

Petras, James, and Henry Veltmeyer. 2001. *Globalisation Unmasked: Imperialism in the Twenty-first Century*. London: Zed Books.

Pianta, Mario. 2001. Parallel summits of global civil society. In Anheier, Glasius, and Kaldor 2001, 169–94.

Scholte, Jan Aart. 2000. Global civil society. In *The Political Economy of Globalisation*, ed. Ngaire Woods, 173–202. London: Palgrave.

Shaw, Martin. 2000. *Theory of the Global State: Globality as Unfinished Revolution*. Cambridge: Cambridge University Press.

Smith, Michael Peter. 2001. *Transnational Urbanism: Locating Globalisation*. Oxford: Blackwell.

Sorel, Georges. 1961. *Reflections on Violence*. New York: Norton.

Waterman, Peter. 1998. *Globalisation, Social Movements, and the New Internationalisms*. London: Mansell.

Wood, Ellen Meiksins. 1990. The uses and abuses of civil society. In *The Socialist Register 1990*, ed. Ralph Miliband and Leo Panitch, 60–84. London: Merlin Press.

# 3.
# The Seattle WTO Protests: Building a Global Movement

## Gillian Hughes Murphy

## Introduction

Early in the morning of November 30, 1999, the normally quiet down-town core of Seattle (Washington State, USA) was flooded with tens of thousands of marching, dancing, chanting, and singing protestors who wanted to make it known that the World Trade Organization (WTO), an institution virtually invisible to the general public, was an undemo-cratic, antilabor, and anti-environmental organization that served the interests of corporations over people and the environment (Cockburn et al. 2000). They accused the WTO of trampling human rights, increas-ing global inequality, and undermining national sovereignty in the pur-suit of capital gain for the few. Protesters carried banners, puppets, and picket signs; they acted out scenes in which WTO officials wreaked havoc on the planet while world citizens tried to save it, they decried human rights abuses in various locations against diverse groups, they wore turtle costumes to highlight one of the WTO's most notorious cases, and they called for global enforcement of labor rights. Some simply walked calmly through what was early in the day a carnival-like atmosphere. Despite the fact that the specific content of their messages varied tremendously, their overall scope—labor and human rights, the environment, and de-

---

The material that informs this analysis is largely drawn from protest-related planning documents, memorabilia, and interviews with protest organizers and participants. Interviews cited in this chapter include Juan Bocanegra and Cindy Domingo, Lydia Cabasco, Denise Cooper, Mike Dolan, Regino Martinez, and Tyree Scott. All these interviews are accessible at the WTO History Project website <www.WTOhistory.org>. The interview with David Solnit is available from the WTO History Project, manuscripts, special collections and university archives, division of University of Washington Libraries.

27

mocracy—was not a fortuitous coincidence. Rather, groups of organizations and individuals consciously developed the protest in such a way as
to minimize conflict among themselves and maximize participation in
the planned protests while cogently communicating their intense dis-
pleasure with the WTO.

Scholars and activists alike have turned to the concept of a developing
global civil society (GCS) to explain the broad-based opposition the WTO
met in Seattle. For activists, identifying legitimate targets to pressure for
global change and motivating local action to reach that target is problematic. Once the WTO, an intergovernmental organization regulating
international trade, was identified as being at least partly responsible for
a broad array of grievances, activists needed a strategy to motivate action. The task was complicated by the fact that neither the causes of nor
the solutions to their grievances could be found or contained within national borders. By linking the fates of distant individuals and ecosystems
to local action, the global justice movement that expressed its opposition
to the WTO has helped create a "global citizen" identity much like other
movements have created identities for women, minority groups, and gays
and lesbians as part of the process of effecting change.

How could a protest in Seattle, whose participants were drawn primarily from the Pacific Northwest play an important role in the development of a GCS? Does GCS even exist? Ronaldo Munck writes that
GCS is a "contested political terrain where different social and political
forces vie for hegemony" (Chapter 2 herein). Much like national landscapes in which different groups vie for power and influence, global politics attracts actors who are motivated by concerns as divergent as maxi-
mizing profits and protecting ecosystems, who have very different
concerns about the effects of trade policies, and who look to members,
stockholders, or even corporations for support.

If defining GCS is our goal, we are likely to be frustrated by inconsistent and even contradictory definitions proposed by politicians, activists,
and scholars, but if we shift our agenda to identifying mechanisms various GCS-building efforts have in common, we may have already made
some progress in understanding the phenomenon. In this chapter it is
shown how the 1999 mobilization in Seattle helped to create an activist
identity that at the very least complements the idea of a GCS. This identity shows promise for future collaborations among diverse groups. First,
attention is directed to the target of the Seattle protest: the WTO.

## The World Trade Organization

Founded in 1995 as an extension of the General Agreement on Tariffs
and Trade (GATT), the goal of the WTO is to provide an institutional

framework for the conduct of trade negotiations among its almost 150 member nations. The WTO has greater influence over multilateral trade than did GATT, having the authority to enforce its rules and governing trade in additional sectors.

Perhaps the most publicly contested aspect of the WTO's trade rules is the requirement that member nations maintain nondiscriminatory trade relationships with all other members. This has the effect of disallowing historical trade relationships based on longstanding preferences and agreements, trade (or trade bans) based on environmental considerations, and many other aspects that are not specifically related to the goods being traded. The policy further requires the increasing elimination of protectionism, such as subsidies to agricultural products. When violations are suspected, the cases are heard by a panel of trade representatives who decide if sanctions should be imposed on the offending country. WTO member nations must submit to the panel's decision, even when doing so is inconsistent with domestic laws. The WTO has been harshly criticized for this policy and accused of undermining national sovereignties, and the mobilization in Seattle prominently featured the claim that the WTO could undermine US laws.

Trade ministers who represent their countries within the WTO meet periodically in negotiations named for the locales that host them to work out details of trade agreements. During the Seattle Round, key issues to be discussed were the Forest Products Agreement, the Multilateral Agreement on Investments (banking and finance), biotechnology, and intellectual property rights. Each of these issues attracted the interest of activists, but an even more serious issue overall was that the social and environmental consequences of trade policies were *not* to be discussed. Moreover, activists found that domestic laws to protect the environment and workers could be considered illegal barriers to trade according to the WTO's rules.

Activists publicized two illustrative cases of contested WTO policies: the hormone-beef and the shrimp-turtle cases. In both, the WTO's dispute-resolution board ruled against countries that had adopted regulations to protect the environment or public health. In the hormone-beef case the United States challenged a European Union (EU) ban on the sale of beef from cattle that had been fed certain artificial growth hormones because this would effectively make some American beef unsalable in the EU. Many Europeans, unsure of the health effects of the hormones, were opposed to their use, but the WTO ruled that this public-health measure was an illegal barrier to trade under the WTO and gave the EU a limited period to open its markets to US hormone-treated beef.

In the shrimp-turtle case the WTO ruled against the United States for banning shrimp from several Asian countries that did not require their shrimping vessels to use nets equipped with "turtle excluder devices" that decreased the risk of endangered sea turtles being caught inadvertently. This policy came about as a result of the US Endangered Species Act, but once the case was brought before the WTO, the United States was forced to consider either abandoning the policy or rewriting its laws to maintain compliance with WTO regulations.

Activists also pointed to the WTO's failure to create enforceable policies related to labor standards. In 1996 WTO members vowed to observe the International Labor Organization's core labor standards without creating official procedures within the WTO to uphold them.[1]

## Main Protest Organizations

As downtown Seattle filled with protestors, many of whom were specifically trying to block delegates from reaching the WTO's opening ceremonies, police in riot gear tried unsuccessfully to secure the delegates' passage. Not only were the police outnumbered, but they faced protestors who used nonviolent protest techniques, such as sitting down and linking arms, that made them difficult to move. While police were effectively blockaded by the crowds, a small and agile group of individuals smashed store windows and spray painted anti-corporate graffiti on shop fronts. Most media attention focused on these actions and largely ignored the fact that most of those individuals fled and police proceeded to beat and pepper spray nonviolent protestors in an increasingly aggressive standoff. Police continued to advance on foot and in armored vehicles, using their entire supply of concussion grenades and pepper spray to clear the streets. Meanwhile, the tens of thousands of labor activists held a planned rally nearby before beginning their own march, which was diverted away from the downtown core as the melee continued into the afternoon.

City officials declared a state of emergency in the late afternoon and designated downtown Seattle a "protest-free" zone, which inspired additional protests throughout the week. Most arrests during Ministerial Week were on December 1, during protests focused on police brutality the day before and the right to freedom of speech.

These events may have seemed random to outside observers, but they were actually the result of careful, if loose, coordination of movement organizations (Lichbach and Almeida 2002). Furthermore, the efforts of these organizations in the mobilization for the Ministerial Week protests resulted in many individuals being prepared for the violent police reaction, which they used to highlight the dominance of corporate trade interests over the rights of individuals.

Although several hundred organizations, many of them based in countries other than the United States, had some role in the lengthy mobilization that preceded the November 30 protest, and more than fourteen hundred registered themselves as opposed to the WTO, three US-based organizations were the primary architects of the Seattle-area mobilization: the People for Fair Trade/Network Opposed to the WTO (PFT/NO!WTO); the AFL-CIO (a federation of American labor unions), with its local affiliate, the King County Labor Council (KCLC); and the Direct Action Network (DAN). Both cooperatively and independently these organizations and their representatives built a framework around which the protests could incorporate diverse interests without diluting the primary message or compromising the general goal of the protest—to force the WTO into the public spotlight. These organizations are discussed in turn.

### People for Fair Trade/Network Opposed to the WTO

PFT, one of the key organizations in the Seattle mobilization, was an outgrowth of the Citizens Trade Campaign (CTC), a coalition of labor, trade, and environment groups based in Washington, D.C., that came together to work on campaigns such as the North American Free Trade Agreement (NAFTA) and Fast Track. The CTC's field director Mike Dolan became the lead organizer for PFT in Seattle, using the resources of Public Citizen and the CTC to provide resources and direction to a significant number of grassroots groups. Soon after the January 1999 announcement that the WTO would hold its meeting in Seattle later that year, the CTC developed a mobilization plan. Organization documents show that an early concern was how to manage the participation of organizations and individuals who had little in common, and whether presenting a unified message would help moderate inter-organizational competition (WTO History Project).

A February meeting that veteran organizer Dolan hosted for Seattle activists to plan a response to the WTO drew eighty participants. Some represented labor, environment, animal rights, biotechnology, debt-relief, religious, or environmental-justice organizations; others were not affiliated with any organization but were integrated into local networks of activists. Motivated by different ideologies and interests, they employed a variety of tactics in their pursuits, ranging from lobbying to nonviolent direct action. Some had little network overlap, while others had ongoing personal and professional contact with one another.

The group selected a steering committee and for the next several months, according to Dolan, its primary activity was to develop a coherent identity for the group. Fundamental differences in goals—some wanted to "shut down" the WTO while others wanted the WTO to "incorporate core labor standards, environmental and consumer protections, into the [WTO's] agreements" (Mike Dolan, interview)—made that impossible. Proposals for the group's name—"People for Fair Trade" and "Network Opposed to the WTO" reflected that inconsistency. When it became apparent that there would be no reconciliation, the group adopted a merger of the two names (PFT/NO!WTO) and became referred to alternately as "People for Fair Trade" and "NO!WTO," depending on the speaker's or audience's political and ideological standpoint.

Later the PFT/NO!WTO name was adopted by an office run by a small group of organizers hired by Dolan, an action that highlighted the feelings of isolation felt by some early participants, particularly those representing minority organizations that tended to have more radical ideologies and wanted the group to take a more radical stance and adopt a confrontational strategy. This "professionalized" incarnation of PFT/NO!WTO welcomed the affiliation of grassroots groups and became a hub of activity and supplied fliers and other mobilization materials for other groups to distribute. Some groups advertised their affiliation with the PFT, and others became branches of the NO!WTO. The staff ran a speakers' bureau and spent the next three months organizing events designed to teach Seattleites about the WTO. Educational events, many of which were either sponsored by PFT or included presentations by PFT representatives, comprised nearly 40 percent of more than 550 public events that preceded Ministerial Week (WTO History Project). Ideational preparation was important in Seattle, a city with a relatively educated population and in which international trade is a significant source of revenue.

The materials produced directly by PFT/NO!WTO were designed to appeal to a politically mainstream audience. Some typical banner phrases on the mainstream materials were No Globalization Without Representation, Mobilization Against Corporate Globalization, and Fair Trade not Free Trade. Onlookers were urged to Be Part of History. The materials PFT produced often included brief summaries of contentious cases brought before the WTO and cartoons that depicted the WTO as a monster in the process of destroying democracy. By framing the issue as a critique of neoliberal trade policies rather than an opposition to globalization, per se, and by celebrating the diversity of participants rather than pressing for conformity, the group advocated creating an environment in Seattle that would enable it to attract the maximum number of participants.[2]

### Organized Labor

As the national economy has shifted away from manufacturing in recent decades, organized labor has experienced significant threats to its economic and political influence and has responded by adopting an "inside-outside" political strategy to reverse its decline. Showing renewed interest in grassroots activism and global justice issues, the participation of organized labor was the critical factor in mobilizing large-scale protest in Seattle (Levi and Olson 2000). This role was unusual for a US labor movement often regarded as conservative, but not so in the Seattle area, which has a strong and radical labor history.

King County Labor Council and AFL-CIO leadership faced pressure from union locals to make a strong statement against the WTO. Seattle-area labor organizations condemned the WTO's policies for undercutting local sovereignty and damaging US wage levels and living standards, and warned the national AFL-CIO leadership that failure to stage a major show of force in Seattle would be a "lost opportunity."[3] Representatives of two hundred international unions condemned the WTO and called on the trade-regulating body to add a clear and enforceable endorsement of worker's rights.

Labor's key demand was that the labor standards established by the International Labor Organization—itself lacking enforcement power—be adopted and enforced by the WTO. This was intended to have a broad appeal across a variety of workers and avoid criticism on grounds of protectionism and nativism. Leaders emphasized rules for—not resistance to—globalization in an effort to attract broad public support. Labor's campaign was facilitated by close cooperation with environmental and citizen's advocacy groups in the CTC.

Organized labor's commitment to opposing WTO policies opened up considerable resources for social movement organizations (SMOs) in the Seattle area. The AFL-CIO purchased advertisements, and produced and distributed placards, buttons, and other materials designed to get union members to attend a planned mass march and rally. Some of these were also distributed by non-labor groups. Thirty AFL-CIO staffers were deployed to Seattle to assist local unions in the mobilization drive. In both the United States and British Columbia (Canada) unions sent out field organizers to arrange an "I'm coming to Seattle" campaign. They organized workshops to teach members about the WTO and the consequences for labor, and some of the more radical members saw to it that they had access to nonviolence training.

At the local level the King County Labor Council and area unions expended additional resources. As KCLC executive secretary Ron Judd recalled, "What happened in Seattle was not an accident. For months, labor led an effort with allies to educate and inform the community about the devastating impacts of the WTO and its policies" (quoted in Guilloud 2000, 51).

The support of the AFL-CIO and its affiliates was crucial for the scale of the protests. The unions organized transportation for thousands to ensure a large Northwest labor turnout to the planned November 30 rally and march, overcoming the inertia that can prevent even those who agree with a plan from participating. The union strategies appear to have worked, because various activist and media sources estimate that between thirty thousand and fifty thousand people attended the rally and march.

At the end of the November 30 rally union members had planned to march through downtown Seattle, but because of the ongoing violent standoff between police and other protestors, labor organizers altered their route to bypass the most congested and turbulent areas of downtown. Frustrated with what they considered an inadequate strategy, and ignoring the instructions of union officials, thousands of union demonstrators broke off from the officially sanctioned march and joined the fray to show their support for other activists. Labor was not a single actor; there were unions, locals, and individuals who did not support the dominant inside-outside labor strategy, preferring tighter links with other groups and a more confrontational approach to protest, such as a general strike.

In the following days, when hundreds of protestors were arrested for violating the city's newly created protest-free zone downtown as they protested violent police tactics and city-sanctioned assaults on freedom of speech and expression, local labor leaders defended the right to protest and to be relieved of ongoing police harassment. At least once, protestors were offered refuge from overzealous police in the downtown Labor Temple, and union leaders were instrumental in negotiating the release of hundreds of protestors and other individuals who had got caught in police sweeps. These unplanned events helped bring activists who had parallel plans closer together while strengthening preexisting inter-organizational relationships.

### Direct Action Network

The DAN was formed specifically to coordinate a mass nonviolent direct action aimed at shutting down the WTO's ministerial meeting in Seattle. Funded primarily by Global Exchange, the Rainforest Action Network, and the Ruckus Society, and founded by another group of veteran activists, DAN supported thousands of activists with the tools they needed to mount a nonviolent confrontation of the WTO. The DAN and DAN-affiliated individuals organized and facilitated public workshops, training sessions, teach-ins, and debates for several weeks before November 30, and helped to organize housing and food for those activists who arrived from outside Seattle to participate. The lead organizers' hope was that the organizational and strategic model developed in Seattle would be used in future mass actions. DAN groups were eventually formed throughout the United States and were central to protests that followed Seattle.

DAN adopted an institutional structure that was intended to be the polar opposite of the WTO's. Decisions were made by consensus after a period of open deliberation, and the structure was horizontal rather than hierarchical. Participants were organized into self-reliant affinity groups of five to fifteen members, each of which had a representative in a central planning group. All participants were required to agree to a set of four action principles that prohibited the use of any form of violence; the use of weapons; the use of alcohol or illegal drugs; and the destruction of property. Commitment to nonviolence was at the core of all activities.

In Seattle, DAN secured a large warehouse space close to downtown where activists could gather for meetings, create props (puppets, banners, picket signs, costumes), eat, and attend training and workshops sessions on a variety of topics ranging from "radical jeerleading" and drumming to emergency first aid. For several weeks the "convergence center" was a major hub of protest-planning activity in Seattle. Interestingly enough, events that will be remembered as the Battle in Seattle because of police repression of activists were conceived of by DAN organizers as a festival of resistance. Indeed, the many DAN puppet-making and "radical jeerleading" workshops did result in a festive start to the November 30 protest. Many of the activists who had attended DAN-sponsored training sessions on the West Coast in the months preceding the "convergence" were veterans of other mass actions of the 1980s and 1990s. Longstanding personal affiliations among some activists played a role in facilitating cooperation among the affinity groups.

As November 30 grew closer, and DAN membership grew larger, relationships between DAN and the more mainstream organizers remained chilly. The AFL-CIO–initiated march and the mass direct action were scheduled on the same day purely by accident. DAN and the AFL-CIO had almost no contact. PFT/NO!WTO was not overtly supportive of DAN either, most obviously by excluding DAN-sponsored events from the public calendar of events it published weekly in print and electronic form. Activists accused the AFL-CIO and PFT/NO!WTO of isolating their supporters from DAN, putting the labor march and the direct action in competition with each other. "We were the bad protestors" (David Solnit, interview). More marginal groups in the labor movement, such as Jobs with Justice and the Industrial Workers of the World, as well as a number of student groups at the various Seattle campuses, were very supportive of and more tightly linked to DAN.

## Building a Global Movement

### Networks and Coalitions

That November 30 was a day of action recognized by tens of thousands of individuals and hundreds of organizations sounding a cacophony of demands and representing diverse interests was no accident. Rather, individuals actively used social and organizational networks in the months preceding the protests to disseminate carefully framed information and ideas. Though the three central groups in the Seattle mobilization (PFT/NO!WTO, the AFL-CIO, and the DAN) mobilized largely separate constituencies, they shared information with one another (and with the authorities), participated together in open and closed strategy meetings, and supported one another, if not always overtly or with maximum gusto. Cooperative efforts sometimes took the form of a coalition, but the dominant form of these relationships is better described as a network. The networks developed during this period strongly influenced the course of the events during Ministerial Week. Furthermore, these networks are the foundation of a global justice movement, defining its character and creating opportunities for protest.

Each group involved drew on its native strengths, many of which were complementary, and indirectly assisted other groups in the network. Labor, for example, used its federated structure to facilitate the mobilization of union locals and dispatched organizers directly to their shops. PFT/NO!WTO counted on labor to provide needed numbers, while the AFL-CIO needed PFT/NO!WTO and DAN to create a base of support among local Seattle activists. PFT's primary resource was the legitimacy it held among "professional" activists, which earned the protest some legitimacy among broader segments of the public. PFT brokered relationships primarily among local non-direct-action–oriented trade, biotech, environmental, and labor groups, while DAN did the same among those who did use direct action.

Strong ties with Ruckus, well known for direct-action training, and Rainforest Action Network, well known for protests, increased DAN's ability to bring together veteran and neophyte activists with diverse backgrounds who all used some form of direct action as a tactic in their specific areas. Using DAN's resources, veterans of the peace, anti-nuclear, environmental, and other movements trained newcomers and veterans alike, sharing their experiences and expertise. Train-the-trainer events were held specifically to enable central individuals to disseminate information.

The participation of the AFL-CIO and PFT increased the likelihood of broad public support for the protests; the efforts of DAN ensured broad support among another core group of activists. Because the use of direct action has the tendency to isolate otherwise supportive individuals, had these activists not been coordinated with one another and with non-direct-action–oriented groups, the protests may have had far less coherence and public support.

Interdependence among these groups facilitated their willingness and ability to work together (where needs were not strong, cooperation and bargaining were less likely). This resulted in an atmosphere that minimized conflict even without developing strong ongoing relationships among key individuals and organizations. However, enabling the expression of the diversity of the opposition to the WTO would have an affect on movement adherents and the public at large. Exposure is the first step toward acceptance or understanding of alternative viewpoints.

Two sociological patterns can be highlighted in the Seattle mobilization: the framing of local action for global results; and the role of trust, credible commitments, and bargaining in the development of inter-organizational relationships. The key to understanding the protests is in recognizing how central groups coordinated their activities and messages. By examining similarities and differences across these groups, we can isolate patterns and mechanisms that inform our understanding of the development of the global justice movement and, by extension, GCS.

### Framing Local Action for Global Results

Individuals are most likely to be motivated to participate in collective action when they have an interest in the goals and believe their effort will have an effect (Klandermans 1984). Sometimes, however, it can be difficult to understand the link between a specific action and a desired goal. For example, it could be difficult to understand that sitting at a lunch counter could help the effort to gain civil rights for African Americans in the United States. Some actions can carry multiple meanings and interpretations. Movements recruit individuals by convincing them of an action's merits and by presenting an interpretation that would appeal to that individual (Snow, Zurcher, and Ekland-Olson 1980). Movements also frame issues to appeal to broader publics (Snow et al. 1986) and gain their support. Frames that identify a problem and attribute blame are called diagnostic frames; those that propose strategies and solutions are called prognostic frames (Snow and Benford 1988).

Movements that are populated by organizations that have different ideologies or that use different tactics can suffer when issue framing is uncoordinated (Staggenborg 1991). Radically different messages can pit activists against one another instead of focusing their energy on a common target. In this respect the SMOs that were active in the mobilization for the Seattle protests were careful to translate their own understanding of the effects of WTO policies into terms that not only would be understandable by broad groups of individuals but also would motivate them to participate. Labor, for example, appealed to concern about how WTO policies could affect working conditions for all laborers to mobilize union members rather than trying to explain how the complexity of global trade affects US jobs.

The message was also worded in such a way that it would not provoke dissent. Other groups agreed that WTO policies that favor corporations have the effect of undermining national sovereignty, endangering the environment, and discouraging democratic processes. The explicit message was that the position of all laborers was jeopardized by WTO policies that favored corporations; the implicit message in labor slogans like "Make the global economy work for working families" was that reforming (or for the more radical unions and locals—abolishing) the WTO would improve their position. Omitting public suggestions for specific concrete changes and using the nonspecific message that the WTO needed "reform," labor increased the probability that it would have the support of other interests.

The effort to create a mass protest against the WTO in Seattle was made possible by conscious attempts to develop diagnostic frames that attributed blame for global social and environmental problems to the WTO without provoking opposition from political allies on the left. This was particularly important because both labor and environmental interests, long distrustful of each others' intentions, were heavily represented among the protestors. The scale of the protests was a direct result of a coordinated mobilization effort among diverse groups that agreed that the WTO was a valid target and that the Seattle meeting presented a political opportunity that they could exploit. By agreeing on the diagnostic framing and limiting or "agreeing to disagree" (Rose 2000) about prognostic frames, SMOs maximized their ability to cooperate. It was important that they agree on a short-term target for action; less important was that they agree on long-term strategies for addressing their grievances.

The central groups reinforced one anothers' messages but were free to ask their constituencies to pursue different strategies of targeting the WTO. Some groups marched with signs and banners, filling the streets with people to register opposition, while others used nonviolent civil disobedience to block the passage of all traffic. Many groups, but not all, agreed that they would have more to gain from reinforcing one anothers' messages than from focusing on the issues on which they disagreed, by complementing one anothers' strategies rather than arguing their efficacy.

The months preceding the Seattle protest were filled with events that served to educate the public about the WTO, presenting expert speakers who shared their knowledge, experiences, and proposed solutions with the audience. These events also brought together the individuals serving on the panels and those sitting in the audiences. The November 30 protest was not the first time that individuals were brought together around these issues—they had been given many opportunities over time to become acquainted. Exposure increases the possibility of some sort of cooperation in the future as individuals develop ties, however weak they are.

## A Global Justice Movement

The 1999 protests were by no means the first to call for limiting the power of corporations or changing the way an intergovernmental organization like the WTO operates, but unlike many others, the Seattle protests can be heralded as being significant in launching a mass movement. Seattle marks the advent of a movement for global justice as a result of the broad framing of the issues presented in the protest. Activist concerns clearly involved global trade issues, although their orientations to the problem varied considerably. Overall, however, activists sought a solution that would be more equitable, distributing a greater share of the benefits of trade more broadly and transferring power from corporate interests to democratic bodies. The Seattle protest built a foundation for a broad movement by creating a template for dissent that enabled cooperation among diverse groups without requiring excessive compromise; it has also become the example to which all other global justice protests are compared.

When the banners were folded, the puppets put away, and the protesters scattered, there remained a legacy of transformed relationships among individuals, movement organizations, and authorities. Where no relationship had existed previously—as between individuals and the WTO, or between DAN and labor activists—one was created. Other relationships, such as those between SMOs, were redefined. These transformations are significant, because the dynamics of relationships can influence the effectiveness of advocacy (Jordan and Van Tuijl 2000).

Agreeing to disagree was important for the course of the protests. While some actors did not receive the support from their compatriots that they desired, there are few if any reports of serious efforts directly to undermine other groups' work. A notable exception is the anarchist-inspired Black Bloc, which smashed shop windows and sparked public outrage that initially was erroneously directed toward the protestors at large. Central organizers broadcast in every medium a message that the protest would be nonviolent and that property destruction would not be an acceptable tactic and would only serve to undermine their intentions. They reinforced the message with training sessions that focused on theory and techniques of nonviolent civil disobedience. In the weeks leading up to the protest, some 25 percent of publicly announced protest-related events were training sessions, a large proportion focusing on the theory and techniques of nonviolent civil disobedience.

That the Seattle protest attracted so many individuals motivated by diverse ideologies and interests is a result of the lengthy mobilization that prominently featured educational events. The sheer number of these events, and the fact that many featured speakers represented diverse interests, also enabled local activists the opportunity to draw (or have drawn for them) the connection between local and global issues (Smith and Johnston 2002). These events did more than help individuals connect symbolically—they helped "to dig deep into layers of advantage, exploitation and oppression done to others in one's name," like efforts involving women on both sides of the Palestinian conflict (Cockburn 2000, 52). By helping local activists identify with distant actors and helping them understand the parallels between local and foreign issues, SMOs helped foster a feeling of mutual fate while suggesting specific action to address social and environmental ills that complements the idea of global citizenship.

## Conclusion

The Seattle events are notable for the diversity of actors and interests that participated (Smith and Johnston 2002). Where broad participation is a hallmark of campaigns that address the process of globalization, we should look to the mechanisms that draw the various actors together. Ongoing relationships among movement actors were clearly important in affecting the course of the Seattle mobilization, but so too were new relationships formed during the mobilization and ensuing protest events. These relationships were developed through communication in multiple mediums—face-to-face contact, websites, email, mass meetings, and so on. The coalition group Mobilization for Global Justice drew on the organizing model developed in Seattle for subsequent campaigns targeting the World Bank, the WTO, and the IMF. Mobilization for Global Justice helped network and coordinate organizations and individuals, developed a central framing for the issues, and spread the word through the training sessions that we now expect to precede large-scale protests.

It is important to note also that Seattle was the birthplace of two organizations that featured prominently in later protests: the DAN and the Independent Media Center (IMC). The latter allows mostly amateur journalists to present accounts of events that often contrast starkly with corporate media accounts. The IMC serves to channel energy into and distribute information about the global justice movement. DAN groups have included legal teams for the legal defense of activists; in Seattle, film archived by the IMC was used in the defense of activists who were accused of committing various crimes during the protests.

The significance of the Seattle protests can also be found in terms of the shifting scale of contention (McAdam, Tarrow, and Tilly 2001), which also has implications for the development of a GCS. Whereas social movements are more often found to target local or domestic institutions, the events in Seattle showed a diverse population of activists using their own political and social liberties to demand changes within the

WTO that would have global social and environmental repercussions, not all of which would be objectively beneficial to the protesters. They accused the WTO of enabling corporations to dominate the process of globalization at the expense of environmental and social welfare. Globalization was therefore both a reason to protest and a means for the protest to have an effect. Removing activists from the streets was a job for the local authorities, not the WTO, but the Seattle protest had a modified "boomerang" effect (Keck and Sikkink 1998), empowering nations less powerful than the United States to press for change in the WTO.

A logical next step would be to look for movement-building features in other events that form part of the global justice movement, and to compare how the mechanisms that combined to produce the Seattle protest operate in these circumstances and contexts. The concept of a GCS is not novel, but the mechanisms that are currently shaping its development will affect the way it is perceived and acted upon. For activists and scholars alike the Seattle protest forms a central part of any understanding of the current state of GCS, for in Seattle there developed an issue frame and a strategy that could unite multiple divergent interests into a single campaign.

Activists in Seattle framed the issues in such a way as to link the fates of local activists to the fates of people they had never met and places they had never been, and they reached that understanding by working with other activists who had different concerns but a common target for their grievances. The protest model developed in Seattle—with its central features being information sharing among diverse organizations, public education, and activist training—has been used in many subsequent protests. As much a result of conscious effort as unforeseeable events, activist networks have grown broader and deeper, which should facilitate them as their efforts also increase in scope. The protest that took place on the streets is but the tip of the iceberg that represents a movement for global justice. The protests showed that the strategies to unite the public were successful. What remains to be seen is whether the behind-the-scenes work is cooperative as well and how activists are able to translate the public lessons into strategies for developing agreeable solutions to grievances.

### Notes

[1] These standards include the right to organize and bargain collectively, prohibition on the use of any form of forced or compulsory labor, a minimum age for the employment of children, acceptable conditions of work with respect to minimum wages, hours of work, and occupational safety and health.

[2] It seems that PFT/NO!WTO was not totally inclusive. In interviews with the WTO History Project, a number of activists expressed the opinion that the

mobilization was ill suited to attracting US minorities (WTO History Project, especially interviews with Juan Bocanegra and Cindy Domingo, Lydia Cabasco, Denise Cooper, Regino Martinez, and Tyree Scott). See also Martinez 2000.

[3] See statement in International Association of Longshore and Warehouseworker Union, President's Report, ILWU president Brian McWilliams, May 1999.

### References

Cockburn, Cynthia. 2000. The women's movement. In *Global Social Movements*, ed. Robin Cohen and Sharin Rai, 46–61. London: Athlone Press.

Cockburn, Alexander, Jeffrey St. Clair, and Allan Sekula. 2000. *Five Days That Shook the World: Seattle and Beyond*. London: Verso.

Guilloud, Stephanie, ed. 2000. *Voices from the WTO*. Olympia, Wash.: The Evergreen State College.

Jordan, Lisa, and Peter Van Tuijl. 2000. Political responsibility in transnational NGO advocacy. *World Development* 28, no. 12: 2051–65.

Keck, Margaret E., and Kathryn Sikkink. 1998. *Activists Beyond Borders: Advocacy Networks in International Politics*. Ithaca, N.Y.: Cornell University Press.

Klandermans, Bert. 1984. Mobilization and participation: Social psychological expansions of resource mobilization theory. *American Sociological Review* 49, no. 5: 583–600.

Levi, Margaret, and David Olson. 2000. The battles in Seattle. *Politics and Society* 28, no. 3: 309–29.

Lichbach, Mark I., and Paul Almeida. 2002. Global order and local resistance: The neoliberal institutional trilemma and the battle of Seattle. Department of Political Science, University of California, Riverside. Available online.

McAdam, Doug, Sidney G. Tarrow, and Charles Tilly. 2001. *Dynamics of Contention*. New York: Cambridge University Press.

Martinez, Elizabeth. 2000. Where was the color in Seattle? Looking for reasons why the great battle was so white. *Monthly Review* 53, no. 3: 141–48.

Rose, Fred. 2000. *Coalitions Across the Class Divide: Lessons from the Labor, Peace, and Environmental Movements*. Ithaca, N.Y.: Cornell University Press.

Smith, Jackie, and Hank Johnston, eds. 2002. *Globalization and Resistance: Transnational Dimensions of Social Movements*. Lanham, Mass.: Rowman and Littlefield.

Snow, David A., and Robert D. Benford. 1988. Ideology, frame resonance, and participant mobilization. *International Social Movement Research* 1: 197–217.

Snow, David A., E. Burke Rochford, Jr., Steven K. Worden, and Robert D. Benford. 1986. Frame alignment processes, micromobilization, and movement participation. *American Sociological Review* 51, no. 4: 464–81.

Snow, David A., Louis A. Zurcher, and Sheldon Ekland-Olson. 1980. Social networks and social movements: A microstructural approach to differential recruitment. *American Sociological Review* 45, no. 5: 787–801.

Staggenborg, Suzanne. 1991. *The Pro-Choice Movement: Organization and Activism in the Abortion Conflict*. New York: Oxford University Press.

# 4.
# Understanding the Genoa Protest

## Massimiliano Andretta
## and Lorenzo Mosca

## Introduction

The increasing problem of world poverty, the structural gap between the rich countries of the North and the countries of the so-called Third World, the politics of economic over-consumption, the reduction of the public debt of poor countries, and the conditions of environmental degradation that plague the whole planet have found ample space in the international mass media in recent years. And if nothing else, the birth of a movement that is mobilized on a global scale for the purpose of contesting the socioeconomic and environmental imbalances created by neoliberal globalization sheds new light on public debate of such issues.

Until quite recently elite-led intergovernmental meetings seldom attracted media or public concern. Since the battle in Seattle, however, the spotlight has fallen on a new spectral presence, a new movement of contention that has materialized around the world, haunting the cosmopolitan elite who meet time and time again to decide what should be done, or perhaps more fittingly, what is opportune *not* to do with respect to the economy, trade, welfare, employment, and environment. This movement has been labeled "Seattle's soul" and is embedded in a broader and

Although the authors share responsiblity for the whole chapter, Massimiliano Andretta wrote the "Introduction" and "Understanding the New Movement" sections, while Lorenzo Mosca wrote the "Key Features of the Genoa Protest" and "Conclusion" sections. The Department of Political Science and Sociology of the University of Florence, Italy, sponsored this research. This study forms part of a broader project focused on European social movements and protest being conducted by the Group of Research on Collective Action in Europe, coordinated by Donatella della Porta.

emergent global civil society that is concerned to create a better world (Shaw 1994).

Though some features of the collective action that took place in Genoa, Italy, in July 2001, have some continuity with post-Seattle anti-globalization protests, it can be said that a definite quantitative and qualitative shift took place. For example, on Saturday July 21, 2001, there were 300,000 people shouting out against the G8 in Genoa, whereas previous protests against neoliberal globalization had never approached this level of mass participation. Moreover, the Genoa Social Forum (GSF)—the main network of networks that organized the protest—was the first attempt to coordinate properly actions among such a wide array of individuals and organizations. As a further point, in Genoa a collective mourning on a massive scale was held over the tragic assassination of a twenty-three-year-old demonstrator, Carlo Giuliani, by the bullets of a *carabiniere*.

The first official street demonstration, led by Genoa's immigrant communities, took place on Thursday, July 19, with a peaceful march in favor of freedom of movement. Notwithstanding the huge tension provoked by negative media hype and a very large police presence, around fifty thousand people marched across the city. Over the following days, when the G8 meeting started, the main networks of protest engaged in precisely coordinated demonstrations. The destructive activities of the anarchist-inspired Black Bloc attracted particular media attention and police surveillance, but all peaceful demonstrations also encountered repressive policing. Then, on the night of July 21, the police raided the main office of the GSF, destroying and confiscating computers. On the pretext of taking action against the Black Bloc, police also raided a building being used as a dormitory and proceeded to arrest ninety-three people, over two-thirds of whom were brutally assaulted. Furthermore, media reports documented ill-treatment of those imprisoned, and the Italian police were denounced by Amnesty International.

Although it was never openly declared by the demonstrators that their protest was also directed against the new center-right government—led by Silvio Berlusconi *(Forza Italia)* and Gianfranco Fini (president of the post-fascist party *Alleanza Nazionale*), the scale of the protest has to be understood within this national political context. To put this in terms of the political-opportunity–structure perspective of social movement scholars (e.g., McAdam, McCarthy, and Zald 1996), on the one hand the state radicalized its repressive attitude toward mass protest (della Porta and Reiter 2001), and on the other, the very fact that the center-left coalition was in opposition provided the opportunity for its supporters to bring to the protest issues such as social justice and environmental protection. Thus, the Genoa protest played itself out as both protest against neoliberal globalization and a popular reaction against the national police's repressive tactics. The Genoa protest also opened a new course for the global justice movement; since Genoa, focus seems to have shifted from a counter-summit strategy to a more autonomous strategy centered on negotiating its own agenda within world and continental social forums.

To further understand the Genoa protest this chapter draws on our own research into events that occurred in the city. From July 16 to July 21, 2001, we administered one thousand questionnaires to demonstrators, made direct contact with the mobilization organizations, and participated in meetings and actions of protest.[1]

First, we proceed to highlight some principal features of the new movement, applying key concepts drawn from mainstream social movement literature (della Porta and Diani 1999; Melucci 1996; Tarrow 1994). Here, the units of analysis are the organizations that networked for the purpose of coordinating the demonstrations in Genoa. Subsequently, we analyze the findings of the questionnaire to draw out some of the main sociological features of the Genoa protest movement—probing to see if interactions among individuals are working to further collective identity and if a form of solidarity and mutual trust is emerging.

## Key Features of the Genoa Protest

To form a better understanding of the movement against neoliberal globalization, this section focuses on a meso-level analysis that takes into account the most important anti-G8 networks in Genoa during the July 2001 G8 summit. The intent is to describe their interpretative frames, forms of action, organizational structures, and relationships with the GSF—the main network that organized the Genoa protest. Particular consideration is given to Rete Lilliput, ATTAC, White Overalls (*Tute Bianche*), and the Network for Global Rights (NGR)—all of which were coordinated under the broad umbrella of the GSF. In addition, attention is given to the Black Bloc, an organization—if it is possible to call it one—that, without belonging to the GSF, was undoubtedly one of the main protagonists of the Genoa "battle."

### Interpretative Frames of GSF's Network

According to Snow and Benford, a frame is "an interpretative schemata that simplifies and condenses the 'world out there' by selectively punctuating and encoding objects, situations, events, experiences, and sequences of actions within one's present or past environments" (Snow and Benford 1992, 137). Framing is essential for social movement formation and mobilization (Snow and Benford 1988), and this is especially true for very heterogeneous movements, such as those analyzed here.

The introduction of the GSF framing document states:

> The world in which we are preparing the G8 summit in Genoa is one full of deep injustices. 20% of the world population—in countries with advanced capitalism—wastes 83% of the resources of our planet; 11 million children die every year of malnutrition; and 1.3 billions live on less than one dollar per day. This situation does not improve: it is worsening continuously. (GSF 2002, 39)

The GSF position, short and vague in nature, created the space to allow hundreds of different organizations to join the network. A key part of the document is that relating to the rules of work agreement. All signatory organizations were required to commit themselves to conscientize people; to ask institutions to respect the right to demonstrate; to coordinate their actions; and to respect all pacifist and nonviolent forms of action.

The GSF was organized as a network of networks with a very flexible structure aiming to synthesize the huge variety of networks, organizations, and groups mobilized against the G8 summit. As shown in Figure 4–1, the GSF was not the only actor in the Genoa protest. On the one hand, Catholic groups, and on the other, more radical groups (Black Bloc, Anarchists Against G8,[2] and Anti-imperialist Coordination), took part in the protest without coordinating their actions with the GSF.

FIGURE 4-1. KEY GENOA PROTEST GROUPS

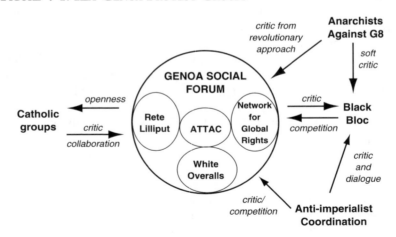

At the heart of Figure 4–1 is the French-initiated association ATTAC. ATTAC was created in 1998 to impose democratic control on institutions that lead the world system. Today, it relies on more than thirty thousand adherents and hundreds of local groups (Ancelovici 2002). The principles on which it was constituted were published in an Ignacio Ramonet editorial under the title "Disarming the Markets" (*Le Monde Diplomatique*, December 1997). The author proposed the constitution of "a new worldwide nongovernmental organization, called Association for a Tobin Tax to Assist the Citizen (ATTAC)," with the objective of modifying the existing economic system through some technical reforms, such as the Tobin Tax—a tax on monetary transactions, first proposed in 1972 by Nobel laureate James Tobin. This proposal has become one of the most widely known and shared goals of the global justice movement.

ATTAC defines itself as an "international movement for democratic control of financial markets and their institutions." It aims to promote concrete alternatives and to build international campaigns. The association declares itself democratic, pluralist, and open—it is composed of a variety of individual and group members. ATTAC's novelty consists in promoting the creation of affiliated organizations around the world (for example, Argentina, Australia, Brazil, Chile, Japan, Morocco, Québec, and Senegal), and in trying to spread the struggle for global justice to countries that to date have been only marginally involved.

Rete Lilliput was begun at the end of 1999 to organize Italian protestors against the World Trade Organization (WTO) in Seattle.[3] It was promoted by some campaigns (Drop the Debt, Campaign to Reform the World Bank, "Stop Millennium Round" campaign) and associations (Fair Trade, WWF-Italy, and Pax Christi), and was joined within a few months by hundreds of groups.

Lilliput's manifesto enunciates its principles, strategies, forms of action, and objectives, the contents of which must be shared by those who decide to join. Lilliput characterizes itself as seeking radical goals through moderate forms of action (Gulliver 2001, 53–59). The manifesto declares a long-term objective of creating a world where all inhabitants "can satisfy their own material, social and spiritual needs"; as a more immediate objective the network sets itself in opposition "to economic choices that inhibit democracy, destroy the environment and condemn billions of people to poverty."

The White Overalls (WOs) and the NGR are very unusual networks consisting primarily of Italian squats (*centri sociali*, self-managed "social centers") that are spread throughout the country. The history of Italian squats begins at the end of the 1970s, inspired by the phenomenon of the German *Gemeinschaften*.[4] After a period of crisis in the 1980s, the following decade brought a new wave of illegal occupations of public and private unused buildings (Marincola 2001, 61–72). Currently, Italian social centers number approximately two hundred and represent a complex phenomenon in terms of cultural references (from anarchist and libertarian to neo-communist and autonomous ideas) and relationships with institutions (particularly local government). Moreover, their objectives and forms of action vary notably (Dines 2000, 107). In the last few years approximately half of the social centers joined the WOs and reached an agreement with either the owner of an occupied building or with institutions of local government. Nevertheless, a significant number of social centers criticized this decision and rejected a legalization and institutionalization process (Berzano and Gallini 2000, 59).

The idea of the WOs was inspired by Subcomandante Marcos and the EZLN (Ejército Zapatista de Liberación Nacional—Zapatista National Liberation Army). The Italian collective of Ya Basta! (a transnational organization in solidarity with the EZLN) was one of the main groups contributing to the creation of the WOs.[5] The WOs compare the cruel conditions suffered by Native Americans with the inhuman situation of the "invisible" and "voiceless" of the European continent. Therefore, the WOs consider themselves to be an army fighting for minority rights. The white overall is symbolic of social transformation; it expresses the transition from a society based on the industrial model of production to one characterized by the leading role of knowledge and communication. The traditional blue overall of Fordist production becomes white in post-Fordist society. Productive activities no longer dwell only within the four walls of the factory but are extending outward to all aspects of life. Therefore, the white overall symbolizes a new productive subject whose work is decreasingly manual and increasingly intellectual, affective, and communicative.

The NGR emerged in March 2001 with the Naples' mobilization against the United Nations summit on the digital divide. Its specific purpose consists of linking the battles of the anti-neoliberal globalization movement with local conflicts. The NGR emphasizes three main aspects of this struggle: employment (for guaranteed salary and against flexibility); immigration (equal rights and freedom of movement); and the environment (against pollution and genetic manipulation).

The Black Bloc is the radical wing of the social movement that—from Seattle to Genoa—has become the protagonist of a new cycle of protest. The Black Bloc was influenced in its way of dressing and in its forms of action by German *autonomen*, violent leftist autonomous groups that were theoretically inspired by Italian *Autonomia Operaia*. The call to "blockers" in Genoa was made by the International Genoa Offensive (IGO) platform, which stated: "We do not want to be limited by GSF guidelines. The State uses all means available against us; therefore we will use all means available to fight against it. We created the IGO to organize on our own terms."

Accordingly, Black Bloc relationships with other sectors of the movement against neoliberal globalization have not been good and have over time become worse. During the Seattle protest some activists from the nonviolent sector of the movement tried to stop "blockers" engaged in property destruction. This attempt was harshly criticized by the "blockers," who labeled nonviolent activists "peace police."[6]

### Spectacular and Media-Oriented Forms of Action

Forms of actions constitute the political repertoire of a social movement (Tilly 1978), their variation from moderation to violence may depend on both organizational structure and frame of a movement. The global justice movement as a network of different movements comprises different repertoires. Nevertheless, the process of networking includes a negotiation of means as well as a negotiation of goals.

The GSF was able to attract more than eight hundred signatures to the work agreement—an agreement that recognized "all the forms of expression, of demonstration and of direct nonviolent actions declared in a public and transparent form" (GSF 2002, 39). The GSF also issued a press release (June 5, 2001) that stated, "We choose to act in a respectful manner towards the city and towards all people, whether they wear a uniform or not."

Before the G8 summit the GSF tried to establish a dialogue with institutions and to establish rules for the anti-G8 protest. Hence, a meeting between GSF spokespeople and some representatives of the Italian government took place. Nonetheless, this attempt did not succeed in avoiding the repressive and tragic events that transpired.

The organizations that joined the GSF expressed varying forms of action and attitudes regarding the issue of violence, as shown in Figure 4–2.

FIGURE 4-2. GENOA PROTEST NETWORKS' FORMS OF ACTION

| GENOA SOCIAL FORUM (work agreement) | | | | |
|---|---|---|---|---|
| Gandhian nonviolence | Peaceful media-oriented direct actions | Protected civil disobedience | Violence on symbolic targets | Violence on property |
| Rete Lilliput | ATTAC | White Overalls | Network for Global Rights | Black Bloc |

Some organizations inspired by the Gandhian philosophy of nonviolent action refused all defensive and offensive tactics and considered the smashing of a shop window violent. Other organizations decided to adopt only tools of self-defense to protect themselves from police violence and declared publicly that they were not going to bring offensive instruments with them and that they would respect the city and its inhabitants—including the police. Still other groups openly declared the possibility that they would carry and use "stones, batons, helmets and anything useful to avoid a massacre" (*La Repubblica*, June 21, 2001).

The GSF succeeded in reaching an agreement on scheduling the counter-meeting to the G8 summit. It organized a public forum with important guests from all around the world (July 15–22), including an international demonstration with claims for immigrant rights (July 19), the isolation of the red zone (July 20),[7] and a mass demonstration (July 21). The most interesting event was the day of the red-zone isolation: a collective initiative with multiple and diversified actions "including contestation and disobedience, with the verbal and physical encirclement of the zone and disobedience to the denial of access."

Recalling the Prague experience—where the first major European protest against neoliberal globalization took place in September 2000—the GSF organizations decided to promote a clear division of streets and squares according to each network's specific form of action. This was an innovative and intriguing experiment based on a type of mutual respect pact. Nonetheless, the Black Bloc was not considered part of the agreement, a fact that ultimately caused many problems for GSF networks.

ATTAC derives its action repertoire from Greenpeace, choosing to perform symbolic and spectacular media-orientated protests.[8] Over the Genoa days of protest, ATTAC militants wore a specific shirt and distributed stickers with the association's logo and some effective slogans. ATTAC organized a humorous soccer match pitting the Italian ATTAC team against the French one; the match took place in the red zone and was refereed by a policeman. During the red-zone isolation day, ATTAC occupied a square and penetrated the "wall of shame" with music, noise, balloons, banners, eggs, and garlic.[9] Only ATTAC managed to violate the red zone; two people from its square passed the "wall of shame," but they were quickly stopped and arrested by the police. The day after Giuliani's death, ATTAC led the mass march, displaying a sort of "service of order" in directing the demonstration.[10]

If ATTAC's square was primarily joined by leftist parties and trade unions, Lilliput's square contained a wide spectrum of groups, including Catholic and secular associations. ATTAC's and Lilliput's forms of action are not very different. ATTAC has a more pragmatic attitude toward protest, Lilliput a more ethical approach. The most important feature of Lilliput's network is its nonviolent method of action. Lilliput's strategies are derived from the predisposition of the various subjects that compose its network. The manifesto makes clear a concern to promote "people's awareness and to weaken power centers; critical consumption and the boycott to condition enterprises; alternative economy experimentation and more sober life styles in order to show that an economy of justice is possible."

During the G8, Lilliput activists wore shirts displaying the network's logo and the well-known Porto Alegre slogan "Another world is possible." On the day of red-zone isolation, Lilliput occupied a square to perform its symbolic actions. To make evident its nonviolent action, activists painted their hands white and raised them in front of the police; they did so again when the Black Bloc entered their square. This action was quite effective and had satisfactory visibility, even though Lilliput suffered low media coverage during the protests for lack of charismatic leadership.

Lilliput activists make intensive use of the Internet to spread information and to discuss themes of relevant interest through a system of national, regional, and local newsletters and mailing lists. Some weeks before the G8 summit a chat line had been activated to promote discussions in real time among web users. Lilliput promotes online surveys among its activists to ascertain their positions on different issues. Hence, Lilliput uses technology to promote democracy and participation among its supporters.

The WOs represent one of the most visible parts of the global justice movement in Italy that in the last few years has experienced an interesting evolution in its action repertoire. The WOs inhabit the border between violence and nonviolence, as these concepts are not seen to represent an ideological choice to defend in every place and time. Their innovative concept of civil disobedience is of an action form that is protected, collective, and self-organized. Their method of action is like a performance, a simulation of a clash with the police. The WOs believe that the symbolic staving of a police line is intriguing for the mass media and also useful for gaining the support of public opinion by exposing the system's structural violence.

The action consists of taking the head of a demonstration up to the lines of police officers. WOs advance with their bodies covered with protection; they use tire inner-tubes to maintain distance between the police and the head of the march, and helmets and Plexiglas shields disposed like a "tortoise" to protect them from police cudgels. Advancing with hands lifted in a sign of nonaggression, the WOs are prepared to suffer police repression without using offensive violence, only protecting themselves with non-offensive tools. The WOs are very aware of the working of today's information society, and this helps to explain some of their clamorous, unpredictable, and spectacular actions.

Before the G8 summit the WOs promoted public training for their activists (Velena 2001, 133–39) and held an online referendum to decide on the forms of action and the goals of the Genoa protest.[11] Taking into account the results of this referendum, and just after Italian Vice-premier Fini declared that the army would provide order in Genoa during the days of the G8 summit, the Italian WOs' spokesperson, Luca Casarini, declared war on "the world's powerful people." Casarini made clear that WOs do not submit to police repression: "If we have to choose between meeting your troops of occupation and resignation, we don't have any doubts. . . . We are an army destined to disappear, but only after having defeated you."

This declaration caused problems for GSF unity because it seemed to violate the work agreement on forms of action. This was the reason that, some days later, the WOs submitted a new press release declaring "peace toward the city of Genoa and its citizens" and committing themselves not to break any shop windows or make any provocative gestures. Another somewhat astonishing act of the WOs was the decision to remove their white overalls on the day of the red-zone attack. They stated that the civil disobedience model "was so widespread that it could not be considered a WOs' tactic anymore but a tactic belonging to everybody" (*Il Manifesto*, August 8, 2001). That act permitted the formation of a mass demonstration of about ten thousand marchers. All the same, the police charged this march even before it reached the red zone, thus violating the informal nonaggression pact between protestors and police. A large number of people were beaten severely, and this event was the beginning of the violent battle in which Carlo Giuliani was killed (Chiesa 2001, 39–55). After Genoa the WOs decided to dissolve and participated in the formation of The Disobedients (Disobbedienti), a broader network that includes social centers from the south and center of Italy. The Disobedients had earlier been very critical of the WOs.

Before the Genoa protest, radical activists encountered marginalization; they were not allowed to join marches organized by more moderate groups. This separation forced radical protestors to assume responsibility for their own actions and made it more difficult for them to avoid police reaction (Marincola 2001, 63–64). Accordingly, radical protestors decided to unite to strengthen their position through the newly established network combining Cobas (Italian radical unions, independent from parties and official trade unions) and the radical squats, namely, the NGR.[12] This network represents the most hardened sector of the GSF; it encountered problems in accepting the content of the GSF work agreement, and many who reject the WOs' innovative tactics are from this network. They distinguish themselves from the WOs in both their forms of action—they do not accept WOs' clash simulations with police lines— and by advocating the institutionalization of occupied houses (Caruso 1999). Many social centers that joined the NGR consider it effective to use violence in some circumstances, primarily because it guarantees mass media attention for the protest (Berzano and Gallini 2000, 74).

Before the G8 summit the NGR reached an agreement with other networks of the broader movement in order to enhance visibility and to exploit new opportunities. This pact was achieved through guaranties about the moderation of its forms of action. Also prior to the G8 summit, the NGR sought a high media profile by engaging in visible actions in the style of the WOs. For example, during the day of the meeting between representatives of the Italian government and GSF spokespeople, a letter was sent to the interior minister containing a bullet. This followed the shooting of protestors at the EU summit in Gothenburg, Sweden, and the stunt was intended as a dramatic request that the minister not provide live ammunition to the police in Genoa.

The radicalism of the NGR can be partially explained by being rooted in the south of Italy, an area characterized by high rates of unemployment and job insecurity (Dines 2000, 107). As one of the NGR's spokespeople affirmed: "We reject the concept of civil disobedience. For unemployed and precarious workers disobedience can only be uncivil" (*La Repubblica*, June 20, 2001).

In Genoa the Black Bloc did not use forms of action that corresponded directly to those previously used by the "blockers." This time direct action was not limited to the private ownership of banks and multinational enterprises but also included small shops and private cars. Moreover, some members of the Black Bloc even attacked the GSF demonstrations (for example, the NGR march).

Immediately after "bloody" Friday, the day on which Carlo Giuliani was killed by an Italian *carabiniere*, the GSF decided to find a way to protect the following day's peaceful mass demonstration from the violent protestors' tactic of hiding themselves in the GSF march. This attempt, however, was unsuccessful. After performing their direct action, violent demonstrators simply changed their black clothes and joined the GSF march as if they were peaceful protestors.

The future success of the broad movement will depend on the capacity to develop proper means to avoid violent escalation of protest. Here, a major obstacle has certainly been the Black Bloc's continued rejection of agreed-upon forms of action with other sectors of the movement.

### Open, Flexible, and Multicentric Organizational Structures

The impetus of the movement against neoliberal globalization inspired local level coordination among various sectors of the Italian-based movement. Until the G8 summit, this was more or less a spontaneous process, but since Genoa local social forums have come to assume a more stable and formal structure.

Genoa's G8 summit spurred the formation of ATTAC-Italia in June 2001. ATTAC-Italia is structured around fifty-seven local committees.

The statutes of the Italian association allow for enrollment of individual and collective members but excludes parties and other organized political movements. Payment of an annual subscription quota is obligatory. Compared to the other networks of protest, ATTAC's organizational structure is more formalized. In fact, ATTAC is the only one—of all the networks we analyzed—that has a rigid set of rules and a formal membership. It is remarkable that an association such as ATTAC—which has adopted an organizational structure closer to that of traditional political parties than to social movement organizations—has succeeded in gaining mass support. ATTAC's success suggests that the crisis of parties is not due mainly to their methods of organization but to their forms of action (conventional and institutionalized), the way they select relevant issues to build their agenda, and the relationship they adopt toward their constituencies.

Lilliput, consistent with its non-hierarchical and participative approach, structures itself in local "knots" that comprise groups, associations, and individuals. Therefore, the national network characterizes itself as a network of local knots. The Lilliput knots express great heterogeneity; they follow a consensual form of decision-making typical of direct democracy, which gives more value to participation than efficacy. Every local knot has its particular concerns and focuses on different issues while granting support to actions and campaigns promoted by the national network.

Currently the directive organ of the Lilliput is formed by two components: (1) it is based on the Tavolo Intercampagne, a group of different associations that has been criticized for being rather exclusive and resistant to change, but (2) it also recognizes the role of local knots that are represented in the decision-making of the organization by some spokespersons. At present, seventy-five local knots exist in Italy. In terms of geographical spread the Lilliput network is strongest in northern regions (thirty-seven knots), well rooted in central ones (twenty-eight knots), and less well represented in the south (ten knots).

Neither the WOs nor the NGR have any real organizational structure to compare to that of ATTAC (more formal) or Lilliput (more informal). The WOs and the NGR are formed by some squats that agree to coordinate their activities in a very loose way.

The lack of a clear organizational structure makes the Black Bloc volatile and hard to define. No recognizable organization exists, and the Black Bloc affirms that "there is no standing Black Bloc organization between protests. . . . The BB is a tactic, similar to civil disobedience." Hence, there is no stable organization, and there are no leaders. It is a weakly coordinated network linking small affinity groups of trusted people (from five to fifteen) in clusters. A cluster requires general agreement on tactics and styles of protest. The affinity group is the organizational model chosen by the Black Bloc's anarchists because it allows them to perform autonomous actions while granting safety and security at the same time (VV. AA. 2000).

## Researching the New Movement

To research the new movement we administered a structured questionnaire (with one open question) to activists over the period from July 16 to July 20. The questionnaire attempted to represent the different components of the movement by covering the areas where individuals and networks organized the protest, the major meeting points, and the places where people stayed in accordance with their membership in, or support for, each group in the main network. We collected 763 completed questionnaires out of the one thousand distributed.

To assess the representative nature of our survey in terms of the principal organizational networks involved, we compared the returns with overall estimates of participation for each main component (see, e.g., *Limes* 2001). Among those who claimed to currently belong to one organization (45 percent), 32 percent belonged to Lilliput, while the overall estimate was put at the same percentage (out of eighty thousand people). Those who belonged to one of the organizations with traditional ties to the workers' movement constituted 58 percent (as against an overall estimate of 62 percent), and 10 percent belonged to one of the radical social centers (as against 6 percent). Thus, even though it was not possible to work with a statistically representative sample, our findings are fairly well balanced. The research reveals important findings with respect to activists' social location, formal organizations and informal ties, and collective identity formation.

### Activists' Social Location

Research into new social movements has emphasized either the cross-class feature of contemporary collective action or the fact that collective action is no longer organized around the working class but around a new middle class that has emerged under the conditions of late capitalism (Offe 1985; Touraine 1977). With respect to the global justice movement a similar heterogeneity emerges but, as Table 4–1 reveals, students are quite significantly the most mobilized social actors in the protest.[13] Generally students acquire cognitive tools for criticizing society and are socialized in a context where public debate is more frequent, and this finding is consistent with recent surveys of Italian students that reveal a newfound interest in social and political issues (Cartocci and Corbetta 2001).

TABLE 4-1. RESPONDENTS' SOCIAL LOCATION

| Social Location | Percentage |
|---|---|
| Students | 49.9 |
| Private-sector and public-sector workers | 12.6 |
| Unemployed, precarious, pensioners | 10.7 |
| Upper classes | 7.1 |
| Intellectual workers | 6.8 |
| Autonomous workers | 2.3 |
| Others | 10.6 |
| TOTAL | 100 (N=746) |

Taking this one step further, in terms of the social location of the parents of the student activists, the findings in Table 4–2 reveal that—as is the case for new social movements—those involved in the Genoa protest were not primarily from the working class, even when broadly defined. In fact, among students, many of those most mobilized were found to have an upper-class family background.

Given that the survey findings also reveal that 19 percent of people are under twenty-one years of age, 50 percent are between twenty-one and twenty-nine, and 31 percent are older than twenty-nine (mean age in the first category is 18.7, in the second 24.7, and in the third 41.0),

TABLE 4-2. PARENTS' SOCIAL LOCATION

| Social Location | Percentage |
|---|---|
| Private-sector and public-sector workers | 31.5 |
| Upper classes | 25.3 |
| Intellectual workers | 14.3 |
| Unemployed, precarious, pensioners | 12.7 |
| Autonomous workers | 11.6 |
| Others | 4.6 |
| TOTAL | 100 (N=371) |

generation emerges as an important factor. The new movement represents, at its core, a new phase of youth protest in the public sphere.

## Formal Organizations and Informal Networks

Social movements are generally defined in terms of "informal networks, based on shared beliefs and solidarity" (della Porta and Diani 1999, 16).[14] The movement against neoliberal globalization, however, is more a network of networks. Networks involve both formal organizations and informal personal ties.

Organizations offer resources in order to get people involved in collective action, such as information and social spaces for participation. This is confirmed by the fact that 26 percent of respondents came to an awareness of the movement through a formal organization, and 36 percent became informed about the Genoa protest in this way. Respondents also stressed the importance of informal networks, with 23 percent encountering the new movement through friends and colleagues, and 15 percent getting to know of the Genoa protest though such contacts. It is clear that organizations as well as informal networks are important in the mobilization process, and it is by combining these two channels of socialization and communication that the potential for new forms of collective action becomes greater.

Moreover, within the new movement it is not necessary that individuals be exclusively linked to a single organization in order to explain their activism. Overlapping membership facilitates political participation. As far as the Genoa protest is concerned, only 16 percent of activists declared themselves to have *ever* just belonged to only one organization; 50 percent have belonged to two to four organizations; and 19 percent to more than four organizations (15 percent of respondents did not answer this question). Overlapping membership, then, is a main feature of this movement and can be considered to be a form of social capital (Bourdieu 1986; Putnam 1993). When individuals belong to more than one organization horizontal socialization is likely to result; that is, individuals' values and opinions (including protest attitudes) are influenced by different types of collective experiences, which, in turn, provide informal resources (contacts and so on) for consolidating joint action.

## Collective Identity Formation

As a network of formal organizations and informal ties, the movement finds its strength in combining different political traditions, varying forms of action, and diverse resources. To what extent and in what ways, though, does this work to build a shared identity, or at least a degree of mutual trust? To address this question we chose to ask activists what they thought about the movement, how much they identified themselves with the movement's organizational networks, and how much they trusted them.

According to activists the movement is primarily considered a "set of organizations that share some common goals" (75 percent). Only 11 percent consider the movement to be "a set of different organizations with different goals." At the same time, however, only 14 percent consider the movement to be a "movement with homogeneous goals." What can be drawn from this data? The movement is not considered homogeneous, but neither is it seen as overly fragmented. It would appear that we are in a nascent phase of movement building, with individuals and groups endeavoring to form a broader collective identity; as such, the movement itself is a space of creative and competitive contestation.

Collective identity is defined as a process through which individuals and groups interact, to negotiate a "cognitive definition" concerning goals, means, and the external environment. It implies a certain degree of "emotional investment"—feeling oneself to be part of a "we"—in a "system of active relationships" (forms of organization, communication channels, leadership models, and so forth) (Melucci 1996). If activists think that the movement is still in a nascent phase, the possibility for collective identity-building success greatly depends on the efforts each one makes—on the level of "emotional investment" involved. From this point of view, as indicated in Table 4–3, more than three-quarters of the Genoa activists surveyed claimed that they identified "enough" or "much" with the movement as a whole, certainly more than with any single network.

Each network—with the exception of Anarchists Against G8—receives a lot of trust, Lilliput above all. The fact that all those networks involved in the GSF received more trust than those that shunned it (for example, anarchists) shows that a process of boundary building is at work.

As mentioned, the overlapping membership of movement activists represents a form of social capital; belonging to multiple organizations may facilitate trust and the building of a shared identity and solidarity. In order to test this, we crossed the degree of overlapping membership of each activist with the mean sum of the scores each individual gave according to his or her degree of trust for each network. We did this first for those networks cited in Table 4–3 belonging to the GSF only (namely, Lilliput, WOs, and NGR), and then for all networks mentioned (adding Anarchists Against G8).[15] The results, shown in Table 4–4, indicate that there is a positive correlation between the level of trust and the number of overlapping memberships. This is the case for both GSF networks and all networks.

Beyond the question of internal trust we can also consider the import of external generalized trust. As Sidney Tarrow has stated, protest may bring "activists further into the realms of tolerated and prescribed poli-

TABLE 4-3. IDENTIFICATION WITH AND TRUST IN THE MOVEMENT
AND MOVEMENT NETWORKS

| | "Enough" or "Much" (%) | Mean* | Standard deviation | "Missing" & "Don't know" |
|---|---|---|---|---|
| Identification with the movement as a whole | 75.3 | 2.10 | 0.70 | 40 |
| Identification with a specific network of the movement | 64.7 | 1.88 | 0.88 | 117 |
| Trust in Rete Lilliput | 68.8 | 2.05 | 0.90 | 124 |
| Trust in White Overalls | 47.6 | 1.49 | 0.91 | 120 |
| Trust in NGR | 47.7 | 1.74 | 0.87 | 263 |
| Trust in Anarchists Against G8 | 23.7 | 1.01 | 0.93 | 188 |

* The mean was calculated by assigning the following scores to the answers: "not at all" = 0; "little" = 1; "enough" = 2; "much" = 3.

tics and make possible relations of *working trust* with public officials" (Tarrow 2000, 289, emphasis added). It may be added that the more people participate in different sectors of collective action the more likely they are to be involved in this "working trust." As Table 4–5 shows, however, we find no evidence of a clear relationship between internal and external trust.

All else considered, institutional actors receive very little trust—and this is not affected by the degree of overlapping membership. There is

TABLE 4-4. MEAN SCORES FOR LEVEL OF TRUST PER DEGREE
OF OVERLAPPING MEMBERSHIP

| Overlapping Membership | Trust in GSF Networks | Trust in All Networks |
|---|---|---|
| Only 1 | 3.83 | 6.38 |
| From 2 to 4 | 4.02 | 6.71 |
| More than 4 | 4.45 | 6.99 |

only a slight positive correlation between trust in Parliament and over-lapping membership, and a slight negative correlation with respect to trust in the United Nations and the police. What does emerge is that national institutions, such as Parliament, are generally less trusted than global ones, despite the lack of democratic accountability of the latter. This is a finding confirmed by the data we received on the readiness of each individual to negotiate with different institutions. While 50 per-cent of demonstrators would be willing to negotiate with the EU and 48 percent with UN organizations, only 35 percent were in favor of negoti-ating with national government. The findings in Table 4–5 show clearly that what this movement requires is a more democratic global order.

TABLE 4-5. MEAN SCORES FOR LEVEL OF TRUST IN DIFFERENT
ACTORS PER DEGREE OF OVERLAPPING MEMBERSHIP

| Overlapping Membership | Trust in . . . | | | | |
| --- | --- | --- | --- | --- | --- |
| | Local Institutions | European Union | United Nations | Parliament | Police |
| Only 1 | 1.35 | 1.07 | 1.04 | 0.86 | 0.45 |
| From 2 to 4 | 1.26 | 0.96 | 0.98 | 0.92 | 0.41 |
| More than 4 | 1.32 | 0.99 | 0.96 | 0.97 | 0.34 |

## Conclusion

In this chapter—through stretching the existing frontiers of social move-ment theorizing—we have traced the key sociological features of activ-ists and organizations involved in the Genoa protest of July 19–21, 2001. What has emerged as a main characteristic of the new movement is its heterogeneity, and such pluralism has not, due to the creation of a com-mon interpretative scheme, represented an obstacle to unitary action. Our survey findings confirm that the social dynamics of the movement foster a new solidarity. Central to this is the role of the network. Every-thing from different forms of organizations to frameworks, from indi-viduals to experts, are located in networks, and these networks them-selves are located in a larger network, illustrating the congruence of this new movement with the globalized "network society." Far from being only a contingent coalitional tool, the network is also capable of foster-ing an open and flexible collective identity, one whose stability and strength is witnessed by subsequent events, such as the European Social

Forum and worldwide antiwar mobilization on February 15, 2003, against US military intervention in Iraq.

At a time when all the traditional indicators of political participation—such as electoral behavior, party membership, and public discussion—seem to indicate a mass exit of people from the public sphere, the recent rise of new forms of social activism, as evidenced in the Genoa protest, represents the emergence of a new global mass politics.

## Notes

[1] We distributed the questionnaires to people in selected places in Genoa: the three main points where people gathered and were accommodated on the basis of their political affinity (Carlini Stadium, Sciorba Stadium, and GSF center), and the key meeting spots where assemblies and seminars took place.

[2] An official coordination of anarchist groups based on the Federazione Anarchica Italiana (Italian Anarchist Federation). This network criticized both the media-oriented actions of GSF networks and the violent actions of the Black Bloc.

[3] The name of the network is derived from the well-known novel *Gulliver's Travels*, written by Jonathan Swift and first published in 1726. It was chosen "to describe the type of strategies necessary to capture globalization's giants in the net" (Meloni 2000, 69).

[4] Communities managed by young people (mainly students and unemployed) that leave their families and occupy unused buildings because they cannot afford to pay rent.

[5] The Italian section of Ya Basta! was founded mainly by Italian activists of social centers who attended the first Intercontinental Encounter for Humanity and Against Neoliberalism in Chiapas in 1996.

[6] As reported in the "N30 black bloc communiqué," written by the ACME Collective.

[7] The red zone was the name given by the media to the historical center of Genoa where the G8 summit took place. The Italian interior minister prohibited demonstrators from entering this area.

[8] As, for example, the winter swim of some activists to symbolically save the European Charter of Fundamental Rights in December 2000, during the European Union (EU) summit in Nice, France.

[9] In order to secure the red zone, the Italian government decided to build a wall of iron gratings and to defend it with police. It was named the "wall of shame" by demonstrators because it symbolized the exclusion of civil society from places where powerful people made decisions affecting the whole globe.

[10] Italian political parties and unions often use a "service of order" to avoid infiltration by external groups interested in a violent escalation of the conflict and to limit police repression.

[11] The online referendum, written in four different languages, attracted a large response. However, it was not technically valid, as it was possible to vote more than once.

[12] Some of the groups that joined NGR were part of the "blue block" in Prague, the protest march that fought Czech police using stones, Molotov cocktails, and batons (VV. AA. 2000).

[13] This compares to the 1965–74 protest cycle in Italy, in which students were involved in 38.6 percent of 4,980 protest events (Tarrow 1990, 71).

[14] The importance of informal relationships to political participation in nonconventional groups has been made apparent in student movements (McAdam 1988), environmental movements (Diani 1995), and violent political groups (della Porta 1990).

[15] Degree of trust is calculated on a Likert scale with scores from 0 = not at all, to 3 = much. If, for example, an individual gave "much" for Lilliput, "little" for WOs, and "enough" for both Anarchists Against G8 and NGR, his or her score would be calculated as $(3+1+2+2) = 8$. The score can vary from 0 to 9 if we do not include trust in Anarchists Against G8, and from 0 to 12 if we do.

## References

Ancelovici, Marcos. 2002. Organizing against globalization: The case of ATTAC in France. *Politics and Society* 30, no. 3: 427–63.

Berzano, Luigi, and Renzo Gallini. 2000. Centri sociali autogestiti a Torino. *Quaderni di Sociologia* 22: 50–80.

Bourdieu, Pierre. 1986. The forms of capital. In *Handbook of Theory and Research for the Sociology of Education*, ed. John G. Richardson, 241–58. New York: Greenwood Press.

Cartocci, Roberto, and Piergiorgio Corbetta. 2001. Ventenni contro. *Il Mulino* 5: 861–70.

Caruso, Francesco. 1999. *Le nuove forme dell'antagonismo sociale*. Thesis. Naples: Oriental Institute, University of Naples.

Chiesa, Giulietto. 2001. *G8/Genoa*. Turin: Einaudi.

Della Porta, Donatella. 1990. *Il terrorismo di sinistra*. Bologna: Il Mulino.

Della Porta, Donatella, and Herbert Reiter. 2001. Protesta noglobal e ordine pubblico. *Il Mulino* 5: 871–82.

Della Porta, Donatella, and Mario Diani. 1999. *Social Movements: An Introduction*. Oxford: Blackwell.

Diani, Mario. 1995. *Green Networks: A Structural Analysis of the Italian Environmental Movement*. Edinburgh: Edinburgh University Press.

Dines, Nicholas. 2000. Centri sociali: Occupazioni autogestite a Napoli negli anni novanta. *Quaderni di Sociologia* 21: 90–111.

GSF (Genoa Social Forum). 2002. *Genova: Il libro bianco*. Milan: Nuova Iniziativa Editoriale.

Gulliver. 2001. Il mondo alternativo dei lillipuziani. *Limes* 3: 53–59.

*Limes*. 2001. I popoli di Seattle. No. 3 (special issue).

Marincola, Elisa. 2001. La galassia dei centri sociali. *Limes* 3: 61–72.

McAdam, Doug. 1988. *Freedom Summer*. Oxford: Oxford University Press.

McAdam, Doug, John D. McCarthy, and Mayer N. Zald, eds. 1996. *Comparative Perspectives on Social Movements, Political Opportunities, Mobilizing Structures, and Cultural Framing*. Cambridge: Cambridge University Press.

Meloni, Maurizio. 2000. *La battaglia di Seattle*. Naples: Editrice Berti.

Melucci, Alberto. 1996. *Challenging Codes*. New York: Cambridge University Press.

Offe, Claus. 1985. New social movements: Changing boundaries of the political. *Social Research* 52: 817–68.

Putnam, Robert D. 1993. *Making Democracy Work: Civic Tradition in Modern Italy*. Princeton, N.J.: Princeton University Press.

Shaw, Martin. 1994. Civil society and global politics: Beyond a social movement approach. *Millennium* 23, no. 3: 647–67.

Snow, David A., and Robert D. Benford. 1988. Ideology, frame resonance, and participant mobilization. In *From Structure to Action: Comparing Social Movement Research Across Cultures*, ed. Bert Klandermans, Hanspeter Kriesi, and Sidney Tarrow, 197–218. Greenwich, Conn.: JAI Press.

———. 1992. Master frames and cycles of protest. In *Frontiers in Social Movement Theory*, ed. Aldon D. Morris and Carol McClung Mueller, 133–55. New Haven, Conn.: Yale University Press.

Tarrow, Sidney. 1990. *Democrazia e disordine*. Rome: Laterza.

———. 1994. *Power in Movement: Social Movements and Contentious Politics*, Cambridge: Cambridge University Press.

———. 2000. Mad cows and social activists: Contentious politics in the trilateral democracies. In *Disaffected Democracies: What's Troubling the Trilateral Countries?* ed. Susan J. Pharr and Robert D. Putnam, 270–90. Princeton, N.J.: Princeton University Press.

Tilly, Charles. 1978. *From Mobilization to Revolution*. Reading, Mass.: Addison-Wesley.

Touraine, Alain. 1977. *The Self-Production of Society*. Chicago: University of Chicago Press.

Velena, Helena. 2001. *Il popolo di Seattle*. Rome: Malatempora.

VV. AA. (various authors). 2000. *S 26—Praga 26 settembre 2000*. Turin: Velleità Alternative—CSOA Askatasuna.

# 5.
# Grassroots Movements as Transnational Actors: Implications for Global Civil Society

## Srilatha Batliwala

The rise in number of internationally orientated civil society actors over the past two decades has been exponential. An entirely new range of social movements, networks, and organizations has emerged at the transnational level, often collectively—and somewhat inaccurately—described as global civil society (GCS), in what has clearly developed as a sort of global civic space. This phenomenon is a cause-effect spiral generated by several forces in recent history, generally described collectively as globalization.

## The Rise of Global Civil Society

The unregulated practices of transnational corporations in particular, and of global capital in general, provided the earliest catalysts for civil society groups to join hands across national borders to demand accountability.[1] By the late 1970s global networks focusing on the environment, human rights, and gender equality had emerged, recognizing the universality of these issues and the need for unified international policy mechanisms. Worldwide, there was growing acknowledgment that governments could not achieve development goals without the participation of civil society. The United Nations (UN) Conference Decade of the 1990s accelerated the global associational revolution by affirming the right of nongovernmental actors to participate in shaping national and global policies on the environment, population, human rights, economic development, and women.[2] On their part, civil society actors had also discovered the power of international support, resources, and intervention in strengthening local work or fighting local repression.

The increasing integration of the world's economies into a vast global market has provided further fuel for the growth of global civil society. A whole range of old and new economic and financial institutions and mechanisms, operating across borders and regions, is increasingly shaping the development policies and priorities of individual nations. At no time in world history has the local been more influenced by the global. At the vanguard of the economic and financial globalization process is a set of institutions that have growing influence on the economic health, development agenda, and policies of individual nations—especially poor nations. They include the World Trade Organization (WTO), the International Monetary Fund (IMF), the World Bank and regional development banks, and regional trade organizations (NAFTA—the North American Free Trade Agreement, the European Union—EU, and the Association of Southeast Asian Nations). The global economic arrangements ushered in or supported by these institutions are highly complex, generally opaque, and have largely eclipsed—if not replaced—the power of the UN system. They have formed a virtual quasi-state at the global level because they are reshaping national policies and pushing forward legislative and fiscal reforms that will serve global market interests (such as lowering trade barriers, loosening labor laws, and adhering to new copyright laws).

These institutions, however, have no democratic base or direct accountability to citizens. Their awesome and largely unchecked power has provided a powerful catalyst for the formation of transnational citizen activism. Consequently, a number of associations have formed at the global level specifically to engage and advocate with institutions like the World Bank, to protest the power and lack of accountability of arrangements like the WTO, and to monitor the social impacts of debt and debt servicing, and of new trade and investment agreements, particularly on poor nations.

Moreover, the unprecedented possibilities unleashed by new information and communication technologies have further accelerated the globalization of civil society. Individuals and organizations can exchange information, network, forge transnational alliances, and respond to new challenges and developments with unprecedented speed and ease. This has helped both to create and to expand access to an autonomous global civic space—a space that even the most authoritarian states and regimes, hostile to civil society, cannot control.

## Transnational Grassroots Movements

With the emergence of transnational movements and campaigns, there has been both a broadening and a deepening of citizen formations. Individuals, groups, organizations, networks, and federations, with vastly different attributes, structures, and ways of functioning, can be found within each of these movements at different locations—from the local to the global. The focus of activity is also highly diverse: from lobbying and advocacy-specialist groups, to research and documentation centers, to direct mobilization and organization of populations most directly affected by a given issue. Regardless of activity focus, however, there are very few movements or citizen networks that do not recognize the necessity—some might say urgency—of organizing across borders and dealing with the range of international institutions that are increasingly influencing their local realities.

Although it is very comforting to view this panorama—what Ann Florini describes somewhat unflatteringly as "a loose agglomeration of unelected activists" (Florini 2000, 3)—through the rosy lens of "social movement," the fact is that these different actors enjoy varying levels of power and privilege in shaping the debate, speaking for the affected, and gaining entry into the policymaking arena. This is why a distinction must be made between those who are negotiating the adverse impacts of economic changes in their own homes, communities, and lives—who can be termed *direct stakeholders*—with those who are less directly affected, no matter how committed to the plight of others. This is important not for moral but analytical reasons, especially in the context of social movements. Also important is the distinction between movements that adopt obscurantist ideologies and strategies of violence and those that are committed to progressive and peaceful agendas, even if equally militant. As Arjun Appadurai says:

> Among the many varieties of grassroots political movements, at least one broad distinction can be made. On the one hand are groups that have opted for armed, militarized solutions to their problems of inclusion, recognition and participation. On the other are those that have opted for a politics of partnership—partnership, that is, between traditionally opposed groups, such as states, corporations and workers. (Appadurai 2002, 22)

As the most important "popular" force pushing for greater democratization and accountability of global governance and financial institutions, it is vital that "good" global civil society—that is, the segment committed to peace, equity, democracy, and tolerance—reflect on its own level of democracy and representativeness. It is in this context that transnational grassroots movements manifest an important force for democratizing global society's structure, agendas, and strategies. And it is in this regard that four propositions can be advanced to establish the rationale for this concern and the implications of transnational grassroots movements for discussions about GCS.

**Proposition 1.** *In a globalized world, the understanding of who and what is* grassroots *has changed; hence, the characterization of* grassroots *movements is also changing.*

The concept of *grassroots* was once very specific: it meant the basic building blocks of society—small rural communities or urban neighborhoods where the "common man" (or woman) lived. In some contexts it was used to signify the poor, labor, or working class as opposed to dominant social elites; in others, it was applied to rural, village-level communities rather than to urban ones. But today, globalization and the emergence of a global citizen have changed the way in which the term *grassroots* is used. Consequently, the meaning of *grassroots movements* is also undergoing a sea change. Recent articles by Kenny Bruno (2002) and Joshua Karliner (2002), for example, about both the protests at the World Economic Forum in New York City and the deliberations at the World Social Forum in Porto Alegre, are clubbed under the heading "grassroots globalization." Both authors make it clear that they consider these very separate activities, attended by very few of the really poor or marginalized, as expressions of grassroots voices. So it would appear that in a national or local context *grassroots* means one thing, and in the context of global activism quite another. This creates conceptual and analytical problems in our attempts to understand grassroots movements at the transnational level, and we must move toward greater clarity about whom we want to include in the grassroots category. Thus, *grassroots* and *non-grassroots* should be differentiated in terms of the *degree of vulnerability* to global policy and economic shifts. In other words, *grassroots* can be a relative rather than static term but should always refer to those who are most severely affected in terms of the material condition of their daily lives.

**Proposition 2.** *This broadening of the term* grassroots *and* grassroots *movements disguises the very real differences in power, resources, visibility, access, structure, ideology, and strategies between movements of directly affected peoples and those of their champions, spokespeople, or advocates. These imbalances have a direct bearing on who can effectively access advocacy opportunities or participation spaces for civil society at the international public policy level.*

GCS is a microcosm, in many ways, of the imbalances of power, resources, and access that characterize the world at large. Northern groups and networks—even if they have Southern organizations in their membership—occupy much of the space for citizen input at the multilateral institution level and "elite" NGOs at the national level. As Michael Edwards puts it:

> NGOs and citizen networks . . . feel they have the *right* to participate in global decision-making, yet much less attention has been paid to their *obligations* in pursuing this role responsibly, or to concrete ways in which these rights might be expressed in the emerging structures of global governance. (Edwards 2001, 146)

Elsewhere, Edwards writes that "only 251 of the 1,550 NGOs associated with the UN Department of Public Information come from the South, and the ratio of NGOs in consultative status with ECOSOC [United Nations Economic and Social Council] is even lower" (Edwards 2000, 18). Global NGOs and civil society networks, while representing the issues and concerns of poor or marginalized people in global-policy realms, often have few formal or structured links with direct-stakeholder constituencies. Their "take" on issues and strategic priorities is rarely subject to debate within the communities whose concerns they represent. When interrogated closely, one finds that their priorities and positions are not necessarily derived through any convincing process of grassroots debate and legitimization.

For instance, several grassroots women's groups (identities withheld at their request) who recently attended a Commission on the Status of Women meeting in New York were exasperated when an international coalition of NGOs kept deleting the term *women* from their draft, substituting *gender*, without bothering to determine whether the women's groups had consciously chosen to use the former term. It was simply assumed that they were using outdated language. Similarly, during the mass protests during the meeting of the WTO in Seattle in November-December 1999, the NGOs that were "regulating" spaces for public meetings declined to allot the space requested by members of GROOTS (Grassroots Organizations Operating Together in Sisterhood). The reason was apparently their less than hard-line stand—these poor third-world women were demanding equal access to global markets. These are obviously extreme examples. Most transnational NGOs are subtler than this and far too savvy to practice such outrageous discrimination against grassroots groups. The point is that the growing sophistication and complexity of global policy debates—especially regarding economic policy and financial flows—create their own pressures and assumptions of expertise among those who frequent these arenas. Again, the speed at which some of these processes occur often requires rapid-fire interventions that may not allow for extensive debate among affected constituencies.

The case is quite similar at the national level. Advocacy spaces for influencing public policy are often occupied by more elite NGOs that may or may not have direct links with or accountability to the constituencies affected by such policy—and often have distinctly different perceptions of the nature of the problem. Several Indian scholars have analyzed, for instance, the differences in priorities between direct stakeholders, conservationists, political parties, and other environmental activists in recent environmental struggles (Baviskar 2001, 3–6; Guha 2000). Government authorities often collude and reinforce the exclusion of direct stakeholders by inviting the elite NGOs into policymaking processes rather than the loud, militant, and difficult to control grassroots groups who do not speak the same bureaucratic language that elite social advocates have learned. In older civil societies, or countries with longer histories of organizing and more democratic space for citizen participation in policy formation, however, larger numbers of grassroots or community-based organizations have gained direct access to policy processes.

On the other hand, grassroots constituencies and their formations often feel used by their NGO kin in many ways. Links with them—often extremely perfunctory—are used to establish legitimacy and credibility for NGOs claiming to speak for the masses. Issues are often taken out of the hands of the grassroots stakeholders, who might have been the first to mobilize around them, sometimes with negative results for their communities. The example comes to mind of a lawyer's collective that took the state government to court over the eviction of pavement dwellers in Mumbai in India. After promising that they would fight for alternative settlements for them, the lawyers disappeared for several years as the case wound its way through the courts and failed to offer an explanation to people when they lost the case and the municipal authorities began mass demolitions. The pavements dwellers felt betrayed—this high-profile, precedent-setting case had actually impaired their ability to negotiate with local authorities (Batliwala 1987).

**Proposition 3.** *There is a need to advance and sharpen theory and analysis of social movements. We need to rebuild our definitions and theories of social movements to address not only transnational movements but cross-border grassroots movements.*

The term *movement* has become so *au courant* and loosely used in current discourse as to be almost devoid of meaning. So, before we can address the question of grassroots movements and their role in public policy, we need to revisit our definition of *movement* and be clear about what is and what is not a movement. It is somewhat troubling how many different phenomena are described as movements: agglomerations of organizations working on a particular issue (women's empowerment, child labor, peace and security, land rights, and so forth); single organizations mobilizing people around a single issue (preventing the construction of a large dam or nuclear power station, demand for political autonomy or statehood, abolition of bonded labor, and so on); and federations or networks of organizations with different aims but affiliated in pursuit of some generic or sectoral interests (such as nonprofit umbrella organizations, businesses, trade associations).

Classic social movement theory seems almost irrelevant juxtaposed with the current array of transnational claimants to the movement title. Sanjeev Khagram, James Riker, and Kathryn Sikkink, quoting Doug McAdam, refer to the "myopically domestic" focus of movement theorists and call for greater attention to the emergence of transnational movements, particularly through more interdisciplinary work—such as between social movement and international-relations theory (Khagram, Riker, and Sikkink 2002, 5–6). Even McAdam's theory of political process (McAdam 1982), which at least acknowledges both political environment and organizing capacity as essential to movements, does not account for the way in which some movements—such as the ones examined later in this chapter—*create* a political ambiance. The slum-dwellers movement in Mumbai gained strength and became a national movement at a time when the political environment was particularly hostile to the claims of slum dwellers. They helped change government policy toward the resettlement rights of pavement dwellers at a time when the regime in power had an unbroken record of antipathy and subtle violence toward slum dwellers. As Mimi Sheller (2000) argues, "Fluid metaphors operate in relation to social-movements," and there is a need to put the "movement" back into social movement theory—to view and understand movements in more fluid, mobile ways.

There is thus a need to build new frameworks out of the experience of the range of global movements that has emerged in the past twenty years, given the growing phenomenon of grassroots-based movements. The search for fresh theoretical and analytical constructs will have to address several issues: the causal, structural, and strategic distinctions between grassroots movements (such as of the urban poor, home-based workers, poor grassroots women, the Roma) and other types of movements (such as the landmines campaign, anti-globalization); the new forms of homogeneity and heterogeneity that coexist within movements (e.g., geographically and culturally dispersed groups like slum dwellers or indigenous people forming associations and new identities across borders); the differences in organizing and advocacy strategies principles between domestic (Chiapas) and transnational (landmines or freedom from debt) movements; characteristics of short-term (campaigns against nuclear installations) and long-term struggles for change (disarmament, rights of informal sector workers), and between single-issue (reproductive rights) versus more broad-based transformation-type movements (anti-globalization); and the phenomenon of participation in multiple movements, that is, the fluidity and mobility that makes the boundaries between movements more porous than in the past.

**Proposition 4.** *Grassroots movements—movements of, for, and by people most directly affected by the consequences of public policies—are emerging as global movements and forming structures to sustain their movements. They are challenging the rights of non-grassroots organizations to lead and represent them, especially in the public policy arena at both national and international levels.*

For all the reasons cited earlier, there are a growing number of grassroots, direct-stakeholder, as well as ascriptive or identity-based associations that have emerged as global entities—home-based workers, child workers, self-employed women, small and marginal farmers, fish workers, shack or slum dwellers, grassroots women, indigenous people, *Dalits*, and other racially, ethnically, or religiously based associations. More important, many are critically questioning the right and need to have their issues and concerns represented by others. Their analyses, strategies, and tactics often differ radically from those of the usual global actors—some could be far more militant (such as Latin American peasant movements or the Movement to Save the Narmada), and others far more pragmatic and less "ideological" (such as the home-based workers and slum dwellers) than their counterparts would like.

Transnational grassroots movements are struggling with several ironies, including the resistance to resourcing them from funders who have pigeonholed them as local and cannot see a role for them in the global arena, and the struggle to enter global advocacy spaces dominated by more elite representatives who have been speaking for them. Several are tired of being the "little brothers and sisters" of dominant global NGOs, or the "mass-base tokens" used to lend these NGOs credibility.[3] These groups are often impolite and impatient with their NGO colleagues and have raised important questions of legitimacy, right to representation, and other uncomfortable issues (Batliwala 2001). Their capacity to affect public policy at the international level is growing, but not yet fully realized.

These movements are also inventing new kinds of partnerships, institutional arrangements, and relationships with state and private-sector actors to sharpen their engagement with public policy processes at both national and transnational levels.

## Going Global

Although there are many effective transnational grassroots movements, the following two case studies relating to Women in the Informal Economy Globalizing and Organizing (WIEGO) and Slum/Shack Dwellers International (SDI) best illustrate the power and potential of grassroots movements that "go global."

### *WIEGO*

In 1994, unions of home-based workers in both developed and developing countries, led by SEWA (Self Employed Women's Association) in India, joined hands to form HomeNet, the International Network of Home-based Workers. The intention was to provide an international network and voice for these workers, who had not been welcomed by existing national or international trade union federations. Their aims were to build an international network for home-based workers and their organizations, as well as allies from among NGOs, cooperatives, trade unions, researchers, and women's groups who were committed to improving the conditions of such workers; to coordinate an international campaign for the improvement of working conditions for home-based workers at national, regional, and international levels; and to strengthen home-based workers themselves through information and technical assistance.

It soon became apparent, however, that these goals could work against each other. For instance, the task of making home-based workers more "visible" internationally, and of influencing international labor standards, could undermine the "on the ground" strengthening and capacity building goals. More important for the purpose of the analysis here, they realized that research and enumeration, macroeconomic and labor-policy analysis, and international advocacy campaigns would require building and managing relationships with a diverse range of actors, and that this process could overwhelm the network. HomeNet also began to recognize that there were other types of informal-sector work with large numbers of women who needed similar visibility and policy advocacy—street vendors, for example, who are continually vulnerable because of city zoning and vending regulations that work against them.

Thus, WIEGO was formed in 1997 to take on these tasks—to become the international research-and-advocacy platform for women in informal employment. WIEGO strives to improve the status of women in informal employment by compiling better statistics, conducting research, and developing enabling programs and policies. WIEGO's steering committee includes representatives from three different types of organizations: grassroots organizations (HomeNet and SEWA), research or academic institutions (Harvard University, where WIEGO's secretariat is located), and international development organizations (the UN Development Fund for Women). The research-and-advocacy agendas of WIEGO are generated and monitored through annual meetings in which all its different constituents are present, but privileging the priorities and concerns of its grassroots members for whose benefit it exists.

This innovative arrangement—of separating the grassroots organizing entity and the international advocacy entity, but ensuring the latter is accountable to the former—has enabled both HomeNet and WIEGO to have immense impact on the public policy environment in a relatively short space of time. For example, HomeNet and SEWA's successful lobbying led to the adoption by the International Labor Organization (ILO) of a new Convention on Home Work in June 1996. Now WIEGO works closely with allies within ILO to improve and strengthen the basic framework of the convention—such as sharpening definitions of home-based work—and also monitoring; HomeNet and its members campaign at the national level for both ratification of the convention by their governments and implementation and enforcement of the standards and protections within their countries. To support these initiatives in one region—

South Asia—HomeNet and WIEGO organized a regional policy dialogue on home-based workers in which mixed delegations of representatives from government, NGOs, and worker organizations from five South Asian countries participated.

In the case of informal workers, especially women, statistical invisibility has facilitated policy apathy. WIEGO has made great strides in a short number of years in enhancing visibility and thus forcing policymakers to address workers' issues. It has developed a close working relationship with the UN Statistics Division and the ILO Bureau of Statistics in order to help improve the definitions, enumeration, and database on informal workers. It sponsored the preparation of five technical papers for the international Expert Group on Informal Sector Statistics, and it was commissioned to write two papers on informality, poverty, and gender for the World Development Report (2000). To help estimate the size and shape of the informal sector in Africa for the national accounts of African countries, WIEGO works with the Economic Commission for Africa. It has similar working relationships with national statistical institutes across Asia and Latin America. Recently, WIEGO was commissioned by the ILO to prepare a booklet of all existing statistics on the informal economy worldwide. WIEGO's uniqueness lies in having created a single space in which a diverse range of actors with different capacities and interests can work together to improve the situation of informal workers—statisticians, economists, activists and organizers, policy analysts, and academics from different disciplines.

## Slum/Shack Dwellers International

SDI was the outcome of a process of lateral learning and strategic-planning processes undertaken from 1988 to 1996 between organizations of slum and shack dwellers and their partner NGOs in Asia and Africa. These included the NGO SPARC (Society for Promotion of Area Resource Centres), the National Slum Dwellers Federation (NSDF) and Mahila Milan (literally, "women together") in India, and the Asian Coalition for Housing Rights based in Bangkok. The exchanges soon extended to African groups through the South African Homeless Peoples Federation. SDI was founded in 1996 and formally registered in 1999; it comprises federations representing over one million urban poor in eleven countries. The network is interesting because while federations of the urban poor—such as the NSDF of India and the South African Homeless Peoples Federation—are its primary members, it includes a handful of NGO partners, such as SPARC in India and People's Dialogue in South Africa. The NGO members, however, are required to play a supportive rather than a leadership role. For instance, they are typically involved in monitoring and analyzing public policy developments; opening spaces for the urban-poor federations with local, national, and international policy bodies; managing the formidable database generated by the federations through their settlement surveys; and fund-raising. They are not allowed to represent the grassroots federations at any public policy forum unless they have been authorized to do so alongside federation leaders.

Initially the focus of SDI activities was to build and strengthen community-based organizations of the urban poor and their negotiations with local and national authorities to find sustainable, community-driven solutions to their housing and livelihood needs. Their strategies include savings and credit groups to provide consumption loans, build their creditworthiness for future housing loans, and develop the "bridging social capital" to form federations of slum organizations, as well as rigorous, community-managed enumerations of informal settlements and slum populations so that official data could be contested as a basis for resettlement planning. Quite rapidly, however, the locus of advocacy and negotiation had to be expanded to include multilateral institutions. As some of SDI's founders state:

> Choices as to how investments are made in development are increasingly influenced by a wider spectrum of actors than they were decades ago. While decentralization has moved decision-making and resource utilization from the national to the local level, paradoxically, many of the organizations that influence these resource flows are located beyond national institutions in the global development arena. (Patel, Burra, and D'Cruz 2001, 47)

SDI's structure comprises national and regional federations of the urban poor (most of which have more than 50 percent women members and women in their leadership structures), a governing committee of five federation representatives and two representatives of partner NGOs, and a series of networking activities that focus on sharing the strategies and learning of member groups in their local area's efforts to help one another. SDI also uses successful partnerships with state actors such as local bureaucrats and elected officials in one of its areas of operation to leverage similar support or cut through red tape in other countries and cities. Among its great successes in the policy arena is the growing acceptance by government and city authorities across its countries of operation that coercive forms of slum clearance and ignoring the claims of poor urban dwellers in urban infrastructure projects is simply not sustainable. Specifically, SDI has been able to push through formal recognition of the claims of pavement dwellers to government-supported resettlement programs for the first time in India's history, to gain legitimacy for slum census data generated by its member federations as the basis for official resettlement policy rather than government data, to secure acceptance from local and national authorities of low-cost housing and community sanitation block designs developed by its members (as opposed to the more expensive and less appropriate designs developed by the state), and to enable affected communities to select their resettlement sites (from an approved menu of choices) in cases where existing settlements are to be cleared.

At the international level, too, SDI has begun to change policies. The World Bank in India has opened up its tendering system for development of urban sanitation projects to NGOs and community federations, whereas earlier only construction companies with adequate "technical" expertise could bid for these. Through sustained lobbying, SDI convinced the World Bank that social expertise and an organized base within communities counted for more in urban sanitation projects. The United Nations Habitat Program sought out SDI as its partner in launching its Secure Urban Tenure Campaign in 2000. Most recently, SDI was asked to design and convene the Urban Poverty Forum in Nairobi (May 2002), which ran alongside the Urban Forum, an outcome of the Habitat Conferences. Several European bilateral donors have agreed to resource SDI's idea of a venture fund for poor communities to experiment and develop pro-poor, community-led, and controlled infrastructure projects in urban areas.

Interestingly, this very success at the transnational level has created new tensions in the network about the balance between local and global work. Members hold different views on what this balance should be, and the current phase is one of debating this issue and finding a formula that works for all constituents.

## Implications for Global Civil Society

These two cases bring out several critical elements that go to the heart of current debates about GCS—particularly regarding its legitimacy, accountability, and right to have both a voice and a vote in global policy. These elements, which have made these two movements particularly successful in terms of policy impact, are considered in turn.

*They have been created by a mass base of direct stakeholders and enjoy high levels of legitimacy and right to representation.* These are not movements that need to establish their credentials or mass base. As organizations, they did not mobilize a constituency; rather, their constituents created them. When SDI or WIEGO leaders represent their movement in any forum, it is clear to all concerned that hundreds of thousands of their members are standing behind them. This has enormous impact, particularly in their capacity to engage and negotiate with formal institutions.

*They are women-centered and have evolved a genuinely "gendered" approach.* Although WIEGO's founding networks are women driven, they do not exclude men, because obviously men also form a substantial segment of informal workers. Their priority areas for research and action reflect this—the emphasis on social security measures, for instance, rather than on wage issues. SDI's organizing strategies at the community and federation level are focused on building women's savings and credit groups, and women lead both the federations and all negotiations with local, state, national, and international agencies. Mahila Milan is a co-founder of SDI. Consequently, their approaches to informal work and the urban poor are deeply and fundamentally gendered. This is an important feature, given the fact that many of the more visible and articulate transnational advocacy groups are often either blind or weak in their gender analysis (Dhanraj, Batliwala, and Misra 2002).

*They take an empowered stance.* Neither of these movements suffers from the "poor me" syndrome nor positions its constituents as poor, exploited victims, appealing to the world's conscience. These movements do not ask to be heard because they are downtrodden and deserving, or out of some moral obligation on the part of the powerful. They see themselves as populations playing vital roles in both macro- and microeconomic contexts, providing critical services to their cities and to the local, national, and global economies. This is a subtle but important psychological shift for both themselves and the institutions they seek to engage; it is an empowering mind-set, demanding to be taken seriously rather than pleading for a place at the table. It is also dramatically different from how they are often represented by those advocating on their behalf.

*They have made powerful use of research and data to empower their members and challenge public policy.* Generating data to challenge and force a shift in mainstream perceptions of their role and as a basis for awareness building and developing people-centered solutions has been a fundamental strategy of both WIEGO and SDI. Data are used not only to increase visibility but as the basis of both challenge and partnership with state and multilateral actors.[4] They hire or otherwise acquire the necessary research expertise, but the data are owned and controlled by the movement and used strategically by its leaders—not by remote researchers or outside institutions. This challenges the assumption that grassroots actors are incapable of engaging sophisticated, complex policy debates without experts interceding for them in this capacity. And they do not allow access to or manipulation of their data by outside researchers to build their professional profiles or out of academic interest unless these activities bring strong and clear benefits to the movement.

*They have created new forms of partnership between grassroots actors and NGOs, other private and public institutions, scholars and researchers, and state and multilateral agencies.* Again, what distinguishes these relationships is

their fundamentally democratic character. These are partnerships between relative equals—each brings to the engagement a different source
of power, but that power is recognized and acknowledged by the other.
This recognition is forced by their strong organizational—"mass"—base
and their database. There is little subordination, condescension, or pa-
tronage in these engagements.

*These partnerships with high-caliber expertise, combined with a solid
grassroots base, have enhanced their access to and impact on public policy, especially at the international level.* Both SDI and WIEGO are taken very seriously by international policy institutions because of their capacity to
straddle the worlds of global, national, and local policies; to speak the
required language; and to bring to the negotiating table solid data, analysis,
and alternatives. This capacity, in turn, arises from the creative ways in
which they have built partnerships and alliances with other epistemological communities.

*They come to the table with concrete strategies, not with problems. They
demonstrate that sustainable solutions are possible only through partnership with
them.* Both these movements have been extremely creative in the way
they develop solutions and strategies in specific locations and then use
these to push for changes at other locations and levels. For instance, at
national and city levels SDI's members have proved that sustainable solutions to slum rehabilitation are possible only when slum dwellers are
actively involved in designing and implementing the solutions.[5] WIEGO's
member networks have demonstrated viable ways of providing health
and unemployment insurance for informal women workers, thus challenging the neglect of these vital benefits for this group.

*They have changed definitions, debates, and policy dialogues about their con-
stituents.* WIEGO has helped transform the earlier very narrow,
economistic definition of informal employment and gained endorsement
for a broader definition from an international body like ILO. SDI has
changed definitions of the urban poor, altered urban infrastructure construction and tendering norms, and pushed through policies such as joint
housing tenure for men and women that have far-reaching transformative implications.

*They have changed the traditional relationship between researcher and ac-
tivist.* Both WIEGO and SDI demonstrate a radical alteration in the
power equation between practitioners and scholars. They do not lend
themselves as passive subjects of research; they *initiate* research, and they
invite and control engagements with a whole range of experts, fully realizing the importance of research in their long-term struggle. The information and analysis that emerges, as a result, is knowledge generation in
the most powerful sense.

*Size and spread matter.* The World Bank and multilateral agencies
like the ILO take these movements very seriously largely because they

represent serious numbers across a significant number of countries and regions. It is doubtful if they could have had the same access, voice, or negotiating space without these two attributes. This again distinguishes them from a number of the transnational NGO networks.

## Conclusion

Transnational grassroots movements are an emerging force in the global arena. It is clear that some—such as the two examples presented here— have developed equal or even greater capacity (than their more elite coun- terparts) to influence public policy at the international level. There is evidence that more such movements are on the rise. Together, they are breaking the stereotype that grassroots movements are locally or domes- tically focused, or concerned only with building local alliances that strengthen their membership and agenda. These actors are forging links across borders, making common cause with their counterparts regard- less of the cultural and contextual differences that were once thought to be barriers to such associations. They demonstrate the capacity to have visions, agendas, and identities that are transnational and even global in every sense.

More important, they are "different from most other transnational citizen networks [because] the locus of power and authority lies and is kept in the communities themselves rather than in intermediary NGOs at the national and international levels" (Edwards 2001, 145). Thus, while both SDI and WIEGO are undoubtedly strengthened by the presence of such NGOs in the partnership, the priorities and agendas are gener- ated by the grassroots member organizations and their leaders, such as the South African Homeless People's Federation, the NSDF, HomeNet, and StreetNet.

The challenge they represent to other transnational civil society ac- tors is that they enjoy a greater degree of legitimacy in the eyes of policymakers and multilateral institutions because of their grassroots base. As Edwards would have it, they have gained the right to participate in global and local decision-making by having met their obligation to de- rive this right from a concrete base of grassroots constituents (ibid.). This, in turn, is because they contain within their structure and charac- ter the four elements that Edwards identifies as critical: they have legiti- macy and the right to represent their members; their structure is balanced (between North and South, between grassroots and non-grassroots mem- bers, and so on); they have expertise on the issues and demonstrated solu- tions, strategies, and policy alternatives; and they have effective links and balance among their local, national, and global work (Edwards 2001, 146).

Other transnational civil society actors—particularly those involved in global and regional policy advocacy—must consider the implications of these grassroots movements for their own strategies. Given the increasingly strident attacks on the legitimacy of CSOs, especially at the global level, the role of transnational grassroots movements has become critical, and their organizing principles contain many important clues and lessons for other transnational civil society actors. A growing number of grassroots movements have also developed the capacity to represent themselves and influence public policy at all levels, but particularly in international arenas. Those transnational actors who have achieved high degrees of access, visibility, and voice in global arenas need to make links with such movements and make way for them in forums where they could ably represent themselves. In issues and campaigns where such entities are yet to emerge, existing global advocacy groups need to link up more consciously with local movements and develop their positions and agendas in more "bottom up" ways. In fact, it is vital that all CSOs and networks engaged in both local advocacy and global advocacy build strong and accountable relationships with grassroots constituencies—and with grassroots organizations and movements wherever they do exist.

Sundaramma, a grassroots women's leader, told me more than a decade ago that to empower the voices of the poor in policymaking, outside activists must reposition their leadership roles over time: "In the beginning, you may walk in front of us. After a while, as we grow stronger, you must walk beside us. But finally, you must learn to walk behind us."[6] Clearly, there are a growing number of transnational grassroots movements that are already walking in front.

## Notes

[1] For example, the worldwide boycott of Nestlé products to protest that multinational corporation's marketing of infant milk formula to poor rural households (using salespersons dressed as nurses), which resulted in countless infant deaths. This was an effective boycott, in the days of "snail mail," which led to a change of marketing strategy. Also, the Bhopal gas disaster helped unearth evidence of the unethical practices of the multinational Union Carbide, causing civil society organizations (CSOs) of the North and the South to unite in a joint campaign demanding accountability from multinational corporations.

[2] The 1990s witnessed a number of major UN world conferences, spanning the key developmental challenges of our times: the environment conference at Rio in 1992; the human rights conference in Vienna in 1993; the population conference in Cairo in 1994; the World Summit for Social Development in Copenhagen in 1995; the women's conference in Beijing in 1995; and the Habitat II conference in Istanbul in 1996.

[3] Personal communication with Arputham Jockin, president of the National Slum Dwellers Federation of India and co-founder of Slum/Shack Dwellers International.

[4] In India, local federations discovered early that government data about slums was highly inaccurate and biased toward under-enumeration. They demonstrated this through their own census of India's largest slum in Mumbai, which showed 80 percent under-counting in the official census, and then challenged the state government to undertake a joint census to see which one was accurate. WIEGO has demonstrated similar under-counting of informal workers in virtually all national economic surveys.

[5] SDI's Indian member, the NSDF, has successfully worked with local authorities to clear and resettle over ten thousand households formerly living in slums along Mumbai's railway tracks and roads. More important, these slums have not reappeared, as they have usually done, within months of forced evictions, because the new settlements were located and designed by the affected groups, keeping in mind their social and economic infrastructure needs.

[6] Personal communication with Sundaramma, Mahila Samakhya Sangha (women's collective) leader of Bagdal village, Bidar District, Karnataka State in South India, February 1991.

## References

Appadurai, Arjun. 2002. Deep democracy: Urban governmentality and the horizon of politics. *Public Culture* 14, no. 1: 21–48.

Batliwala, Srilatha. 1987. Women and housing. *Lokayan Bulletin*. July.

———. 2001. Acting for change: Trends and challenges in citizen movements. Background paper for CIVICUS General Assembly, Vancouver, Canada. Available online.

Baviskar, Amita. 2001. Red in tooth and claw: Looking for class in struggles over nature. Department of Sociology, University of Delhi. Available online.

Bruno, Kenny. 2002. The whole world was watching: New York stages a peaceful protest against the World Economic Forum. *CorpWatch*. February 6. Available online.

Dhanraj, Deepa, Srilatha Batliwala, and Geeta Misra. 2002. A South Asian perspective on future challenges for the global women's movement. Paper presented at the Ninth Association for Women's Rights in Development Forum, Guadalajara, Mexico, October 3–6. Forthcoming publication of Association for Women's Rights in Development and Mama Cash. Available online.

Edwards, Michael. 2000. *NGO Rights and Responsibilities: A New Deal for Global Governance*. London: The Foreign Policy Centre.

———. 2001. Global civil society and community exchanges: A different form of movement. *Environment and Urbanization* 13, no. 2: 145–49.

Florini, Ann, ed. 2000. *The Third Force: The Rise of Transnational Civil Society*. Washington, D.C.: Carnegie Endowment for International Peace; Tokyo: Japan Center for International Exchange.

Guha, Ramachandra. 2000. *Environmentalism: A Global History*. Delhi: Oxford University Press.

Karliner, Joshua. 2002. Porto Alegre: Globalizing hope. *CorpWatch*. February 6. Available online.

Khagram, Sanjeev, James V. Riker, and Kathryn Sikkink, eds. 2002. *Restructuring World Politics: Transnational Social Movements, Networks and Norms*. Minneapolis: University of Minnesota Press.

McAdam, Doug. 1982. *Political Process and the Development of Black Insurgency 1930–1970*. Chicago: University of Chicago Press.

Patel, Sheela, Sundar Burra, and Celine D'Cruz. 2001. Slum/Shack Dwellers International: From foundations to treetops. *Environment and Urbanization* 13, no. 2: 45–59.

Sheller, Mimi. 2000. The mechanisms of mobility and liquidity: Rethinking the movement in social movement theory. Department of Sociology, Lancaster University, UK. Available online.

# 6.
# Global Civil Society
# and the New Labor Internationalism:
# A View from the South

## Robert Lambert and Edward Webster

## Introduction

The emergence of the World Social Forum (WSF) as a counter to the World Economic Forum (WEF) says much about the notion of a global civil society (GCS). Civil society is not a unified entity outside of the state; it is a site of struggle over competing perspectives reflecting competing interests in globalization. The anti-globalization movement that emerged out of Seattle, of which the WSF is one expression, has demonstrated that a GCS, bound by broad values that run counter to the values embodied in the WEF, is in the making, as various civil society groups across the global form coalitions in the fight against corporate dominance and the consequences of this for the environment, the status of women, and the question of labor standards.

This global movement has empowered and emboldened these civil society groups and united them in an anti-neoliberal globalization project. Naomi Klein identified the spirit of this shift when she wrote of one of the protests:

> "We are here to show the world that another world is possible!" the man on the stage said and the crowd of more than 10,000 roared its approval. What was strange is that they weren't cheering for a specific other world, just the possibility of one. We were cheering for the idea that another world could, in theory, exist. (Klein 2001, 1)

This new movement makes its presence felt at a time when organized labor is in worldwide decline. Hence theorists of global change have written off unions. In volume 2 of his major new work, *The Information Age: Economy, Society and Culture*, Manuel Castells writes:

> The labor movement seems to be historically superseded. . . . Labor unions are influential political actors in many countries . . . yet the labor movement does not seem fit to generate by itself and from itself a project identity able to reconstruct social control and to rebuild social institutions in the Information Age. Labor militants will undoubtedly be part of new transformative social dynamics. I am less sure that labor unions will. (Castells 1997, 360)

If we were to take just a couple of examples, national trends would appear to confirm this pessimistic assessment. For example, the Australian Council of Trade Unions (ACTU), one of the world's long-established trade unions, with a reputation for militancy, is in dramatic decline. Australian unions appear to be in free fall with membership down to a mere 23.1 percent of the work force in August 2002. This slide needs to be viewed against the backdrop of their relative historical strength, which had remained above 50 percent for all but thirteen years (eleven of those years following the Great Depression: 1931–41) between 1920 and 1980 (Peetz 1998). While membership loss is not as dramatic, the Congress of South African Trade Unions (COSATU) faces a similar predicament. A Report to the Central Committee notes, "For the first time COSATU's overall membership has declined . . . from 1,819,871 to 1,707,646" (Johannesburg, April 14–16, 2003, 3). This has created an "unprecedented organizational challenge" as declining membership leads to a declining subscription base and hence to "real cuts in income." Seven of the sixteen affiliates are now in deficit (ibid., 18).

Corporate restructuring has played a significant role in the decline of traditional national trade unionism. When, for example, the Arcelor Steel plant in the Liege industrial heartland of Belgium was bought out by an American multinational corporation, closure was announced, leading to a loss of ten thousand jobs. The corporation plans to relocate production to Brazil and China. A Belgium steel worker fighting the closure was acutely aware of the link:

> This is worse than a war, much worse than death—this is the dismantling of the solidarity of the working class.
>
> The MNC [multinational corporation] sees itself as building history and becoming so powerful that its power extends beyond regions and continents. They see themselves as the real masters—masters of countries, police forces, citizens.
>
> They have only one aim—to become a leading global steel corporation. To achieve this they are willing to break any laws, conventions

and rights on their way to building their power base. They don't take account of human beings and communities.

They don't discuss or negotiate. They only present a monologue. (Presentation at the meeting of the World Social Forum, Belgium Branch, Brussels, May 10, 2003)

Global restructuring challenges the legitimacy of national trade unionism, for if these organizations cannot defend workers against casualization, job loss, and closure, why join? Why should the victims of change, who often face personal financial catastrophe, pay membership fees to an organization that appears to have no answer to the predicament confronted?

We would argue that trade unions alone cannot challenge global restructuring. They need to become part of the GCS movement. In the absence of their involvement, that movement will itself be fatally flawed. Our argument is that traditional collective bargaining unionism, with an exclusive work-place focus, is unlikely to pay more than lip service to this promising GCS development. Only if unions reclaim their social movement dimension is their any prospect of a creative synergy between the new global social movements and the unions. In our view the creation of a new labor internationalism (NLI) is critical to such a venture. This chapter explores these issues.

## Revitalizing Labor

The need to revitalize the labor movement has been the central focus of a group of labor scholars in recent years. The most extensive research has focused on the reawakening of the American labor movement under new leadership and new strategic directions (Turner, Katz, and Hurd 2001; Voss and Sherman 2000). Some unions, such as the Service Employees International Union, Hotel and Restaurant Employees, and the United Food and Commercial Workers, have begun to organize new members, using a variety of confrontational tactics including street demonstrations, direct action, worker mobilization, and sophisticated corporate campaigns.

At the heart of this revitalization strategy is an attempt to shift labor away from traditional business unionism to a new social movement unionism. At the core of Lowell Turner's and Richard Hurd's (2001) argument on union revitalization in the United States is the understanding that, while the leadership of the AFL-CIO and many of its member unions is generally older and traditional, many campus and work-place leaders have activist experience outside of the labor movement. As Kim Voss and Rachel Sherman contend in their case studies of union renewal in Southern California, this latter group has "brought broad visions, knowledge of alternative organizational models, and practices in disruptive tactics to the locals that became fully revitalized" (Voss and Sherman 2000, 333).

The concept of a "political generation" is a valuable insight into the forces shaping social movements and is used effectively in these studies.[1] However, *social movement unionism* is defined rather vaguely and narrowly as a type of unionism that mobilizes the rank and file for specific actions and gains (Turner and Hurd 2001, 23).

Importantly, the authors distinguish between "a social movement" and "social movement unionism," arguing that "labor activists in the United States promote social movement unionism in the absence of a broader social movement" (Turner and Hurd 2001, 23). The result, Harry Katz concludes, is that "in spite of intensified efforts, greater expenditures, and significant changes in the style and modes of organizing; to date these efforts have produced limited increases in membership" (Katz 2001, 346). Indeed, at the end of 2000, union density remained at 13.9 percent overall and had dropped to 9.5 percent in the private sector (Turner and Hurd 2001, 24).

The need to link the "revitalization debate" to broader agendas of social transformation is acknowledged by Paul Johnston, who sees "the resurgence of social movement unionism" in the United States as an attempt to "defend, exercise, and extend the boundaries of citizenship" (Johnston 2001, 35). But Johnston qualifies his assessment by suggesting that this potential can be realized only if the labor movement works to-gether with other democratic social movements and encourages its mem-bers to "act not only as workers but as members of a community with multiple interests and identities" (ibid., 36). This "citizenship frame," he suggests, "resonates" with social movement unionism in countries where labor movements battle for human rights and social justice.

With the exception of Kim Moody (1997) and Dale Hathaway (2000), the absence of this global dimension is the most striking omission in the revitalization problematic in the United States. As Katz notes in his con-clusion to the *Rekindling the Movement* study:

> Ultimately, the labor movement will have to find a way to extend revitalization into the international arena. . . . The problem now confronting labor movements all over the globe is that they con-front the need for cross-national unionism, yet their efforts to cre-ate such unionism face incredible barriers. These barriers include divergent interests (i.e., each labor movement wants the employ-ment) and national differences in language, culture, law and struc-ture. (Katz 2001, 348)

The idea of internationalizing labor struggles is not new; indeed, it was present at the very origins of the labor movement in nineteenth-century Europe. At the time Europe was dominated by a free-market ideology not dissimilar to that of the current era. This spurred contacts between English and French workers in an effort to challenge the employer practice of importing lower-paid workers as "scabs" into England. In spite of this ambitious strategy, labor internationalism failed to gain momentum and consolidate (Olle and Schoeller 1977, 55–75). Instead, as legal recognition was won by unions and national bargaining systems emerged, the view that problems could be fought and resolved at the national level, without reference to the international context, dominated. The result was a "rather feeble" internationalism that could best be seen as a form of national protectionism (ibid., 70). The deep political divisions in twentieth-century labor following the creation of the Soviet Union brought complicated and tragic divisions to bear on an already fractured movement. Furthermore, the Cold War interventions in Asian labor and elsewhere by the United States created divisions that shape today's labor map (Deyo 1987; Scipes 2000).

This pessimism was reinforced by the advent of the new international division of labor that emerged in the 1970s, which, it was argued, deepened the nationally based conflict of material interest in a divided international movement (Haworth and Ramsay 1986; Ramsay 1999). The relocation of jobs from developed to developing nations where labor was cheap overrode any sense of solidarity with the workers suffering under these regimes (Olle and Schoeller 1977, 68–71). Furthermore, "jobs and work lost in one country may benefit workers in another." Hence, there was "no natural affinity between union movements across the developed world/third world divide" (Haworth and Ramsay 1984, 63, 81). In such circumstances workers in the North see workers in the South as their main enemy rather than as potential allies.

Despite this somewhat bleak history of failed initiatives, neoliberal globalization and the advent of informational capitalism has ironically led to opportunities to transcend past constraints. The old International Trade Secretariats now call themselves Global Union Federations. Cold War divisions have all but dissipated. The technological revolution brought about by globalization can be used to the advantage of activists—email, websites, databases, and many other computer applications are being widely used around the world to find, store, analyze, and transmit information.

Cyberspace communication systems provide the opportunity to coordinate global campaigns and integrate organization across national boundaries. Indeed, the widespread supply chains inherent in global production introduce new vulnerabilities to enterprises, exposing them to international campaigns (Ramsay and Bair 1999). The emergence of global norms of work-place rights, especially the notion that there are certain core labor rights, creates opportunities for pressure to be exerted on multinational companies breaching these rights. Codes of conduct are reemerging as responses to these pressures (Sable, O'Rourke, and Fung 2000).

These opportunities have attracted the attention of an older as well as a new generation of scholars (Hathaway 2000; Lee 1997; Moody 1997; Munck 2002; O'Brien 2000; Ross 1997; Waterman 1998; Waterman and Wills 2001). They have begun to signal a new logic at work in the global economy, a logic that argues that international labor standards must be introduced to prevent a "race to the bottom." The disruption of the World Trade Organization (WTO) Ministerial Meeting in Seattle in late 1999 publicly highlighted this new logic. The holding of the WSF in 2001 in Porto Alegre, Brazil, and its rapid expansion annually since then provides further evidence of alternative visions of globalization (Cock, Chapter 10 herein). These developments point to the emergence of an alternative, counter-hegemonic "globalization from below" that seeks to challenge the forces of neoliberal globalization (Sandbrook 2003).

Importantly, these scholars see the new global economy as an opportunity for labor to realize its historic goal of worldwide working-class unity (Waterman and Wills 2001). They argue that the new information technology provides workers worldwide with the opportunity to communicate quickly and cheaply through networks. However, to achieve this goal, Peter Waterman and Jane Wills suggest that labor needs to think of itself once more as a social movement rather than as a mutual benevolent society (ibid., 4).

In Ronaldo Munck's (2002) overview of this new global social movement, he identifies two distinct phases of labor internationalism, the "old" and the "new." The former has a "nation-statist" perspective, is based in the established trade unions of the North, and sees labor internationalism as a form of trade union diplomacy. For many trade unionists, labor internationalism is simply an extension of the foreign policies of their respective national governments, a form of "trade union imperialism" (Munck 2002, 135–153). Munck sees the successful developmental solidarity given to the emerging trade union movement in apartheid South Africa as a precursor of the "new labor internationalism" (ibid., 151–52).

In contrast, the new form of internationalism "has moved beyond a conception of transnational collective bargaining, involving a more social movement unionism" (ibid., 154). This broader conception involves coalitions among labor, environmental, and social-justice interests, as well as alliances with NGOs, consumer organizations, and community groups. These alliances cut across the boundaries of national/international, production/consumption, and labor/community (ibid., 154–73). They take advantage of information technology to communicate instantly, directly, and globally around a campaign style of organization that targets "the weak links in capital's chain" (ibid., 162). Above all, it is more genuinely global and promotes the idea that trade and labor rights should be linked, notions that emerged in the so-called social clause debate (ibid., 128–34).

The claims that a NLI has arisen in response to the impact of globalization have led to a cautious response by some scholars. Beverly Silver and Giovanni Arrighi argue that a North/South divide continues to be the main obstacle "to the formation of a homogenous world proletarian condition" and are skeptical of the post-Seattle claims of a NLI based on a Red/Green alliance between Northern and Southern workers (Silver and Arrighi 2001, 530). Indeed, Silver raises the question of "whether struggles by Northern workers aimed at reforming supranational institutions are more likely to be steps towards the formation of a global working class 'for itself,' or signs of an emergent new form of national protectionism" (Silver 2003, 13). Gay Seidman (2002) expresses a similar skepticism highlighting the potential tensions between a language of universal rights and citizenship claims within the nation-state. Seidman articulates the distrust that many developing countries hold of US campaigns for human rights in the Third World, in particular the problem of whether transnational monitoring campaigns empower global managers and consumers in advanced industrial societies rather than workers in the factories and unions in the South.

A critical weakness in much of the literature on the NLI is the lack of evidence advanced to confirm that new strategic directions are indeed emerging. There is often an absence of creative interplay between theoretical analysis and actual struggles to build a new form of internationalism as a pathway to union revitalization. As we indicate in the next section, our chosen method of research has meant that our theoretical insights are grounded in and grow out of concrete struggles for change.

We achieve this by analyzing one instance of the NLI—the rise of the Southern Initiative on Globalization and Trade Union Rights (SIGTUR). SIGTUR is a campaign-oriented network of democratic unions in the South committed to resisting the negative aspects of globalization and to constructing an alternative paradigm of global economic relations. This new formation contrasts with traditional forms of international labor organization as well as a variety of NGO-type initiatives such as the Transnational Information Exchange, created in the 1970s to encourage communication among workers employed by the same transnational companies but living in different countries (Hathaway 2000, 20). A number of similar networks attempt to bring together trade unions, labor NGOs, and campaign organizations. Some of these, such as Global Network, formed in June 2001, link labor activists in the South through seminars and study circles that discuss strategies for improving labor rights and socioeconomic conditions under globalization. In this context SIGTUR is distinctive in that the network is grounded in democratic unions in the South.[2] It is best defined as a form of network organization attempting to build a global movement.

We argue that this still embryonic and fragile initiative reflects the beginnings of labor movements reinventing themselves. At the same time as the destruction of craftwork through mass production threatened the old craft unionism, it created the basis for a new form of worker organization—industrial unionism. Through a global restructuring of work, informational capitalism in the era of neoliberal globalization has generated a similar crisis for industrial unionism. However, this challenge to traditional industrial unionism is opening up the possibility of a new form of union organization, one that seeks to transcend the national through creative, dynamic linkages between the local and the global. This new form is embedded in coalition building and the difficult task of transnational campaigning.

What is new in the emergence of SIGTUR is the way the movement seeks to combine the strengths of networking, a social movement orientation, and established unionism in a transformative project. SIGTUR is grounded in, and accountable to, traditional established trade union organizations and therefore bears all the marks of the varied strengths and weaknesses of these organizations.

There is, of course, the danger of overstating the newness of the NLI and downplaying its continuities with the old. Throughout the history of labor new forms of communication such as railways, telephones, and fax machines have accelerated the possibilities of union organization. It could be argued, therefore, that the Internet is merely another advance in this process. The counter-argument is that cyberspace communication heralds a quantum leap in terms of capacity to organize in a new way. This has certainly been the experience of the SIGTUR leadership, where the new communication's potential has been utilized as a vehicle of revitalization and transformation. This lies at the very center of the project. Existing movements are brought together in a new synergy to transform local organizations through global linkage, new coalitions, and new forms of global campaigning. Furthermore, the form of SIGTUR is new. To consolidate a participative, movement orientation, SIGTUR consciously eschews hierarchy and structures of control. Debate is open, and action is decentralized, flexible, and participative. Yet at the same time, SIGTUR's grounding in union organizations means that the formation has the potential to avoid the obvious pitfalls of pure networks.

The weaknesses of networks stem from their socially disembodied character. Networking may generate protest politics, as happened in Seattle in 1999. However, to translate these significant and possibly defining moments of protest into effective power politics requires grounding in established unions and civil society organizations. This linkage makes it easier to sustain a network, especially if trade unions are democratic and open to change. These organizations also provide a firm financial base on which to build a new global movement that integrates these two organizational forms—social organization and networking—into a coherent whole that draws on the respective strengths of both.

Drawing on our argument of the centrality of the network and social movement nature of the NLI, as well as its Southern orientation, Table 6.1 presents, in ideal-typical form, five differences between the old and the NLI.

TABLE 6–1. CHARACTERISTICS OF OLD AND NEW LABOR
INTERNATIONALISM

| Characteristic | Old Labor Internationalism | New Labor Internationalism |
|---|---|---|
| Predominant type of worker | Established Northern workers in unions institutionalized in industrial-relations systems and parliamentary political parties | Struggling Southern (African, Asian, and Latino) workers building social movement unionism as a dynamic interplay between workplace organization and civil society |
| Officials | Career officials | Political generation of committed activists |
| Structure | Bureaucratic, hierarchical, centralized, restricted debate | Decentralized network |
| Orientation | Diplomatic | Mobilization and campaign |
| Focus | Work place and trade unions only | Coalition building with new social movements and NGOs |

SIGTUR's grounding as a network of existing democratic labor organizations creates the opportunity for revitalization by building creative connections between the local and the global, and by infusing a global social movement orientation through its distinctive leadership. In other words, it is an example of the "new" attempting to revitalize the "old" through the introduction of new strategies and new forms of organization.

## Research Strategy

The study of a global network organization with social movement features such as SIGTUR raises conceptual and methodological challenges. We agree with Karl Von Holdt that

> the really interesting question is to discover how different trade unions with different traditions and histories combine, as most of them do, movement dimensions (mobilization for contentious politics) with institutional dimensions (participation in industrial relations machinery and the negotiation of order); how the tensions between these different dimensions is manifested, and how they change in response to changing historical conditions and vary in different national contexts. (Von Holdt 2002, 298)

SIGTUR is an example of an attempt to reassert a movement dimension in different nationally based labor movements that commit to combining in a Southern global network. These national organizations have distinctive histories, organizational cultures, and traditions forged within the local state. While there are notable differences among these union organizations, SIGTUR has consciously selected only those unions that could be classified as democratic and independent according to ILO conventions. With the exception of Australia, this style of unionism in the South is committed to a movement orientation, to building broader civil society alliances, and to collective action. These unions are therefore open to the need for a NLI.

Over the past decade SIGTUR congresses have attracted around two hundred delegates from sixteen Southern countries: Australia, Bangladesh, Brazil, China, India, Indonesia, Pakistan, the Philippines, Malaysia, New Zealand, South Africa, South Korea, Sri Lanka, Thailand, Vietnam, and Zimbabwe. Global Union Federations as well as a network of academics have attended various congresses. Participating unions include those established and recognized by the state as well as new and unrecognized ones.

SIGTUR therefore brings together unions with common values and organizational principles that differ markedly in their stage of development and the ways in which their history and organizational culture have been marked by their particular national experience. Researching such a global movement is both a conscious choice of sociological orientation and a test of methodological inventiveness. We believe that what is required is what Michael Burawoy (2002) has described as a critical and public sociology. Thus, in this chapter we step beyond the traditional boundaries of sociology to engage directly with "the public" and a critical evaluation of SIGTUR's activities.

The other strategic choice we have made as researchers is the adoption and adaptation of Alain Touraine's (1983) method of sociological interventionism, which is designed to study movements. In his classic study of Solidarity in Poland, Touraine suggests that this approach "seeks to define the meaning which the actors themselves attribute to their action. Because a social movement challenges a situation it is always the bearer of normative values and orientation" (Touraine 1983, 7). Sociological intervention has two phases: the direct intervention of researchers helping participants to move toward self-analysis, and an analysis of its own practices and those of the movement on the basis of the hypotheses introduced by the researchers (ibid., 7–8).

The biannual SIGTUR congresses are an ideal setting for sociological interventionism. The congresses are deliberately structured as weeklong, live-in meetings at remote locations. This provides a variety of opportunities to actualize interventionist processes (engaging with delegates and sharing the results of research analysis), a method complemented by participant observation, interviews, and surveys of delegates. Linking such research to regular movement congresses provides a longitudinal dimension to the work that is invaluable in critically assessing the social dynamic of movement. We collected basic demographic data on the participants by conducting two conventional surveys. The first survey was undertaken in Johannesburg, South Africa, in 1999, and the second in Seoul, South Korea, in 2001.

The surveys were based on a self-administered, semi-structured questionnaire; the same questions were used on both occasions. The questionnaire was distributed to all trade union delegates at the beginning of the congresses. Forty-two returned the 1999 questionnaire (40 percent response rate) and 55 returned the 2001 questionnaire (27.5 percent response rate). The response rate was roughly proportional to the size of the individual country delegations. The largest number of respondents came from India, followed by Australia, and then South Africa, who together represented over half of the respondents.

A key feature of a social movement is its leadership—its vision and commitment. In order to understand this dimension of the movement we developed narratives of struggle and personal biographies through in-depth interviews. This included conversational types of discussions with groups of participants. Finally, in order to understand the experience of the participants and to capture the rituals of protest, the discourse and repertoire of the activists, we observed and participated in the activities of SIGTUR.

This sociological orientation and research strategy enabled us to probe the character of SIGTUR as a global movement of the South and to assess the degree to which this new internationalism has the potential to contribute to union revitalization. We now turn to SIGTUR's origins, where from the outset certain strategic choices were made with the express purpose of building a certain kind of movement—one that would differ markedly from the old internationalism.

## The Social Movement Origins of SIGTUR

In the late 1980s the West Australian labor movement (a state branch of the ACTU) was concerned about the likely impact of globalization and tariff reductions on union rights in Australia. Economic deregulation posed a dilemma for unions: should they turn inward and search for national protectionist strategies, or should they establish links with unions struggling for recognition in Asia and search for an internationalized response to the challenge of globalization? A strategy was needed that addressed the new reality. Economic deregulation exposed the rights and conditions that unionized Australian labor had won to Asia's cheap, controlled labor, a situation that clearly threatened these historical gains (Lambert 1998; 1999a).

After considerable debate, Australian labor adopted the outward-looking strategy. Establishing contact and building enduring relationships with democratic unions in the Asian region became a priority. Individuals who were part of a political generation of committed activists in Asia and South Africa were identified and encouraged to become part of this venture. A visit was made to the Philippines, Malaysia, and Indonesia, where it was found that these organizations faced circumstances similar to those that pertained during the South African labor movement's long and difficult struggle for recognition in the 1970s and 1980s (Lambert 1997).

SIGTUR initiators discovered that a new unionism was emerging in these countries, similar in many respects to that which had occurred in Brazil and South Africa (Seidman 1994). This social movement unionism resonated with the vision of the NLI that SIGTUR's founders articulated. Indeed, it was felt that given the scale of the challenge unions faced in a deregulated environment the only way to engage was through extending the social movement model beyond the bounds of one nation. Problems surrounding the realization of this have preoccupied SIGTUR's leadership over the past decade or so.

The first tentative steps toward constructing a global social movement in the South were taken in May 1991 when a small congress of democratic unions from the Indian Ocean region was organized in Perth. Importantly, it was decided to invite representatives from COSATU to this foundational meeting. South African unions had traversed a social movement as a form of empowerment against the exclusionary and repressive apartheid state (Adler and Webster 2000). Because of this, it was felt, they could provide valuable lessons on how to organize and mobilize workers in a situation where no rights existed and where both state and employers were extremely hostile.

As SIGTUR's founding document shows, the goal of the initiative was to respond creatively and positively to the challenge of globalization:

> The idea of a network of democratic unions needs to be seen as an integral and essential component of the restructuring process within Australia itself. . . . The experience of workers in Johannesburg factories, in the scarred shack lands of Manila, in the vast ship yards of South Korea and in the dense cities of India, will be shared on a continuous basis. . . . The response of Australian workers has been positive because they recognize that global issues do connect with their everyday experience in the factories, the mines, the construction sites and the waterfront.
>
> Within Australia we are all too aware of the decisive character of the present decade of global restructuring. How are the Australian unions to compete in a region based on ultra-cheap labor power, secured through severe trade union repression? We can restructure until the cows come home, but we will never hold our ground on existing conditions, while levels of exploitation in the region are so high. This is the point of convergence between the current agenda of Australian trade unions, and the unions in the region. There is an objective basis to the merging of our interests with their interests. (SIGTUR 1998, 2)

On the basis of these common objectives the initiative grew at a modest but steady rate. When delegates met again in 1992, it was proposed that a Regional Coordinating Committee be established that would meet once a year under what was initially known as the Indian Ocean Initiative. A third meeting was held in Perth in November 1994. The next year marked a turning point for the network when the recently elected Conservative government in Western Australia intensified its anti-union stance. This radicalized the West Australian union movement, generating strong resistance to the proposed changes to labor law. Pressures on the government, including a threat by the Indian and South African members of the Initiative to initiate a shipping and trade boycott, led the West Australian government to withdraw the proposed legislation.

The fourth congress, held in Calcutta, India, in 1997, was organized by the Centre of Indian Trade Unions (CITU). At this first meeting outside Australia the dynamic style and procedures were shaped by the Indian leadership. Banners and posters lined Calcutta's crowded streets, and more than twenty thousand workers participated in the opening events. CITU organized factory and community visits that revealed the union federation's social base in West Bengal's working class. The meeting demonstrated the vitality and organizational capacity of a union movement that was deeply rooted in a broader social movement. This was a learning curve for many delegations, bringing to the fore the importance of cultural awareness in the construction of a new internationalism. The success of the Indian meeting consolidated the vision of a Southern rather than a geographically bound network of democratic unions.

The Calcutta meeting brought to the fore the devastating effect downsizing, outsourcing, casualization, and the privatization of state assets was having on the conditions of working people in the South. This meeting also highlighted differences in approach to labor standards, captured in the so-called social clause debate that proposed linking trade and labor rights. The Australian delegation was surprised to find the Indian delegates arguing that India could not get rid of child labor because families were locked into it. They were also surprised and disturbed by the fact that there seemed little engagement with occupational and safety standards in the factories that they visited (Murie interview).

By 1999 the venture was renamed SIGTUR. The fifth congress was held in Johannesburg, South Africa, where the meeting took a new direction. A limited set of objectives was established prior to the meeting; the focus was on formulating modest, realizable goals and campaign tasks. The sixth SIGTUR congress was held in Seoul, South Korea, in November 2001. This was the first time SIGTUR had met in a non–English speaking country. It was also the first time SIGTUR had met since the 1999 protests in Seattle and the emergence of an international protest movement against neoliberal globalization.

The Seoul congress provided SIGTUR with an opportunity to redefine its role in light of the emergence of the growing anti-globalization movement. Indeed, on the second day of the congress the delegates from the fourteen countries represented in SIGTUR were asked to indicate whether an anti-globalization movement existed in their country and to describe their relationship with it. Delegates concluded that an anti-globalization movement in which labor was a central actor had emerged in all countries represented at the congress.

One may distinguish four organizational traditions within SIGTUR that reflect distinctive strategic approaches and histories. First, three key constituents of SIGTUR—Brazil's Central Única dos Trabalhadores (CUT), COSATU, and the Korean Confederation of Trade Unions (KCTU)—have been at the cutting edge of developing social movement unionism (Lambert and Webster 1988; Seidman 1994; Webster 1988). Seidman contends that in the case of South Africa and Brazil, similar patterns of rapid labor process transformation, despotic systems of labor control, lack of social infrastructure in the community, and restricted access to political power under authoritarian rule were key objective conditions creating opportunities and stimulus for a social movement response to the predicament of the working poor. Seidman's account of the rise of social movement unionism during the 1970s and 1980s stresses the key role of leadership in forging links between the new unions and emerging movements in the community (Seidman 1994, 202). The KCTU followed a similar pathway.

The second organizational tradition relates to the newly emergent democratic unions in Southeast Asia, a region where US-inspired systems of labor control are most evident. In the setting of hostile and authoritarian states, new democratic unions that have a social movement orientation have emerged in Indonesia, Pakistan, the Philippines, Sri Lanka, and Thailand. With the exception of Pakistan and the Philippines, these unions are still embryonic and struggling against great odds. Many union leaders have spent long periods in prison for their endeavors.

A third tradition is drawn from the left of CITU and the All Indian Trade Union Congress. These unions have taken the lead in the anti-globalization movement on the subcontinent, organizing mass campaigns and general strikes embracing a wide range of organizations in civil society.

The fourth tendency is the ACTU in Australia. Here the left unions have played a critical role in the formation and sustenance of SIGTUR in keeping with their rich history of labor internationalism. In periods of conflict such as the 1998 maritime dispute, these unions have evidenced social movement characteristics, which have not been sustained.

Drawing on our research, we now attempt to probe the nature of SIGTUR more deeply as a way of exploring what is new in the NLI.

## Characteristics of NLI: The Case of SIGTUR

SIGTUR illustrates five defining features of the NLI (see Table 6–1), each of which is discussed in turn. Analysis of these characteristics demonstrates their synergy in forging a global social movement that lies at the heart of this new approach.

### A Southern Social Movement of African, Asian, and Latino Workers

SIGTUR has been shaped by the struggles of Southern workers. These struggles have been located within an identity marked by the historical experience of colonialism and racism, an experience in which "coercion—direct and persistent—was an essential element in organizing a labor force" (Munck 1988, 27). Munck notes, "Today, the descendants of Indian and Chinese forced laborers are a sizable portion of the working population of Southeast Asia, Africa and parts of the Americas" (ibid.,

30). This Southern experience was further conditioned by political independence struggles and the disillusionments of the post-colonial era. Our leadership interviews capture this distinctive Southern identity.[3]

These political changes occurred at a time of quite profound transformation in the world economy as the old colonial division of labor gave way to a new international division of labor and the emergence of a substantial manufacturing sector in parts of Asia. The relocation of production from the developed Northern economies to these newly industrializing societies was the paramount feature of this new economic map, a shift that has become ever more prominent with the deregulation of the past two decades. The new industrialization created a new working class in Asia, youthful and desirous of transcending grinding rural poverty. However, their aspirations were soon eroded by the harsh conditions of the new factories, and they became open to the new democratic unionism that was being advanced in the region (Lambert 1997; 1999b). These were the unions that SIGTUR contacted from the outset.

There is a further dimension to this Southern identity. Our research over the past number of years at SIGTUR congresses in India, South Africa, and South Korea reveals that the consciousness of Southern workers is marked by the negative impact of neoliberal globalization. The surveys highlighted a common experience of work restructuring in the new era, where insecurity overwhelmed workers as a result of downsizing, casualization, and privatization. For those who managed to retain employment, conditions changed dramatically with restructuring—as they experienced work intensification, deterioration in the quality of jobs, working, and living conditions; reduced real wages; and the erosion of culture.

The surveys' bleak picture of restructuring was reinforced by the view that privatization is leading to a crisis in the reproduction of labor itself. The reduction of public expenditure in areas such as health, education, and social welfare, as well as the "user pays" principle of decentralization of financing to communities and families, is leading to widespread poverty and social exclusion. There is increasing use of child labor, school dropouts have increased significantly, and families have disintegrated under the pressures.

Significantly, this harsh reality underpinned the delegates' perspective that there is no solution to their predicament through reliance on traditional modes of organizing, hence the stress on the need to build social movements committed to challenging rent evictions, electricity cutoffs, lack of access to public health, and poor transportation. Evidence of concerted collective action in the work place and in the community led delegates to conclude that the most vigorous and determined resistance to neoliberal restructuring had indeed come from the South.

Thus the first and most significant characteristic of the NLI is a commitment to social movements at a global level. However, this commitment needs to take account of different national histories and organizational cultures. A starting point for understanding social movement unionism is the identification of its key characteristics. In our view, these include work-place organizations that seek independent political solutions to their problems in the form of alliances with other social formations and not just as the "labor arm" of a left party; develop forms of decentralized decision-making and autonomy more akin to the loose structures of social movements than to the formal authority relations of trade unions; are willing to embrace forms of collective action in and beyond the work place, against both the employer and the state; and broaden the scope of unionism to include involvement in wider social movements such as the civics and other community-based organizations that are traditionally seen as outside the labor movement.

### Political Generation of Committed Activists

Prior to its formation in the early 1990s, those who initiated the idea of the movement actively sought out a certain type of leadership in the region as the key element in constructing a social movement–oriented NLI. The search was for committed labor activists; long-serving union bureaucrats from company and state-sponsored unions were avoided. This strategic choice led to the discovery of a generation of labor leaders who had fought to win trade union rights in the South, often at a high personal cost. Many in the SIGTUR leadership have endured prison terms, torture, and other types of victimization.[4]

These persons had formed personal identities centered on a resolve to struggle for the empowerment of working people. Our interviews reveal that these identities are grounded in value choices: service to the community rather than individual careerism; collective solidarity in place of upward mobility; service above personal material reward; freedom, democracy, and participation over hierarchy and control; social, economic, and political equality against elitism; and social control above market logic.

Given that these activists hold such values, it is not surprising that SIGTUR has emerged as a movement with the organizational characteristics listed in Table 6–1. Critical to the building of this network is the fact that these leaders also have a long-term perspective of their own value orientation and organizational engagement, seeing these as a life-long commitment. Identity theorists have stressed the importance of this long-term horizon in giving a person the capacity to intervene creatively in society, mastering experience (achieving ego synthesis), rather than being disoriented, estranged, and passive in the face of social forces. In stressing the significance of continuity Erik Erikson (1968) has theorized the way in which individuals link former experiences that are always within us to grasp future experience in a way that gives meaning and purpose to existence (also see Breakwell 1986). For example, Malaysian union leader Arokia Dass's personal identity is inseparable from the colonial past and its impact on his father as an indentured laborer. This sense of his own personal history is a factor in his lifelong commitment.

This long-term leadership commitment is critical to the growth, development, and survival of SIGTUR. By their very nature, social movements evidence a low level of institutionalization; hence their continued survival depends upon such commitment. This stability and continuity make for an ongoing building and rebuilding of the movement. Failure in this regard would lead to the movement's rapid decline. The results of our two surveys demonstrate leadership continuity. A core of union leaders from a range of countries has participated in all six of SIGTUR's congresses.

One-third of the delegates at the Johannesburg congress had attended previous congresses. Some 43 percent of the delegates in Johannesburg had heard of the Initiative that led to SIGTUR before 1996; 22 percent heard about it in 1997—these were mostly from India. The results reveal that the small leadership core is connected to a wider layer of participation in SIGTUR. This connection has provided a degree of stability essential to the movement's survival. This feature of SIGTUR continued in South Korea. Of the respondents to the 2001 survey, 8 percent had attended their first Congress in 1991, while 71 percent had first attended in 2001. The majority had heard about the congress before, however, with 21 percent having heard about it in or before 1991, and 26 percent having heard of it between 1992 and 1999.

Through a series of in-depth interviews with SIGTUR leaders, we can identify a distinct political generation whose members were shaped by their experiences of oppression in their formative years. Many are now in their late fifties. The way in which Dass's political commitment was shaped typifies this political generation:

> One day I was walking along the road and there was this person staggering and walking in front of me. Suddenly, he dropped dead. Someone told me he died of hunger. I turned around and saw that there was so much food. Why should this person die of hunger? Then I realized that religion had no answer for this question. I wanted the eradication of poverty. I started reading Marx. A friend in Madras got me onto it. He was reading Marx. I became a socialist and I became involved in various agitations. We were in a procession and got beaten up by the police. In 1967 I became involved in the DMK [Dravida Munnetra Kazhagam] anti-Brahmin movement. (Dass interview)

What is also distinctive about this age cohort is that its members became active in a variety of social-justice movements in their youth in a similar way to union activists in Southern California (Voss and Sherman 2000). They then carried their vision and organizational experiences into the labor movement. Importantly, they brought to the trade union movement a broader conception of labor that mobilizes workers in the totality of their lives.

Rubina Jamil, president of the All Pakistan Federation of Trade Unions and leader of the Working Women's Organization, illustrates this process. Jamil stressed that it was not possible to recruit women workers into the union movement without a close relationship with the family. Furthermore,

> if there's any problem inside the factory, we try our best to resolve the family problems, too. If the father of the girl needs a job, we try our best with the help of our male colleagues to find him a job. If the father or the mother are suffering from any disease we help them to go to the hospital and we assist them, so we are very much in touch with the family members of the women workers and we organize family counseling programs because we think it is really important for the family members to know why trade unions are important. (Jamil interview)

The crucial point about these activists is that they recognize the importance of culture and that it is not possible to organize women workers in Pakistan without connecting with their families.

At the center of the leadership style of these activists is a commitment to union democracy and accountable leadership. A struggle against bureaucratic and corrupt leadership has been at the heart of trade union struggles in Asia in the postwar period. This is captured in the interview with Dass:

> When we took over leadership we did participatory action research. We got some help from a friend at the University of Malaysia and we developed a questionnaire on what workers expected from the union. Three to four thousand workers were interviewed. They all said that decision-making must be left to the members; the union must be democratic and independent; it should not be affiliated to political parties. (Dass interview)

### Decentralized Network

The third characteristic of the NLI is its decentralized, network character that empowers through open debate. This generates a global movement orientation, rendered possible by cyberspace technology.

A high degree of participation is essential to a movement-building project. This is consonant with the activist leadership style just described.

Cyberspace communication has greatly enhanced the swift dissemination of images of commitment and action, thereby building and reinforcing a common organizational culture that transcends national divides. The activist leadership has instant access to information and photographs of action that they can then communicate to their own constituencies. The communications that flow across SIGTUR's constituencies in the South through the Internet embrace wide-ranging issues and actions. Cyberspace images have included an All India general strike against the privatization of essential services involving millions of organized workers and other social movements; young Thai women workers staging a three-month protest action against a Nike closure; militant mass marches and strikes in South Korea; export processing zone women workers in Sri Lanka striking against a Hong Kong multinational—to mention but a few recent examples.

Cyberspace communication has significantly enhanced the transnational organizational capacity of SIGTUR. In the early years of its existence the Internet and the possibility of electronic communication were not yet available. The first systematic use of electronic communication took place in late 1996, just before the fourth regional congress in Calcutta. Prior to this, communications were based on the relatively expensive, time-consuming, and inefficient use of fax transmissions. It was virtually impossible to get faxes through to countries such as Pakistan, where infrastructure was rudimentary. The impact of the new technology became more apparent during the organization of the fifth congress in South Africa. This is clear from the high proportion of delegates that regularly used email (see Table 6–2).

TABLE 6–2. FREQUENCY OF EMAIL USE

| Response | 1999 | | 2001 | |
|---|---|---|---|---|
| | Frequency | Percent | Frequency | Percent |
| Often / once a week | 21 | 50 | 32 | 60 |
| Sometimes / once a month | 6 | 14 | 6 | 11 |
| Seldom / less than once a month | 4 | 10 | 4 | 8 |
| Never | 11 | 26 | 11 | 21 |
| **Total** | 42 | 100 | 53 | 100 |

Source: Survey of SIGTUR members, fifth congress, October 1999, Johannesburg, and sixth congress, November 2001, Seoul.

SIGTUR's evolution as a networked organization built by committed activists has logically included the development of a decentralized, participatory structure that seeks to advance open debate and democratic decision-making in all spheres. This characteristic contrasts markedly with the old internationalist structures, which are bureaucratic, centralized control structures that minimize genuine debate—the format of their conferences tends to include lengthy speeches from the podium, prearranged resolutions, and the absence of large numbers of delegates from the conference hall.

The Regional Coordinating Committee of SIGTUR is the leadership structure of the movement. The committee comprises delegates from five regions in the South: Australia (ACTU); East Asia (KCTU); Latin America (CUT); Southeast Asia (Kilusang Mayo Uno, KMU); and Southern Africa (COSATU). Over the past decade meetings and congresses have been characterized by vigorous debate on issues such as the nature of democratic unionism and relationships with political parties; trade unionism and the nature of the Chinese state; political divisions in the labor movement in the South; the most appropriate strategic response to the WTO; the role of the United States in the South; and responses to war and terrorism.

### Mobilization and Campaigning

The ability to mobilize workers for a particular period and thereby move them beyond their everyday roles and patterns of interaction is crucial to building a movement. Our survey results show that this is expected by those who participate in SIGTUR. They indicated strong support for a particular style of internationalism—one that is action oriented. In analyzing the first characteristic of the NLI, we highlighted the fact that the survey revealed that workers' experience of neoliberal globalization has been largely negative. The survey also shows a desire for "concrete action against globalization." SIGTUR is viewed as a means to promote this struggle through "building solidarity," "formulating a common approach to global issues," thereby strengthening local organization. We draw on two examples to illustrate characteristics of this action orientation and the challenges it poses.

#### Globalizing May Day

Delegates at the 1999 SIGTUR congress agreed to work toward a common May Day throughout the South. May Day was viewed as an opportunity to highlight the impact of neoliberal globalization on job security and conditions. Participant countries that subsequently mobilized on this common issue were Australia, India, Indonesia, the Philippines, South

Africa, and South Korea. India, South Africa, and South Korea organized a general strike. These actions highlight significant facets of the NLI. SIGTUR does not organize action at the national level. National unions take these decisions. Appropriately, CITU, COSATU, and KCTU were solely responsible for the general strike decision. SIGTUR's role was to utilize cyberspace communication to ensure that common national actions were linked across the South, so that workers in each of these countries who decided to resist felt part of a wider movement for change rather than being isolated at the national level.

The mass actions were for job security and humane conditions, and against the effects of economic globalization. Again, SIGTUR's role was to capture this shift and communicate effectively so that individual national movements were not left isolated when their own power elites challenged their loyalty to the nation's well-being. The elites asserted that such action damaged the nation's competitive interests, placing investment-driven job creation at risk. Future jobs, they claimed, were at stake as a consequence of these "reckless" strikes. Grounded cyberspace communications allowed a dialogue of common worker interests that challenged this narrow national perspective. This is a counterbalance to intense elite-defined nationalism.

Four million workers responded to the general strike call in South Africa, two million in India, and 100,000 in South Korea. Distinctive in these mass actions is that, first, organized labor is gradually evolving an independent ideological stance; second, far from being a spent force "in the new transformative social dynamics," organized labor is in fact proving to be a leading force (Castells 1997, 360); and third, the labor movement is prepared to take direct action to pressure for an end to the liberal economic policies being pursued by political parties in power.

### Release Prisoners Campaign

The end of four decades of military rule in South Korea and its replacement with the rule of Parliament in 1993 did not usher in a new era of freedom for workers. Paradoxically, repression intensified. The new, democratically elected government instituted market reforms, including the end to lifetime employment, while still retaining comparative advantage in its export-driven growth through a cheap, pliant labor force. When the KCTU led a campaign of mass protest marches and general strikes against the changes, repression was swift. Dan Byong-ho, the KCTU president, its first vice-president, Jeong Yong-cheon, and forty-three senior leaders from all the major affiliates of the KCTU were imprisoned. Many union leaders—1,927 of them—were taken into police custody for interrogation. Many of these were later imprisoned. Union leaders' bank accounts were frozen, placing their families in dire straits. Thousands of

KCTU leaders inside the factories, offices, and service industries were victimized through dismissal from employment.

The two hundred SIGTUR congress took place against this backdrop. The 200 delegates resolved to globalize the cause of the imprisoned leaders. During 2002 the campaign took the form of protest marches to South Korean embassies where mass rallies demanded the release of the prisoners. In many of the actions, protests were widened to include demands for an end to the privatization of essential services in South Korea.

The significance of these moments of protest is that workers chose to act in solidarity with other workers in geographically distant locations, contradicting the notion that narrow self-interest is the prevailing culture. Activist leaders inspired commitment to a wider, borderless vision of solidarity and understanding of restructuring's global character. Dan Byong-ho was released on April 3, 2003.

### Coalition Building

Coalition building across labor movements and other civil society actors is a characteristic of the NLI. In the early phase of SIGTUR's development, historical Cold War divisions in the old labor internationalism were an obstacle. Initially the International Trade Secretariats were hostile, viewing SIGTUR as a World Federation of Trade Unions–sponsored body. However, its nonpartisan politics; its commitment to all democratic unions in the South, regardless of their political orientation; and its strong global campaign orientation, eventually led to close working relationships with certain International Trade Secretariats.

We illustrate the coalition-building dimension of NLI through analyzing SIGTUR's engagement with the global campaign of the International Chemical and Engineering Workers Union (ICEM) against the antilabor, anti-environmental policies of the multinational mining corporation Rio Tinto. SIGTUR's role was to support the ICEM program.

Rio Tinto is one of the world's largest private mining corporations, with sixty operations in forty nations.[5] The company continuously downsized its work force, creating serious workload, health, safety, and environmental problems for workers and their communities (Rio Tinto Global Union Network 2000). In Australia, the Construction, Forestry, Mining and Energy Workers Union has been locked in intense struggles at Rio Tinto mine sites in an attempt to stave off this attack on working conditions. Despite lengthy, bitterly fought disputes, the union eventually concluded that local action alone would not succeed and decided to globalize the campaign through cyberspace communications. The Rio Tinto Global Union Network was formed by the ICEM and was coordinated from California. The Internet was used to promote the campaign, to communicate union actions, and to keep track of the corporation's responses.

ICEM's demands of the corporation included a commitment to core ILO conventions that protect worker rights, the negotiation of a global agreement with effective monitoring mechanisms to give effect to these principles, and the resolution of disputes in the light of these principles.

The strategy confirms our arguments about the effectiveness of grounded networking. Rio Tinto Global Union Network's first task was to embody the network within organization. Cyberspace was used to build new organization and movement around the issue. Two forms were distributed: one was directed to unions on Rio Tinto sites, and the other to community organizations and individuals willing to commit to the global campaign. With regard to the former, individuals were chosen by the union to be global campaign work-site organizers. In assuming this position they accepted responsibility for communicating with workers on site about the global campaign, contributing ideas on the planning of the campaign, making sure that all levels of the union were aware of the campaign, and ensuring that workers on site had access to campaign activities.

With regard to the involvement of community organizations and individuals, an email document entitled "Pledge of Solidarity" asked organizations and individuals to send one fax and one email each month with a solidarity message, to attend campaign activities, and to help organize protest demonstrations.

Protest action against Rio Tinto was extended to the global board room. Union leaders from around the world attended Rio Tinto's annual general meeting in London on May 10, 2000, having formed the Coalition of Rio Tinto Shareholders. The coalition advanced resolutions that demanded the company create the position of deputy chairperson to implement core ILO conventions. At the meeting, union leaders warned that in the new global economy, where cyberspace communications allow for instantaneous communication, "everything the company does is increasingly subject to public scrutiny—not just in the local community, but across the world. Rio Tinto's performance in Indonesia may well affect its right to operate in Canada or the USA" (Maher 2000).

The coalition won support for the resolutions from some major institutional shareholders with over £65 billion in assets. Apart from this pressure, the ICEM-led coalition began to organize protest actions around the globe to pressure for a global agreement.

## Challenges Facing NLI

Five challenges can be identified in this ambitious attempt to build an NLI in the South. The first and most critical is whether the social movement character of the labor movement can be sustained. The "double transition" in South Africa (Webster and Adler 1999)—the establishment of a post-apartheid state and the adoption of neoliberal market economics in engaging globalization—has had a significant impact on a section of the COSATU union leadership. While committed organizers still remain, there are others who appear to have broken with a social movement orientation (Buhlungu 2002). Unionists who have chosen a career or entrepreneurial orientation appear to have abandoned the values central to a committed leadership that is so crucial to social movement unionism. Lucrative opportunities in the post-apartheid state and in business have, to use Richard Sennett's words, led to the "acid erosion of those qualities of character, like loyalty, commitment, purpose, and resolution, which are long term in nature" (Sennett 1998, 30). Globalization has produced, "chameleon values" jettisoned as swiftly as a change of clothing as long-term social commitment dissolves before short-term private opportunity. This "corrosion of character" could spell the decline of social movement unionism in South Africa, and it remains to be seen whether or not the remaining activists are sufficiently influential to counter this drift.

There are, however, counter trends. In contrast to South Africa, the KCTU in South Korea is inspiring new unionism in Southeast Asia by providing a model of militant social movement unionism determined to resist global restructuring. The KMU in the Philippines has also done much in this regard, sustaining a social movement unionism orientation and organizing May Day events. SIGTUR has provided opportunities to strengthen these links and social movement unionism is emerging in Indonesia, Pakistan, Sri Lanka, and Thailand. In India, the left unions have successfully organized mass, nationwide strikes against economic liberalization that have united a splintered union movement and drawn in other civil society movements (CITU 2003).

A second challenge is SIGTUR's attempt to bridge the North-South divide by building an alliance with a traditionally Northern country such as Australia. As a member of the Organization for Economic Cooperation and Development (OECD), Australia is one of the advanced industrialized countries. However, there is a convergence as a result of the sustained attack on trade unionism in Australia in the name of competitive efficiency (Lambert 1998). Conditions in a large part of the Australian clothing industry are no different from those endured in the rest of the South. Much of the manufacturing is moving out of Australia to other countries in the South with less developed labor conditions (Lambert 1999a). While the Australian movement has a strong material interest in participating in SIGTUR, given the way that these changes have undermined unionism, strategic differences remain. There is little consensus within SIGTUR on the linkage of trade access and labor rights—the so-called social clause debate. Some unions in the South support the linkage, while others, most notably the Indian unions, are vigorously opposed to such a strategy, viewing it as little more than a Northern protectionist measure.

Furthermore, there are different perspectives on key issues arising out of different levels of industrialization in the South. Brazil, South Africa, and South Korea have developed sophisticated industrial economies. The Republic of Korea is now in the OECD, South Africa is unlike any other African country in its degree of industrialization, and Brazil has the world's seventh-largest industrial economy. They can be distinguished from the developing nations of Southeast Asia that are striving for such status, from the relatively closed economy of India, and from Australia's established OECD position.

A third challenge is the related issue of diversity in the South. The most obvious differences are those of language. At the 1999 congress sixteen different home languages were identified among the delegates: Afrikaans, Bengali, Bahasa, English, Hindi, Kannada, Korean, Malayalam, Marathi, North Sotho, Sinhala, South Sotho, Tagalog, Tamil, Tswana, and Xhosa. Less than a quarter (24 percent) of those interviewed had English as their home language, although 98 percent had a working knowledge of English. This reflects the trend of English becoming the global language, thereby facilitating new opportunities for transnational discourse, which considerably lightens the task of global movement building.

There are also sharp differences in the degree of union autonomy within SIGTUR. In countries such as India and Pakistan, labor has historically been subordinated to a political party, best described as a form of political unionism. This differs from Australia, where the ACTU has maintained a lesser degree of subordination from the Labor Party or, indeed, COSATU, where the federation has acted against its ally in government, the African National Congress, over privatization (Candland and Sil 2001).

There are also uneven organizational capacities of the unions within the region. A key challenge SIGTUR faces is supporting the growth of independent, democratic unions in the nations of Southeast Asia where US Cold War interventions constructed state-sponsored and employer-dominated unionism. Democratic unions with a social movement–unionism orientation are emerging in the region. Promoting the development of a new unionism in the hostile environment in China is a critical issue SIGTUR has found difficult to engage.

There is also diversity in the leadership of SIGTUR. There are two distinct political generations in SIGTUR—an older generation including veterans of the struggle for independence in India and activist leaders in Southeast Asia, alongside a new generation of young activists drawn largely from South Korea. In the 1999 survey three-quarters of the delegates were over the age of forty; two were over the age of seventy. The industrialization of East and Southeast Asia was founded on young workers who were drawn into the massive factories that were the engine of this "economic miracle." The KCTU built its movement on youth and is culturally oriented toward the needs and the style of young people. Although 70 percent of the delegates at the 2001 Seoul congress were over the age of forty, the rest of this group was under the age of fifty.[6]

On the face of it, the fifth congress reflected a significant gender imbalance. Over two-thirds (69 percent) of participants were men. However, some of the delegations, such as those from Indonesia, Malaysia, and the Philippines, consisted entirely of women, while the South African and South Korean delegations had a high proportion of women. Other delegations, such as Australia and India had very few women delegates. In 2001, 76 percent of the delegates were men and 24 percent were women. This reflects a 7 percent drop in the number of women attending.

A fourth challenge is the growing "informalization" of work in the South, a process that is becoming increasingly "feminized" and threatening to established trade unionism. In spite of resolutions at SIGTUR congresses calling on members to broaden the support base of unions to include those in casual work, those in part-time work, and those in the informal sector, SIGTUR has failed to make any headway. There are innovative responses by trade unions to the informal sector, such as the Self-Employed Workers Association in India and the Self Employed Workers Union in South Africa, but these are exceptions and fall largely outside the formal trade union movement (Lund and Skinner 1999; Munck 2002; Nayak 2001).

This challenge clearly requires a response based on alliances among social movements around gender, environment, and other social issues. The union movement would have to place social justice as a priority if it were to organize in this domain.

A fifth challenge is the need to link the local to the global. In the 1999 survey all respondents stated that they reported back to different levels of the trade union movement, either verbally or in writing. One delegation used a digital camera, which gave it the capacity to develop PowerPoint presentations on the congress. The 2001 survey showed that the respondents reported back to different levels within their own trade union, including the membership, but also to other trade unions and related organizations. Approximately equal numbers of participants said they would produce verbal and written reports. A few participants proposed publishing their reports in journals and newspapers, while a couple said they would post their reports on web pages (see, e.g., Collinson 2001).

This process of reporting back means that the resolutions taken at the congresses have the potential to be integrated into local union strategy. A key to the realization of this challenge is actualizing the concept of global unionism. Can historically defined, nationally based industrial unionism be transformed into global unionism as a new organizational form, or will the demands and the dynamics of national struggle make this fade into an unrealizable dream?

In interviews, activists in Australia stressed that restructuring led to workers becoming preoccupied with local struggles to maintain their own jobs. In such a climate of fear and personal insecurity it has proven difficult to get workers to show anything other than superficial solidarity with workers elsewhere. A Western Australian union organizer described an incident where he had failed to interest Australian power workers in the attack on South Korean power workers. On returning to his office, his union secretary warned, "Don't let your internationalism interfere with your work. You have to bring in the money, organize, and service the members. Internationalism is nice to have, but don't let it get in the way" (Murie interview).

Further evidence of the difficulty of linking the local to the global is contained in recent research of union leaders and rank-and-file members in Western Australia (Harris 2002). When asked how workers were responding to the negative effects of globalization, they focused on the pressures of job insecurity. As one worker said, "I mean even the mention of the union in the work place—people almost whisper it" (quoted in ibid., 79). The report suggests that the values underlying the formation of SIGTUR are yet to penetrate the local union level. When asked what their knowledge of SIGTUR was in the work place, workers responded by saying it was "either minimal to none," or "most members would not know about it." As one worker commented, "Everyone is talking about globalization, whether they realize it or not, but not in terms of workers or union movement, or changes in unionism across international boundaries" (quoted in ibid., 94).

## Conclusion

The transformation of work under capitalism is a contradictory process that closes down options as well as opening up new opportunities. The destruction of craftwork by machine-based production undermined craft unionism, leading to dire predictions in the 1930s in the United States of the disappearance of the labor movement. These predictions were, as Cobble (2001) reminds us, issued literally on the eve of the dramatic upsurge of labor organizing that began in 1933. Instead of labor disappearing, a new form of worker and work organization—industrial unionism—emerged; it grew in strength through much of the past century.

Global informational capitalism has now created a similar crisis for industrial unionism, as the global restructuring of work threatens traditional union organization. Across the South this climate of insecurity is further exacerbated by the direct attack on basic organizing rights. Yet the crisis is opening up the possibility of a new form of network organization committed to coalition building and transnational campaigning. SIGTUR is an example of such a phenomenon, albeit in an early stage of development.

However, SIGTUR's immediate gains are limited. Even in Australia it has not succeeded in stemming the decline in union membership. In the space of two decades of increasing engagement with globalization, union density declined from 51 percent in 1976 to 30.3 percent in 1997 (Peetz 1998, 7).[7] However, there is a conservative bias in the way in which the revitalization problematic is conceptualized as it assumes that the task is to strengthen existing organizations. If union revitalization is understood more broadly as the need to develop a new strategy and new forms of organization in the era of globalization, then what we are witnessing is not the disappearance of the labor movement but the necessity for a new form of organization.

This is a matter of strategic choice within national unions and their federations. The evidence upon which this chapter is based suggests that the response of unions to this challenge is uneven. Furthermore, globalization is having a contradictory impact on the work place. In certain circumstances it is making the "link with the global" a necessity for survival; at the same time, however, it is creating conditions of insecurity leading to a preoccupation with the local.

As a consequence, senior union leaders appear trapped. Key unions across the South have actively participated in building SIGTUR over the past fifteen years. They recognize and are committed to a new campaign-oriented internationalism seeking to empower "the local." Yet these leaders still have to make the difficult strategic, resourcing choices that will facilitate the shift to global unionism. In the absence of such a choice, network organizations such as SIGTUR will continue to present an alternative pathway forward. However, the reconfiguration of power relations from below will remain a distant dream unless these grassroots networks of the South begin to affect the institutions of the new international economic order.

To achieve such a reconfiguration of power relations will require a partnership between activists and scholars in the field. This has already begun in SIGTUR, where a group of scholars are engaging with grassroots activists of the South. The information and analysis that are emerging represent knowledge generation in the most powerful sense as it empowers activists and enables them to influence public policy, especially with regard to globalization.[8]

While there may indeed be many barriers to the development of a new internationalism, an increasing number of workers are discovering that there is no alternative. In the words of a young Australian union organizer who has faced strong anti-union and work-place pressures from multinational mining corporations, "Going global is our only future. We have learned that you have to go international on the big disputes. This is how the world is today" (Fowler interview).

## Notes

[1] The concept of political generation defines an age cohort that is shaped by the experiences of its formative years (ages 20–30) and ready to rely on that learning when it becomes the "ruling generation" (c. ages 40–65).

[2] SIGTUR defines *South* politically and not geographically, as those zones of the global economy that are characterized by various forms of authoritarian statism and corporate dominance. That is, SIGTUR is an initiative that aims to bring together some of the world's most exploited working classes, many of whom find themselves in restricted political situations and are denied basic International Labor Organization (ILO)-defined trade union rights. From the outset SIGTUR only linked with grassroots democratic unions that were committed to social emancipation. The policy document, *Principles for Participation in SIGTUR*, stated that only those organizations that reflected ILO Conventions 87 (freedom of association) and 98 (collective bargaining rights) were allowed to participate (SIGTUR 1999).

[3] Certain Southeast Asian leaders are deeply conscious of their family's experience as indentured laborers on plantations. All evidenced a sense of political betrayal as the exploitative conditions of workers remained largely unchanged while post-colonial states consolidated new elites. Part of this sense of history is shaped by the leaders' view of the United States as a dominant and politically manipulative power in the region, playing a key role in the repression of democratic unionism and the construction of pliant work-place organization.

[4] For example, Malaysian union leader Arokia Dass, who has played a key role in the development of SIGTUR, was detained under Malaysia's Internal Security Act between 1987 and 1989; he was psychologically tortured. Dita Sari, a leader of the independent unions in Indonesia, was imprisoned for three years under Suharto; her campaign against prison conditions resulted in her being placed in isolation (Sari interview).

[5] The company focuses on large, long-term, low-cost mining and minerals processing operations in aluminum, copper, coal, uranium, gold, industrial minerals, and iron ore.

[6] These findings are distorted by the fact that the Indian delegation was the largest at the congress.

[7] Since the publication of David Peetz's study, union density has declined even further, to 23 percent.

[8] Srilatha Batliwala, in the previous chapter, identifies a similar relationship between researchers and activists in the worldwide coalition Women in the Informal Employment Globalizing and Organizing.

## Interviews

Dass, Arokia. November 2001. Malaysian union leader. Interviewed in Seoul, South Korea, by Janaka Binwala.

Fowler, Ric. February 23, 2003. International Secretary of the Construction, Mining and Energy Workers Union. Interviewed in Sydney, Australia, by Robert Lambert and Edward Webster.

Jamil, Rubina. November 7, 2001. President of the All Pakistan Federation of Trade Unions and leader of the Working Women's Organization. Interviewed in Seoul, South Korea, by Sakhela Buhlungu and Edward Webster.

Murie, Jim. February 23, 2003. Assistant Secretary of the Communications, Electrical and Postal Union (CEPU). Interviewed in Perth, Australia, by Edward Webster.

Sari, Dita. November 8, 2001. Leader of the independent unions in Indonesia. Interviewed in Seoul, South Korea, by Ayu Ratih.

## References

Adler, Glenn, and Eddie Webster, eds. 2000. *Trade Unions and Democratization in South Africa, 1985–97.* Basingstoke: Palgrave Macmillan.

Breakwell, Glynis M. 1986. *Coping with Threatened Identities.* London: Methuen.

Buhlungu, Sakhela. 2002. *Comrades, Entrepreneurs, and Career Unionists: Organisational Modernisation and the New Cleavages Among Full-Time Union Officials in South Africa.* Occasional Paper No. 17. Johannesburg: Friedrich Ebert Stiftung.

Burawoy, Michael. 2002. Types of sociology. Paper presented at the Colloquium entitled "Southern Africa in Transition Program," Department of Sociology, University of the Witwatersrand, Johannesburg.

Candland, Christopher, and Rudra Sil, eds. 2001. *The Politics of Labour in a Global Age: Continuity and Change in Late-Industrialising and Post-Socialist Economies.* Oxford: Oxford University Press.

Castells, Manuel. 1997. *The Information Age: Economy, Society, and Culture,* vol. 2, *The Power of Identity.* Oxford: Blackwell.

CITU (Centre of Indian Trade Unions). 2003. *United Struggles and the Organizational Consolidation of the Trade Union Movement.* Calcutta: CITU.

Cobble, Dorothy Sue. 2001. Lost ways of unionism: Historical perspectives on reinventing the labor movement. In Turner, Katz, and Hurd 2001, 82–96.

Collinson, Colin. 2001. Southern unions link up on globalization. *Western Teacher.* December 7.

Deyo, Frederic C., ed. 1987. *The Political Economy of the New Asian Industrialism.* Ithaca, N.Y.: Cornell University Press.

Erikson, Erik H. 1968. *Identity: Youth and Crisis*. New York: W. W. Norton.

Harris, Nigel. 2002. *What's New in the New Labor Internationalism: SIGTUR as a Global Network*. Honours dissertation, Department of Organizational and Labor Studies, University of Western Australia.

Hathaway, Dale. 2000. *Allies across the Border: Mexico's "Authentic Labor Front" and Global Solidarity*. Cambridge, Mass.: South End Press.

Haworth, Nigel, and Harvie Ramsay. 1984. Grasping the nettle: Problems with the theory of international trade union solidarity. In Waterman 1984, 60–87.

———. 1986. Workers of the world untied: A critical analysis of the labor response to the internationalization of capital. *International Journal of the Sociology of Law and Social Policy* 6, no. 2: 55–82.

Johnston, Paul. 2001. Organize for what? The resurgence of labor as a citizenship movement. In Turner, Katz, and Hurd 2001, 27–58.

Katz, Harry. 2001. Afterword: Whither the labor movement? In Turner, Katz, and Hurd 2001, 339–49.

Klein, Naomi. 2001. Farewell to "The End of History": Organization and vision in anti-corporate movements. In *Socialist Register 2002: A World of Contradictions*, ed. Leo Panitch and Colin Leys, 1–14. London: Merlin Press.

Lambert, Robert. 1997. *State and Labor in New Order Indonesia*. Perth: University of Western Australia Press.

———. 1998. Asian labor markets and international competitiveness: Australian transformations. *International Review of Comparative Public Policy* 10: 271–96.

———. 1999a. Global dance: Factory regimes, Asian labor standards and corporate restructuring. In *Globalization Patterns of Labor Resistance*, ed. Jeremy Waddington, 72–104. London: Mansell.

———. 1999b. An emerging force? Independent labor in Indonesia. *Labor, Capital, and Society* 32, no. 1: 70–107.

Lambert, Robert, and Edward Webster. 1988. The re-emergence of political unionism in contemporary South Africa. In *Popular Struggles in South Africa*, ed. William Cobbett and Robin Cohen, 20–41. Trenton, N.J.: Africa World Press.

Lee, Eric. 1997. *The Labor Movement and the Internet: The New Internationalism*. London: Pluto.

Lund, Francie, and Caroline Skinner. 1999. *Promoting the Interests of Women in the Informal Economy: An Analysis of Street Trader Organizations in South Africa*. Research Report No. 19, School of Development Studies, University of Natal, Durban.

Maher, Tony. 2000. Speech by Tony Maher, president of the Construction, Forestry, Mining, and Energy Workers Union's Mining Division, to Rio Shareholders Meeting. May 10. An ICEM communiqué, circulated through Rio Tinto Global Union Network.

Moody, Kim. 1997. *Workers in a Lean World: Unions in the International Economy*. London: Verso.

Munck, Ronaldo. 1988. *The New International Labor Studies: An Introduction*. London: Zed Books.

———. 2002. *Globalization and Labor: The New "Great Transformation."* London: Zed Books.

Nayak, Nalini. 2001. "No women, no fish": A feminist perspective on fisheries in developing countries. *Labor Movements Research Committee Newsletter.* October.

O'Brien, Robert. 2000. Workers and world order: The tentative transformation of the international union movement. *Review of International Studies* 26: 533–55.

Olle, Werner, and Wolfgang Schoeller. 1977. World market competition and restrictions on international trade union policies. *Capital and Class* 2: 56–75.

Peetz, David. 1998. *Unions in a Contrary World: The Future of the Australian Trade Union Movement.* Cambridge: Cambridge University Press.

Ramsay, Harvie. 1999. In search of international union theory. In *Globalization Patterns of Labor Resistance*, ed. Jeremy Waddington, 192–219. London: Mansell.

Ramsay, Harvie, and Jennifer Bair. 1999. Working on the chain gang: Global production networks and their implications for organized labor. Paper presented to the European Sociological Association, Congress entitled "Will Europe Work?" Amsterdam, The Netherlands, August 18–21.

Rio Tinto Global Union Network. 2000. *Rio Tinto Global Campaign Fact Sheet.* Available online.

Ross, Andrew, ed. 1997. *No Sweat: Fashion, Free Trade and the Rights of Garment Workers.* London: Verso.

Sable, Charles, Dara O'Rourke, and Archon Fung. 2000. Ratcheting labor standards: Regulation for continuous improvement in the global workplace. Congress on Citizenship in a Global Economy, University of Wisconsin, Madison.

Sandbrook, Richard, ed. 2003. *Civilizing Globalization: A Survival Guide.* Albany, N.Y.: State University of New York Press.

Scipes, Kim. 2000. It's time to come clean: Open the AFL-CIO archives on international labor operations. *Labor Studies Journal* 25, no. 2: 4–25.

Seidman, Gay. 1994. *Manufacturing Militance: Workers' Movements in Brazil and South Africa, 1970–1985.* Berkeley and Los Angeles: University of California Press.

———. 2002. Deflated citizenship: Labor rights in a global order. Paper presented at the Annual Congress of the American Sociological Association, August, Washington, D.C.

Sennett, Richard. 1998. *Corrosion of Character: The Personal Consequences of Work in the New Capitalism.* New York: W. W. Norton.

Silver, Beverly J. 2003. *Forces of Labor: Workers Movements and Globalization Since 1870.* Cambridge: Cambridge University Press.

Silver, Beverly, and Giovanni Arrighi. 2001. Workers North and South. In *Socialist Register 2001. Working Classes: Global Realities*, ed. Leo Panitch and Colin Leys, 53–76. London: Merlin Press.

SIGTUR (Southern Initiative on Globalization and Trade Union Rights). 1998. *Founding Document.* Personal archives of Robert Lambert.

———. 1999. *Principles for Participation in SIGTUR.* Personal archives of Robert Lambert.

Touraine, Alain. 1983. *Solidarity: The Analysis of a Social Movement, Poland, 1980–1981*. Cambridge: Cambridge University Press.

Turner, Lowell, and Richard Hurd. 2001. Building social movement unionism: The transformation of the American labor movement. In Turner, Katz, and Hurd 2001, 9–26.

Turner, Lowell, Harry Katz, and Richard Hurd, eds. 2001. *Rekindling the Movement: Labor's Quest for Relevance in the Twenty-first Century*. Ithaca, N.Y.: ILR Press.

Von Holdt, Karl. 2002. Social movement unionism: The South African case. *Work, Employment and Society* 16, no. 2: 283–304.

Voss, Kim, and Rachel Sherman. 2000. Breaking the iron law of oligarchy: Union revitalization in the American labor movement. *American Journal of Sociology* 106, no. 2: 303–49.

Waterman, Peter. 1998. *Globalization and Social Movements and the New Internationalisms*. London: Mansell.

———, ed. 1984. *For a New Labor Internationalism*. The Hague: Institute of Social Studies.

Waterman, Peter, and Jane Wills, eds. 2001. *Place, Space and the New Labor Internationalisms*. Oxford: Blackwell.

Webster, Eddie. 1988. The rise of social movement unionism: The two faces of the black trade union movement in South Africa. In *State, Resistance and Change in South Africa*, ed. Philip Frankel, Noam Pines, and Mark Swilling, 174–95. London: Croom Helm.

Webster, Edward, and Glenn Adler. 1999. Towards a class compromise in South Africa's double transition. *Politics and Society* 27, no. 2: 347–85.

# 7.
# New Agendas and New Patterns of International NGO Political Action

## Paul Nelson

## Introduction

A broad set of organizations, including community-based groups, trade unions, international human rights, development, and environmental nongovernmental organizations (NGOs), have assumed increasing prominence in international political debates. Often working in shifting coalitions and networks, they operate in political arenas as diverse as, for example, district, provincial, and national governments of Uganda or India; the halls of the European Union in Brussels; municipal, state, and provincial governments in North America; and the governing bodies of the World Bank and the International Monetary Fund (IMF). They deploy a variety of conventional and radical populist political strategies.

Among the areas in which these networks are most extensive and have gained greatest prominence is international economic, development, and trade policy. This chapter draws on the experience of international NGOs (INGOs), mainly based in the United States or Europe, advocating for changes in policy and practice at the World Bank, and examines challenges that confront some of these organizations in broadening their attention to a wider range of international financial and trade policy issues.

Between 1980 and the present, NGOs developed and learned a set of political strategies that are well adapted to influencing development and environmental policy issues at the World Bank. Here, their approach made consistent use of eight political strategies shaped by the World Bank's institutional, professional, and political environment. The strategies are built

Parts of the chapter are drawn from a report written for consultations on the Global Financial Architecture, sponsored by Oxfam America with the Overseas Development Council (Oxfam America 1999). Oxfam America published the earlier paper in its Oxfam Ideas working paper series (Nelson 2001).

around network advocacy, internationalizing local issues by focusing on the World Bank's role in domestic policy and drawing heavily on the support of the US government to reform and regulate World Bank policy.

By the late 1990s, however, many of the same organizations involved in advocacy at the World Bank had become engaged in a broader set of economic policy and trade issues. These issues have required new and different political strategies, forcing NGOs to relearn—even to "unlearn"—political lessons gained in work on the World Bank. The political and institutional factors that require this political retooling include both the political environment of trade and financial policymaking, and the need to relate to growing anti-globalization social movements whose political approaches differ sharply from those of most NGOs.

In fact, these differences between NGO strategies and posture in these policy arenas suggest that a more rigorous model of NGO international action be developed than has hitherto been the case. For, the character of international political networks, strategies, and relationships to governmental organizations are fundamentally shaped by the political tasks for which they are formed, and theorizing about NGOs as political actors has not adequately taken account of this variability. Not only political strategies, but also the forms and members of coalitions and networks, are profoundly shaped by their political goals and the political environments in which they operate.

## Engaging the World Bank

NGOs' advocacy involves learning political strategies and adopting strategic postures toward powerful governments and international organizations. NGOs working to influence policy and practice at the World Bank employ a diverse repertoire of political methods that conform to the dominant model of NGO advocacy strategies.

This dominant approach highlights the role of transnational issue networks which work to persuade powerful governments or other international authorities to bring international norms to bear on a national policy.

Kathryn Sikkink's account of changes in Mexican and Argentine human rights behavior contains the basis of the theory (Sikkink 1993), which holds that principled ideas, articulated by transnational issue-focused networks (including governmental and nongovernmental actors), mobilize political, economic, and diplomatic pressure to help end systematic human rights violations.

Margaret Keck and Kathryn Sikkink (1998), Thomas Risse, Stephen Ropp, and Kathryn Sikkink (1999), and others have elaborated the framework more fully, primarily with reference to human rights advocacy. Keck and Sikkink (1998) invoke the image of a "boomerang": domestic political actors in one country, finding their own government resistant to their agenda, ally with foreign or international NGOs, which in turn mobilize their governments or intergovernmental authorities to put pressure on the offending government. Risse, Ropp, and Sikkink (1999) outline a five-stage process through which government human rights behavior changes under such pressure.

This "internationalization" aptly frames many NGO network efforts, including many campaigns on World Bank policy. Norms formed in an international arena or institution can be a source of leverage over international institutions such as the World Bank and, in turn, over the World Bank's borrowing member governments.

Basically, NGOs have deployed eight broad strategies to influence the World Bank. These strategies, which have been reinforced by policy successes, involve the NGOs in close cooperative relationships with US government and internal World Bank allies, and conform to the "internationalization" pattern, strengthening World Bank influence over its borrowers' domestic economic, social, and environmental policies. The strategies have been effective in the particular political configuration in which World Bank policy and practice are decided.

Among the United States-based and European-based INGOs that have been active in World Bank advocacy are several focused on environmental policy (Bank Information Center, Center for International Environmental Law, Environmental Defense Fund, Friends of the Earth), and on debt and structural adjustment, social policy and related policies (Bretton Woods Project, Christian Aid, Development Group for Alternative Policies, European Network for Debt and Development; see Bread for the World Institute [1999] and Oxfam International [2000]).[1]

In challenging World Bank policy NGOs have honed a set of reporting and lobbying skills; built networks; developed contacts in the media, governments, and within the World Bank; and cultivated information sources. The campaigns and the growing literature on NGOs and the World Bank suggest eight principal political strategies.

1. *NGOs use the World Bank as an international lever to influence domestic policy outcomes.* Advocates target the World Bank largely because of its influence over its member governments, and the well-being of their citizens and ecosystems. This influence varies, of course, across countries and issue areas. NGOs may see the World Bank as a source of positive leverage, as in education, gender policy, and information disclosure, or as a barrier to change, whose position is to be shifted, as in dam building and structural adjustment policy. In either case NGOs' broad strategy has conformed to Keck and Sikkink's "boomerang," influencing national policy through networked efforts that mobilize international leverage. NGOs seldom explicitly enlist the World Bank as an ally; their campaigns

generally involve vigorous criticism of the World Bank, even when they have had the effect of expanding its authority (Nelson 1996).

2. *NGOs disseminate information and exert political pressure through international networks.* Coalitions and networks among NGOs have been global, national, and regional, and have varied in the breadth of their agenda and their degree of formal institutionalization. These coalitions and networks have been the modus operandi for many advocacy efforts, and their impact (Keck and Sikkink 1998; Rich 1994) as well as issues and problems in their governance and strategy have received considerable attention (Chiriboga 2001; Fox and Brown 1998; Jordan and van Tuijl 2000).

Coalitions have formed around sectoral policies such as mining, forestry, dams, information disclosure; crosscutting issues such as gender and structural adjustment lending; and in support of national or regional issues (The Amazon Coalition is an example, see Selverston-Scher 2000). Each of the above features (or featured) US-based NGOs in coordinating roles, and each has (or had) a representative in Washington, D.C. A handful of organizations, particularly the Washington-based Bank Information Center and the London-based Bretton Woods Project, have specialized in disseminating information in support of advocacy campaigns.

3. *NGOs frame issues to take advantage of international norms.* Successfully framing an issue—defining the frame of reference in which it will be seen—has been important to most NGO advocacy (Keck and Sikkink 1998), and advocacy on resettlement and debt relief illustrate the importance of this strategy. Major dam projects are generally designed to produce electricity, provide irrigation, or control flooding, but international debate over these projects has been only secondarily over these objectives. NGOs have framed the issue as one of minority rights by focusing attention on poor communities' loss of land rights and livelihood, their inadequate compensation when resettled, and human rights abuses during dam construction (Khagram 2000; McCully 2001).

Debt is conventionally understood as a contractual obligation incurred when governments borrow to finance development activities. By focusing attention on the human costs of debt servicing, and on debts incurred by undemocratic regimes no longer in power, the Jubilee 2000 debt-relief campaign reframed the debt of poor, highly indebted countries as an issue of distributive justice, even as debt bondage. A widely quoted statement of the All-African Conference of Churches, for example, states: "Every child in Africa is born with a financial burden which a lifetime's work cannot repay. The debt is a new form of slavery as vicious as the slave trade" (Church World Service, n.d.). Jubilee itself, referring to the ancient Jewish principle that property be restored and debts erased periodically, identifies the issue for listeners in the Judeo-Christian tradition as one of distributive justice.

4. *NGOs mobilize US government support for World Bank reforms.* Pressure by the US Congress became the US-based NGOs' dominant strategy for forcing policy changes in the late 1980s and early 1990s (Wirth 1998). The US legislation directly called for the use of environmental-impact assessments, new measures where indigenous groups or involuntary resettlement are involved, new resettlement and information-disclosure policies, and the creation of an independent inspection panel (Bowles and Kormos 1995). NGOs' demands for new information disclosure policies and an independent inspection panel were met when a US congressional committee threatened, with NGO encouragement, to withhold funding from the triennial replenishment of the World Bank's International Development Association (Udall 1998).

With US funding always politically vulnerable, Congressional concerns are taken seriously at the World Bank. Pressuring the World Bank has proven politically attractive to members of Congress on the political right and left, and US executive-branch agencies, especially USAID and the Environmental Protection Agency, have remained key governmental allies to activists on environment and information policies.

5. *NGOs cooperate with sympathetic staff and managers within the World Bank.* Internal reformers have advanced proposals within the organization, leaked documents and other information to help NGOs' advocacy efforts, and supported and relied upon external pressure from NGOs. These relationships have been demonstrated, for example, in work on resettlement (Fox 1998), and in promoting popular participation in World Bank-financed projects (Miller-Adams 1999).

6. *NGOs form alliances with other international actors, including UN bodies, governments, other civil society organizations, and researchers.* During early debates over structural adjustment, UNICEF helped bring together NGO concerns about social and human impact. Such alliances, which Keck and Sikkink (1998) call transnational advocacy networks, cross government/NGO lines to bring together individuals and agencies with shared values and interests. Most successful advocacy efforts at the World Bank have also enjoyed active support from one or more of the World Bank's major shareholder governments. The British government led the advocacy for debt relief both within the G7 process and at the World Bank, collaborating with Oxfam and other NGO supporters (Evans 1999).

7. *NGOs highlight failed projects to argue for new policies or structures.* Environmental advocates successfully used high-profile "problem projects" to gain media and US Congressional attention. NGOs have leveraged the political and professional costs of these embarrassments to the World Bank to win new hiring patterns and staffing, to bring about procedural and policy reforms, and to create new information-disclosure policy and an investigation panel (O'Brien et al. 2000, 119–34).

8. *NGOs sometimes demonstrate mass support, as in the case of debt relief.* Much of the NGO advocacy on social and environmental policy has involved details of policy and staffing issues, and lacked the compelling images and sweeping themes to inspire mass popular support. NGOs' limited success with attracting mass support began with the 50 Years Is Enough campaign in the United States, which brought student organizations into the World Bank networks for the first time (50 Years Is Enough 1994).

The Jubilee 2000 campaign successfully expanded popular involvement in debt-relief advocacy. The issue of debt relief shares characteristics with the World Bank agenda, in that the World Bank and IMF are important creditors to the most highly indebted poor countries, and are targets of the call for debt relief (Donnelly 2002). But in other ways debt relief resembles the issues of the trade and finance agenda, which, unlike development projects and most World Bank policy, have implications for the global financial order. The G7 (now G8) countries have guided debt-relief policy directly (Evans 1999).

To summarize, INGOs have developed a set of strategies, political skills, and assets—including support from key governments—that has become established practice in advocacy networks addressing the World Bank. These approaches, however, are not applicable to international policy issues, including closely related trade and finance issues.

## Beyond the World Bank: The New Agenda

Events in the 1990s brought financial, monetary, and trade policies to the forefront of international policymaking. The financial crises sparked in Mexico in 1994, and Asia, Russia, and Brazil in 1997; the debates over the World Trade Organization (WTO), North American Free Trade Agreement, and the Free Trade Area of the Americas have contributed to the widely held sense that international trade and financial speculation is now beyond the effective control of governmental or intergovernmental authorities. In 1998 a proposed Multilateral Agreement on Investment collapsed under the strain of deep disagreements among OECD parties to the negotiations (Walter 2001). Trade policy at the WTO, management of currency crises, and international capital flows are among the principal issues of the agenda, here called a "new agenda" in reference to the issues' new centrality and to the expanded involvement of NGOs.

The WTO's 1999 Ministerial Meeting in Seattle brought the trade organization and its critics to the world's front pages, as delegates were unable to resolve key issues and street protests disrupted and upstaged the deliberations (Halliday 2000). A broad set of NGOs as well as labor, consumer, student, and civic organizations have campaigned against the WTO as an emblem of "corporate globalization." They seek to slow, discredit, or modify trade liberalization by undercutting the authority and credibility of the WTO, as in Seattle (Kaldor 2000), or by altering its rules and procedures (Oxfam International 2002). NGOs object to the WTO's rule-making authority, its capacity to limit national labor and consumer-protection measures, and the disadvantages that existing trade rules impose on the poorest countries, particularly those of sub-Saharan Africa. Protests and campaigning continued in 2001–2002, and governments and NGOs won some concessions on the application of intellectual-property rules to HIV/AIDS medicines in November 2001 (Joint statement 2001).

When financial crises strike, as in several Asian countries, Russia, and Brazil in 1997, multibillion-dollar "rescue" programs for governments, and for the international banks that are their major creditors, have become the standard response, patched together under the direction of the US Treasury and the IMF (Wade 2000). Two aspects of the NGO agenda for change in the "global financial architecture" involve reform of the IMF and instituting a tax on global financial transactions.

Until the late 1990s, none of the NGOs' strategies—persuasion, confrontation, attack—made significant inroads on any issue at the IMF (Scholte 1998). But in the last years of the 1990s, weakened by criticism of its work in Russia and Southeast Asia, the IMF became more vulnerable to criticism. The IMF was forced to cooperate in debt relief (Evans 1999) and has altered its information-disclosure standards. But although NGOs have made some inroads at the IMF, the existing ad hoc approach to currency crises has not been changed significantly. The experience of Argentina in 2002 only suggests that an option has been added to the crisis-response menu: tighter policy conditions and smaller loans.

After the 1997 financial crisis sparked debate about a new global financial architecture, NGOs moved to advocate new measures to regulate capital movements, promoting a proposal, long associated with economist James Tobin, for a tax on the roughly one trillion (US) dollars of daily international financial transactions. Proponents argue that such a tax could slow the highly volatile flows of capital that are blamed as a factor in recent economic crises and help finance currently under-funded social or peacekeeping activities (Stecher 1999).

Here, NGO support has been coordinated by a loosely linked group of NGO and academic supporters in Canada, the United States, and Europe. Participants in the US Tax Speculation Action Network include a few long-time participants in the World Bank campaigns, and many labor, legal, and student organizations, including the AFL-CIO, EarthAction, Global Exchange, Rainforest Action Network, and Youth

Action for Global Justice. Advocacy efforts aim to build familiarity and support at every political level, national and sub-national, by encouraging legislatures to adopt resolutions and other nonbinding declarations of support. An effort to mobilize support among parliamentarians around the world resulted in 864 signatures to a pro-Tobin tax resolution by June 2004.

The issues on the new agenda differ in fundamental ways from World Bank policy issues, clearly requiring new strategies and the "unlearning" of some World Bank advocacy lessons by activists and a more flexible theoretical approach by scholars. The configuration, positions, and strategies of the political actors involved in the new issues are markedly different from those involved in World Bank policy debates. Three differences are highlighted here: influential governments, including the United States, perceive their interests differently; the international organizations involved may be less susceptible to NGO pressure; and the range of active citizen organizations involved is broader.

First, global financial policy issues are more central to G8 governments, especially the United States, than is World Bank project lending, and reform proposals have little prospect of winning US support. World Bank policy on which NGOs secured US support—environment, resettlement, transparency, and accountability—is peripheral to US economic priorities. Debt relief to date affects mostly small, poor economies, low priorities in US foreign economic policy. But the US government has shown little support for the NGOs' position on any issues related to international monetary policy or trade. The global financial policy issues at stake are more central to US foreign economic policy, and NGOs find themselves generally in opposition to US government positions. When the government of the United Kingdom supported an NGO-endorsed reform on debt relief, it encountered opposition from other G7 leaders (Evans 1999).

Second, the international organizations themselves are less susceptible to NGO leverage or persuasion. Advocates at the World Bank have a clear institutional target whose managers, staff, policies, and loans can be identified and confronted. But for some financial policy issues—such as financial crisis management and capital flow regulation—it is less clear where to turn. The fact that no institution effectively governs these aspects of the international economy, in fact, is part of the NGOs' concern. NGOs' strategies on the Tobin Tax reflect this absence of a single target: activists have worked since 1999 to expand public awareness and promote support in principle, from governments at all levels, for a tax on international capital flows.

In other cases the target for advocacy is clear but development and environmental norms are not as obviously and directly applicable and NGOs have to overcome a legitimacy and credibility barrier. NGOs have been helped at the World Bank by two presumptions: they speak for otherwise excluded groups, and they are expert in some aspects of the World Bank's mission. These bases of legitimacy may sometimes be problematic (Atack 1999; Edwards 2000; Fox and Brown 1998; Nelson 2002a). But for the present, the point is that NGOs benefit from these presumptions because they, like the World Bank, are in the development field. This and the fact that NGOs are an important constituency in support of development assistance funding have helped them win access and a measure of influence.

NGOs' legitimacy, however, does not automatically transfer to financial or trade policy issues that are not directly related to development aid. NGOs were generally recognized, for example, as experts on the human and social costs of the Asian financial crisis but not as important actors in the debate over causes and solutions. The link between NGOs' local constituency or field-based experience, on the one hand, and international policy on the other, grows more difficult to assert as the agenda moves from development-aid policy and projects toward macroeconomic issues, financial policy, and institutional reforms. The relatively long causal chain between global financial policies and the issues on which NGOs have greatest credibility and legitimacy—poverty reduction, gender equity, and environmental protection, for example—challenges NGOs' efforts to frame the issues convincingly as matters of humanitarian or environmental concern.

Moreover, with regard to new agenda issues, advocacy strategies tend to defend the prerogatives and policy choices of at least some governments. Rather than forcing compliance with international norms, the NGO agenda sometimes tries to shore up national authority. In trade policy, for example, the NGOs' positions have favored national authority to apply environmental and labor regulations to imports, to use selective trade barriers to protect new industries, and to produce generic versions of drugs used in HIV/AIDS therapy (Position Paper on WTO Negotiations by Women from ACP Countries 1999; Sayer 2001). In financial crisis management many NGOs have supported the availability of capital controls, such as those used by the government of Malaysia to prevent wholesale currency speculation in 1997 (Interaction 2001).

The trade and financial policy agendas are not a complete reversal of the NGO strategy of applying international leverage to developing country governments. NGOs still advocate international regulation of a variety of national policies and practices, including child labor, environmental pollution, minimum wages, and labor organizing rights. But the new finance and trade agenda does represent a significant shift toward strategies that support and defend national authorities against international rule making, and this shift requires a reassessment of the political significance of NGO advocacy.

The final factor altering the political dynamics for NGO advocates is the emergence of a new wave of social movement advocates. Social movements have changed the political landscape for established NGOs both by making the World Bank a target of anti-globalization protests and, more decisively, by shaping the political environment for debates on trade and finance. Mass demonstrations against the World Bank, IMF, and WTO have brought trade, finance, and development issues to the headlines since 1999.

The social movement organizations involved—student, trade union, consumer, and radical environmental organizations largely based in Europe and North America—sometimes conflict with established NGOs' advocacy agendas and style. Demonstrators in Washington, D.C., and Prague in April and September 2000, and at World Bank/IMF Annual Meetings since then, focused not on World Bank policy or lending but on the place of the IMF and World Bank in broader global economic trends. They attacked neoliberal globalization and the relative freedom of transnational corporations and investors to buy up privatized industries, to move production sites (and jobs), and to trade speculatively on countries' currencies (Greider 2000).

NGOs' advocacy at the World Bank has been led by NGOs with sustained professional engagement in development policy and environmental issues, and advocacy strategies often depend on NGO staffs' detailed knowledge of specific World Bank policies and activities. The new wave of activism, on the other hand, relies much less on consultation and negotiation with IGOs and has little stake in building working relationships with their staffs. The street demonstrations that grabbed attention in Seattle, Washington, D.C., and Prague were both an asset and an embarrassment to established NGOs. Anti-globalization sentiment strengthened the NGOs' case for debt relief and other reforms but also created tensions among the NGOs and social movement organizations. Oxfam and Greenpeace, for example, dissociated themselves in Seattle from the coalition of organizations demanding the abolition of the World Bank and IMF (Kahn 2000). Some protest coordinators have referred disparagingly to the "backroom lobbying" of NGOs and the "NGO reformist community" (Peoples' Global Action 2000, 23). John Dunning observes that there was "negligible" social capital and trust among civil society actors in Seattle (Dunning 2000, 481).

Disagreement flared again in April 2002, when the international Oxfam network launched a campaign refocusing its trade agenda from anti-free trade to pro-fair trade. The campaign, and its flagship report *Rigged Rules and Double Standards*, calls on "governments, institutions, and multinational companies to change the rules so that trade can become part of the solution to poverty, not part of the problem" (p. 4). Arguing that trade could reduce poverty if conducted under equitable rules, the campaign calls for specific changes in international trade and finance rules to stabilize primary commodity prices, eliminate wealthy countries' barriers to low-income countries imports, end policy conditionality on IMF and World Bank loans, change patent rules, and give poor countries a "stronger voice" at the WTO.

Oxfam has provoked criticism from other NGOs and social movements involved in trade policy work, and the split illustrates the challenges that the INGOs face. Critics of the new Oxfam initiative, such as the US-based Food First Network, charge that Oxfam's position amounts to claiming that "more globalization is what the developing countries need," a position that "echo[es] the position of United States Trade Representative (USTR), the European Union (EU), and the World Trade Organization (WTO)" (Food First 2002). Oxfam is further accused of "undermin[ing] the demands of social movements and think tanks in the South such as *Via Campesina*, MST [the Brazilian landless-rural-workers movement], and Focus on the Global South, which have demanded that governments must uphold the rights of all people to food sovereignty rather than industry-led export-oriented production" (ibid).

Such a conflict among NGO allies is not new. During the 1990s, for example, disagreements flared among NGOs over US-based NGOs' positions with respect to US funding for the World Bank (Nelson 1997). Many governments and some NGOs in the global South have viewed NGO agendas that highlight environmental and labor issues as a Northern agenda inimical to their interests. But these North-South splits are now compounded by the radical positions and confrontational strategies of the social movement organizations that have brought unprecedented public attention to issues of global finance and trade.

## Implications of the New Agenda

NGOs' selective, targeted agendas and well-tailored political strategies have helped to force the adoption of new policies at the World Bank. In the process NGOs have learned complex political lessons and developed political resources that serve them well in advocating World Bank reforms. But global financial and trade policy issues differ from the World Bank policies on which many INGOs cut their political teeth, and the lessons learned to date may not serve NGOs well in the new wave of advocacy.

All of this has implications for NGOs (see Nelson 2001) and indicates that the tendency to explain INGO advocacy as a process of mobilizing international political leverage to address domestic concerns must be reconsidered. NGOs' advocacy on international finance and trade policy confronts a different configuration of political actors and is often focused

on weakening international trade and financial authority or on protecting or restoring national authority to control capital movement or regulate trade, rather than on invoking international authority to shape national behavior.

### Debating the Prevailing Model

The internationalization model has been extended beyond human rights
to shape scholarly understanding of environmental movements (Arts
1998; Fabig and Boele 1999; Keck 1998) and of a variety of NGO advocacy efforts (Florini 2000; Khagram, Riker, and Sikkink 2002), including several focused on World Bank policy and practice (Fox and
Brown 1998; Nelson 1997; 2002a). In these accounts international pressure is triggered by local NGO or citizen organizations in a borrowing
country, whose international allies invoke internationally held norms
about rainforest protection, indigenous peoples' rights, compensation of
resettled communities, and so on. Relationships among NGO participants are sometimes complex, but the mobilization of international authority is the dominant strategy for advancing the issue networks' agendas.

The argument presented here is not the first challenge to the model.
On empirical grounds it has been argued either that non-state actors
have less influence than the NGO proponents imagine (Moravcsik 2000)
or that national social movements are more significant, and international
networking less significant, than the internationalization advocates believe (Tarrow 1998). Several recent discussions of NGOs and international politics argue that an alternative perspective is necessary and seek
to ground NGOs more thoroughly in the social, professional, and political systems in which they have thrived (Görg and Hirsch 1998; Pasha
and Blaney 1998; Roe 1995; Tvedt, Chapter 8 herein; Woods 2001).

Earlier challenges enrich the discussion of NGOs' roles in international policymaking. They suggest possible limits of NGOs' internationalizing strategies and raise important cautions about the assumption
that expanding the NGO voice necessarily expands or deepens democratic debate. Most important, they place NGOs within a social and political system, not outside it. NGOs have, at times, challenged the do-
nor-dominated system in which they exist, but they cannot be assumed
to challenge or transform it.

The findings presented here suggest that the protest movement against
corporate globalization, and NGO advocacy on an important set of international financial, trade, and monetary policy issues are not susceptible to the internationalization approach, either as a theoretical framework or as an advocacy strategy. For these issues the configuration of
political actors—NGO, governmental, and international—and thus the

NGO position and posture with respect to international authority, are significantly different.

## NGO Professionalism and Popular Protest

The tension between NGO professionalism and populist protest is not new, but it is an intensified challenge for the former. NGOs benefit from mass support in advancing their international financial policy agenda. But NGOs' credibility with international authorities—officials of major industrial countries and international organizations—depends as well on their ability to participate in substantive policy debates with these agencies. Labor, student, and consumer organizations benefit from the credibility that established NGOs give to their coalitions. Development and environment NGOs should be prepared to hear occasional stinging denunciations from erstwhile allies, as the recent debate over trade illustrates. But if these NGOs fail to forge successful coalitions with the emerging social movements, they will continue to be the targets of such attacks from the populist left and will be increasingly identified as an elite, professional wing of the NGO movement, with limited claim to mass political support and legitimacy.

The politics of international financial and trade policy render some of INGOs' favored strategies less effective. In particular, neither project-specific campaigns nor US government leadership is likely to be an effective source of political leverage. But other strategies and tools, which were not effective with the World Bank, may also be of greater political value. Human rights–based arguments and strategies, for example, may be more effective in some financial and trade policy domains than with the World Bank. Human rights standards, especially standards of economic and social rights, also serve as common ground in alliances among poor country governments, human rights and development NGOs, and labor, student, and consumer movements, addressing issues such as land reform, access to essential medicines, and access to water (Nelson 2002b).

## Influence Without Invoking International Authority?

A broader and more flexible model is now required to account for the growing variety of strategies and forms of NGO and social movement advocacy. Any such model has to allow for great variability in NGOs' strategic relationships with governments. Christoph Görg and Joachim Hirsch (1998) and Terje Tvedt (Chapter 8 herein) call attention to the deep dependence of most NGO advocacy strategies on governments' initiatives and governmental and intergovernmental action. NGOs are not independent actors creating an alternative political sphere. The emerging populist strategies of social movements in the globalization protests, however, suggest that NGOs and social movements have a broad range of strategic choices to make in positioning themselves with respect to the state. As activists use the Internet as well as the streets to disrupt, distract from, or "delegitimize" official meetings or agreements, it becomes clear that winning governmental support for an NGO-initiated agenda is only one of the available options. A new model should recognize the range of possible postures toward governmental allies, opponents, or targets.

NGOs' approaches to international norms and authority are increasingly varied. Many NGO initiatives in international politics do conform to the model identified by Keck and Sikkink, appealing to international norms to make a domestic policy issue subject to the influence of international organizations and powerful governments. But this approach does not fit all cases of international political action; to account for the increasing variety of NGO initiatives, we need to move toward a model that recognizes both the tendency to utilize international leverage and the growing tendency to work with and support some governments on issues such as debt relief, trade, and capital controls.

Civil society activists collaborate with governments to weaken or change the rules of international organizations (for example, the IMF or the WTO), or to reduce the influence of certain international organizations or norms (for example, neoliberal economic theory). They advocate stronger national capacity to regulate some corporate behavior (such as a tax on international currency transactions or capital controls at the national level). This pattern of advocacy, in which NGOs protect governmental prerogatives and oppose stronger international authority, points to the need for a broader, more varied vision of NGOs as international political actors.

## Notes

[1] The survey of NGO political approaches to the World Bank rests on interviews and participation in NGO strategy meetings between 1988 and 1999. The analysis of trade and financial policy draws on observation of a series of NGO meetings held in 1999, sponsored by Oxfam America and the Overseas Development Council.

## References

50 Years Is Enough. 1994. Conference platform summary. Available online.
Arts, Bas. 1998. *The Political Influence of Global NGOs: Case Studies on the Climate and Biodiversity Conventions.* Utrecht, The Netherlands: International Books.
Atack, Ian. 1999. Four criteria of development NGO legitimacy. *World Development* 27, no. 5: 855–64.

Bowles, Ian, and Cyril Kormos. 1995. Environmental reform at the World Bank: The role of the U.S. Congress. *Virginia Journal of International Law* 35, no. 4: 777–839.

Bread for the World Institute. 1999. *Debt and Development Dossier* 1 and 2 (September). Silver Spring, Md.: Bread for the World Institute.

Chiriboga, Manuel. 2001. Constructing a southern constituency for global advocacy: The experience of Latin American NGOs and the World Bank. In *Global Citizen Action*, ed. Michael Edwards and John Gaventa, 73–86. Boulder, Colo.: Lynne Rienner Publishers.

Church World Service. n.d. *Africa: In Bondage to Debt*. New York: Church World Service.

Donnelly, Elizabeth A. 2002. Proclaiming Jubilee: The debt and structural adjustment network. In Khagram, Riker, and Sikkink 2002, 155–80.

Dunning, John H. 2000. The future of the WTO: A socio-relational challenge? *Review of International Political Economy* 7, no. 3: 475–83.

Edwards, Michael. 2000. *NGO Rights and Responsibilities: A New Deal for Global Governance*. London: Foreign Policy Centre.

Evans, Huw. 1999. Debt relief for the poorest countries: Why did it take so long? *Development Policy Review* 17, no. 3: 267–79.

Fabig, Heike, and Richard Boele. 1999. The changing nature of NGO activity in a globalising world. *IDS Bulletin* 30, no. 3: 58–65.

Florini, Ann, ed. 2000. *The Third Force: The Rise of Transnational Civil Society*. Washington, D.C.: Carnegie Endowment for International Peace; Tokyo: Japan Center for International Exchange.

Food First. 2002. New OXFAM campaign contradicts developing country demands for WTO reform. Press statement. April 12. Available online.

Fox, Jonathan. 1998. When does reform policy influence practice? Lessons from the Bankwide Resettlement Review. In Fox and Brown 1998, 303–44.

Fox, Jonathan, and L. David Brown. 1998. *The Struggle for Accountability: The World Bank, NGOs, and Grassroots Movements*. Cambridge, Mass.: MIT Press.

Görg, Christoph, and Joachim Hirsch. 1998. Is international democracy possible? *Review of International Political Economy* 5, no. 4: 585–615.

Greider, William. 2000. After the WTO protest in Seattle, it's time to go on the offensive: Here's how. *The Nation*. January 21.

Halliday, Fred. 2000. Getting real about Seattle. *Millennium* 29, no. 1: 123–29.

Interaction. 2001. Finance for development, minutes of strategy session for NGOs (April 5). Available online.

Joint statement (Médicins Sans Frontières, Oxfam, Third World Network, Consumer Project on Technology, Consumers International, Health Action International, and the Network). 2001. Green light to put public health first at WTO ministerial conference in Doha. Joint statement. November 14. Available online.

Jordan, Lisa, and Peter van Tuijl. 2000. Political responsibility in transnational NGO advocacy. *World Development* 28, no. 12: 2051–65.

Kahn, Joseph. 2000. Globalization unifies its many-striped foes. *New York Times*, April 15, A5.

Kaldor, Mary. 2000. "Civilising" globalisation? The implications of the "Battle in Seattle." *Millennium* 29, no. 1: 105–14.

Keck, Margaret. 1998. Planafloro in Rondônia: The limits of leverage. In Fox and Brown 1998, 181–218.

Keck, Margaret, and Kathryn Sikkink. 1998. *Activists Beyond Borders: Advocacy Networks in International Politics*. Ithaca, N.Y.: Cornell University Press.

Khagram, Sanjeev. 2000. Toward democratic governance for sustainable development: Transnational civil society organizing around big dams. In Florini 2000, 84–114.

Khagram, Sanjeev, James V. Riker, and Kathryn Sikkink, eds. 2002. *Restructuring World Politics: Transnational Social Movements, Networks, and Norms*. Minneapolis: University of Minnesota Press.

McCully, Patrick. 2001. *Silenced Rivers: The Ecology and Politics of Large Dams*. London: Zed Books.

Miller-Adams, Michelle. 1999. *The World Bank: New Agendas in a Changing World*. London: Routledge.

Moravcsik, Andrew. 2000. The origins of human rights regimes: Democratic delegation in postwar Europe. *International Organization* 54, no. 2: 217–52.

Nelson, Paul J. 1996. Internationalising economic and environmental policy: Transnational NGO networks and the World Bank's expanding influence. *Millennium* 25, no. 3: 605–33.

———. 1997. Conflict, legitimacy, and effectiveness: Who speaks for whom in transnational NGO networks lobbying the World Bank? *Nonprofit and Voluntary Sector Quarterly* 26, no. 4: 421–40.

———. 2001. Globalization, NGO advocacy, and international financial policy: Unlearning lessons from lobbying the World Bank? Working paper. Boston: Oxfam America.

———. 2002a. Agendas, accountability, and legitimacy among transnational networks lobbying the World Bank. In Khagram, Riker, and Sikkink 2002, 131–54.

———. 2002b. Human rights, economic and social policy, and international politics: A new model. Paper presented at the annual meeting of the International Studies Association, New Orleans, March 23–27.

O'Brien, Robert, Anne Marie Goetz, Jan Aart Scholte, and Marc Williams. 2000. *Contesting Global Governance: Multilateral Economic Institutions and Global Social Movements*. Cambridge: Cambridge University Press.

Oxfam America. 1999. Participants. IFIs Global Financial Architecture Workshop. September 22–23. On file with author.

Oxfam International. 2000. A global action plan (GAP) for basic education. Available online.

Pasha, Mustapha Kamal, and David L. Blaney. 1998. Elusive paradise: The promise and peril of global civil society. *Alternatives* 23, no. 4: 417–50.

Peoples' Global Action. 2000. *Worldwide Resistance Roundup: Newsletter "Inspired by" Peoples' Global Action*. London: Peoples' Global Action.

Position Paper on WTO Negotiations by Women from ACP Countries. 1999. Consultation organized by Women in Development Europe (WIDE), November 7–9.

Rich, Bruce 1994. *Mortgaging the Earth: The World Bank, Environmental Impoverishment, and the Crisis of Development*. Boston: Beacon Press.

Risse, Thomas, Stephen C. Ropp, and Kathryn Sikkink, eds. 1999. *The Power of Human Rights: International Norms and Domestic Change*. Cambridge: Cambridge University Press.

Roe, Emery M. 1995. Critical theory, sustainable development, and populism. *Telos*, no. 103 (Spring): 149–62.

Sayer, John. 2001. Outline of speech by John Sayer, executive director of Oxfam International. Inaugural session of the Third United Nations Conference on Least Developed Countries, Brussels, May 14–20. On file with the author.

Scholte, Jan Aart. 1998. The IMF and civil society: An underdeveloped dialogue. Paper presented at a Global Workshop on Global Economic Institutions and Global Social Movements, Centre for Economic Policy Research, London, February 28.

Selverston-Scher, Melina. 2000. Building international civil society: Lessons from the Amazon Coalition. Paper presented at the conference entitled "Human Rights and Globalization: When Transnational Civil Society Networks Hit the Ground," University of California Santa Cruz, December 1–2. Available online.

Sikkink, Kathryn. 1993. Human rights, principled issue networks, and sovereignty in Latin America. *International Organizations* 47, no. 3: 411–41.

Stecher, Heinz. 1999. Time for a Tobin Tax: Some practical and political arguments. Oxfam GB discussion paper. Oxford: Oxfam GB. May.

Tarrow, Sidney. 1998. Fishnets, Internets, and catnets: Globalization and transnational collective action. In *Challenging Authority: The Historical Study of Contentious Politics*, ed. Michael P. Hanagan, Leslie Page Moch, and Wayne te Brake, 228–44. Minneapolis: University of Minnesota Press.

Udall, Lori. 1998. The World Bank and public accountability: Has anything changed? In Fox and Brown 1998, 391–436.

Wade, Robert. 2000. Out of the box: Rethinking the governance of international financial markets. *Journal of Human Development* 1, no. 1: 145–57.

Walter, Andrew. 2001. NGOs, business, and international investment: The Multilateral Agreement on Investment, Seattle, and beyond. *Global Governance* 7, no. 1: 51–74.

Wirth, David A. 1998. Partnership advocacy in World Bank environmental reform. In Fox and Brown 1998, 51–79.

Woods, Ngaire. 2001. Making the IMF and the World Bank more accountable. *International Affairs* 77, no. 1: 83–100.

# 8.
# Development NGOs: Actors in a Global Civil Society or in a New International Social System?

## Terje Tvedt

### The Research Challenge

At the national congress of the African National Congress held in December 1997 in South Africa, President Nelson Mandela attacked NGOs for their critical stance on government and for carrying out the political agendas of foreign interests. A few years later the secretary-general of the United Nations, Koffi Annan, described NGOs as the conscience of humanity. Mandela rebuked the NGOs, whereas Annan hailed them. Mainstream research on NGOs would tend to use Annan's claim as a well-placed argument supporting the notion of NGOs as voices of global civil society and democratic change. Mandela's criticism, on the other hand, will tend to be either overlooked and forgotten as soon as possible or interpreted as a political mistake by an otherwise great man. In fact, such a biased interpretation of two valid statements is unhelpful and misses the role of NGOs in today's world, for the positions of Mandela and Annan can best be acknowledged, understood, and analyzed within what can be termed an international social-system approach, and more particularly, within a donor-state-NGO-system approach, what might be called a DOSTANGO-system approach.

In the last decade or so, NGOs—sometimes under the label civil society organizations (CSOs)—have generally been described as a force of democracy, or in more evocative language, as a movement "advanced by a planetary citizen alliance known as global civil society" (Korten 2000, 1). Some commentators have gone so far as to talk of a new global superpower of consciousness (Dhanapala 2002). The reality of the NGO world is, however, much more mundane and complex, and one cannot understand developments without criticizing such ideological generalizations. Just to mention two examples that challenge prevailing assumptions:

*Example 1.* In 1998 the Kenyan NGO Mercy Relief International was raided by a team of Kenyan police and US Federal Bureau of Investigations agents a few days after the August 7 bombing of the US embassies in Nairobi and Dar es Salaam. Four other organizations—the Al-Haramain Foundation,[1] Help African People, the Islamic Relief Organization, and Ibrahim Bin Abdul Aziz Al Ibrahim Foundation—were deregistered because Kenyan authorities found that they were involved in the blast and in "activities and matters that are not in the interest of state security" (Achieng 1998). Kenyan authorities suspected that materials used for the building of the bombs, each weighing at least eight hundred kilograms, were smuggled into East Africa disguised as relief aid with the help of some Islamic relief agencies.

*Example 2.* In the United States the organization of the Reverend Sun Myung Moon, the Unification Church, has been seeking a major role in the NGO community at the United Nations. A US Congress report has stated that the "overriding religious goal" of this organization is "to establish a worldwide theocracy," a world order that would abolish separation of church and state and "be governed by the immediate direction of God" (US Congress report, quoted in Paine and Gratzer 2001). At the time of writing, three Moon groups have been granted formal NGO status and others have applied. The Moon organization has used the United Nations for conferences and held a mass wedding in a UN conference room. A Moon-sponsored umbrella group, known as the World Association of NGOs, describes itself as an authentic voice of the NGO community.[2] Moon activities have been judged illegal by a court of law in the United States, leading to the Rev. Moon's imprisonment for tax evasion, making false statements, and conspiracy to obstruct justice.[3] Moon organizations keep their finances secret, and the Unification Church has vast business and media holdings. The US Internal Revenue Service ruled for a number of years that it primarily acts as a for-profit corporation.

Influential research literature on NGOs has overlooked these types of organizations when the role of NGOs in society has been analyzed. David Korten's widely cited theory on "generations of NGOs" is a good case in point (Korten 1987; 1990). It is easy to falsify, but the theory, or slightly different variations of it, has long served and still serves as the NGO community's imagined past. This story about NGOs is in reality only about the "good," "progressive," and "humanitarian" NGOs, as if they alone constitute the NGO scene, or transnational civil society, or global civil society. The history of these chosen organizations is further constructed to fit a mobilizing story about maturing NGOs. This type of NGO research can be likened to the role of glorious national narratives produced by nationalist historians in Europe in the eighteenth and nineteenth centuries.

The close relationship between this type of research and activism, which has sustained a large group of consultants for a couple of decades, is a very problematic one (Tvedt 1998). Korten spelled out the reasons for this worry almost twenty years after his "generations" approach was first published. Underlining the historical importance of NGOs and the civil society, he wrote that "most important cultural orientations are grounded in a defining story, often a creation story, that provides the culture with its sense of identity, meaning, and purpose. One key to changing a cultural orientation is to change its underlying story" (Korten 2000, 5). By creating an underlying story, or an imagined past, the researcher-cum-activist hopes to change (the cultural orientation of) the world.

From another point of view the framework of this kind of research can be likened to the reaction of moderate Muslims in the wake of September 11, 2001. They claimed that the Muslims who captured the airplanes were not Muslims or not *real* Muslims. The mechanisms are the same: chasing away those who might destroy both self-image and the way the system or the group of people communicates about itself to itself and to the outside world. The tendency has been, at the same time as the heterogeneity of the NGO scene is rhetorically acknowledged, to describe the field as if "not good," "reactionary," or "fundamentalist" NGOs are not NGOs or not *real* NGOs.

The main challenge to NGO research at this stage, then, is not to develop grand theories or develop another inspirational project but to develop research designs that are able to analytically integrate both the homogeneity and heterogeneity of the NGO scene (in political, religious, institutional, and financial terms), its political role(s) and potential(s) within an agency/structure perspective, and at the same time to identify more systemic conflicts and power relations affecting the arena—both externally and internally.

If the aim is to understand the actual and potential roles of NGOs in transforming societies and the world, it is crucial to establish less-normative conceptual tools and concepts that can objectify the research object. Because research in this field to a large extent has been the continuation of politics by other means, and as it has been much more successful as politics than as science, it also implies that a number of very different questions have been mixed and now need to be unraveled. NGOs and their roles have to be analyzed uninfluenced by the veil of conventions and traditions that the whole system has been wrapped up in. By discursively maintaining the distinctiveness of the research system and its basic constitutive values (true *vs.* false, or good research *vs.* bad research), researchers can genuinely advance understanding.

Moreover, comparative research on NGOs requires deep questioning of whether or not the key concepts and measurement tools are relevant and appropriate in different historical and social contexts. Research should take a universalist, as opposed to relativist or absolutist, stance to the study of the NGO and NGO work in different settings and traditions. It is important to recognize that universalism as an epistemological strategy does not require a balance between "local" and "global" (which is impossible), or a search for "indigenous" concepts and practices, but a research strategy that is able to identify similarities and differences in comparable concepts and practices, and a conceptual and analytical approach that is aware that to analyze is to exercise power (in one way or another).

To date, however, mainstream research on development NGOs has not been very interested in the issue of power. To understand power mechanisms within this field (what may conventionally be called the international NGO world), the role of development NGOs within it, and this system's relation to its externalities raises particular problems, because the aid system's basic legitimacy will be regarded by most people as morally just and a system that ought to be furthered. Research on power relations within this policy field confronts the task of having to unravel the complex relationship between its egalitarian justification and its hierarchical structure, between the discourse of partnership and bottom up, and the reality of donor power and a global hegemonic discourse on development.

## A New International Social System

This chapter advances an alternative to analyzing NGOs as civil society actors or as third-sector organizations with a definite and "morally good" mission ascribed to them. Instead, it focuses on a very powerful organizational category affecting civil society globally—development NGOs as part of a new, much broader international social system. This approach is taken because of the financial and conceptual power and the degree of system integration in the development-aid channel, and because the distinction between actors outside and inside this aid system is important if relations and power issues between NGOs in general and states are to be understood on a national and global level. It should be underlined that a focus on the development-aid system does not imply that informal associations or protest movements outside the development-aid system are not important or are less important than development NGOs. The benefit of acknowledging this distinction is that it will sharpen both the research approach and the delineation of the object of research, and it will enable us to understand how the development-aid system has interacted with and affects the rest of the organizational landscape, and how these organizations again might affect the aid system.

*Angels of Mercy or Development Diplomats?* (Tvedt 1998) was written in opposition to a dominant school of thought that overlooked this distinction or regarded it as unimportant—and thus failed to explain the structural forces forming the global organizational landscape. The proposition advanced was that the NGO channel in aid should be viewed as a distinct, very powerful, and new type of international system reflecting global power relations and continuously developing and framing national NGO subsystems and national organizational landscapes globally. If the aim is to understand the complexity and context of NGO activities and their political role, it is absolutely crucial to analyze and understand the particular role of development NGOs in the global upsurge of non-state organizations.

This new international system should be seen as a system embracing not only NGOs attached to the aid system, but also the donor offices that provide funds and assess their performance and the research milieus that for various reasons serve NGO interests. The NGOs and their members, activists, and employees, the research consultancy businesses that feed on the same NGO-system sources and that provide the language with which NGO experience is described and communicated, and the government offices that deal with them and the UN offices contracting NGOs as implementing agencies, are here regarded in the same way as a river and its feeders. A river system consists of both channels and reservoirs. Research has shown that personnel in public donor offices and NGO leaders share essentially the same ideas about NGO roles and NGO activities (Tvedt 1998). The system is socially integrated through continuous exchange of personnel between NGO leadership and state offices working with NGOs both in donor countries and in Africa, Asia, and Latin America. The strength of the river-system analogy is that this social system consists of both the NGOs as diversion channels and the donor offices and funding sources as reservoirs. As one does not understand the way a river runs without knowing about its reservoirs, it is necessary to understand the linkages that different NGOs have to funding sources in order to understand structures that have influenced the history and function of a particular NGO and its activities.

The system can be seen as consisting of different subsystems, or different tributaries, or deltaic streams. The United States–NGO subsystem is different than the French-NGO subsystem, the Norwegian-NGO subsystem, and so on. When analyzing these national subsystems, the employees working with support to development NGOs in government ministries, and development agencies and people working in NGOs (whether in so-called Northern or Southern NGOs, a terminology that tends to blur and simplify the power structures involved) but paid mostly by the same governments, should be seen as belonging to the same social system. These subsystems are impressed by particular national histories and shifting international relations, but they form parts of a bigger multinational NGO system, together with and mingling with other subsystems having different donor states as the reservoir or core. Our knowledge is still very scant about how these subsystems relate to each other, how they differ, and why—and what kinds of constraints and possibilities NGOs from different donor countries experience in the field, and what implication support from different donor countries has on organizational developments.

This system perspective provides a frame for realistic comparative analyses of the history and character of the NGO landscape in any particular country—of how it is connected to, and affected by, global developments and state power, and of the potential for and limits of action. It also opens up a broad historical dimension. How have organizational landscapes been influenced by national and international aid systems? How has development aid, as a particular way of organizing relationships between states and societies—only some few decades old—affected systemic power relations?

The system itself is primarily produced, reproduced, and defined vis-à-vis the rest of the world and the rest of the organizational landscape by the flow and transfer of funds, and the character of this resource transfer. What today has become a worldwide system was established by an American government initiative in the early 1960s (Smith 1990). The United States asked other OECD (Organization for Economic Cooperation and Development) governments to follow its lead in giving money to NGOs or private voluntary organizations primarily to mobilize them as propagandists (OECD 1983). It was thought that NGOs could be useful in increasing and rooting public support for the official aid project. Gradually the role of the NGOs was enlarged, expanding dramatically in the 1980s and early 1990s. We can now talk of a worldwide system, dispersing billions of dollars every year, engaging tens and thousands of NGOs, and assisting hundreds of millions of people.

The boundaries of this money flow have produced a rather closed system (and by that reproduced its "systemness"), in the sense that the partners or members have formally to apply to be included in it or allowed to cross the "boundaries." If you get money, you are inside. If not, you are on the outside. Today, many are looking—thousands upon thousands of organizations worldwide are knocking at the donors' doors or at a potential partner's door—to join the system. Exactly how boundaries are established and where they are drawn vary from country to country and from time to time, partly reflecting national donor policies and national contexts, but these boundaries are important, since they give different subsystems their particular features. In Scandinavia, for example, for-profit firms have traditionally not been allowed to join this system. In some countries, for example, trade unions and interest organizations are eligible for support through the NGO channel, whereas in Bangladesh and Nicaragua this has not been the case. One important impact of the demarcation of this system is that to join the system, ad hoc organizations or small grassroots organizations have had to transform themselves into more formally established NGOs and to take on the language of the donor subsystem in question. It is thus a boundary that produces the system's distinctiveness in its communication about itself, distinguishing the actors of the aid system from the rest of society and the rest of the organizational landscape.

One of the most important structural properties of this system is the members' discursive internalization of what is very often rhetorically described as "shared values" of the channel. People have employed a common value-laden language as a means of communication while not necessarily internalizing its conflicting norms. In the NGO literature since the mid-1980s the basic, although changing, concepts have been shared.

This does not presuppose that there has always been value consensus among NGO activists and between NGOs and official donors. There has been, however, something that can be called NGO-speak (employed by NGO people, donor bureaucrats, and NGO consultants), that is, a language that has functioned as a "symbolic order" within the whole system, organized around a dichotomy, a rhetoric code with two values: "good" development and "not good" development. In NGO-speak NGOs have been seen as the embodiment of good development.

The symbolically powerful NGO language may change over time, but it always tends to serve as an identity marker for the system vis-à-vis the external world. The system is extremely dependent on how the rest of society perceives it, and therefore also on image management and image production.[4] The fact that it feeds on gift money has created a system that does not develop according to laws or rules in the marketplace or in political life but rather according to how the system itself manages political and moral dilemmas and conflicts within the channel itself. In spite of the real or potential contradictions among, for example, NGOs aiming at mobilizing the poor through project or advocacy work, mission organizations, and secular NGOs organizing business leaders, or between NGOs and public funding institutions, there are sufficient overlapping interests to provide common ground for consensus.

The actors in this system are structurally integrated, primarily through resource transfers and communication exchange.[5] Its "systemness" has also been produced and reproduced through many local and global gatherings and conferences where NGO leaders, from the so-called North and South, meet donors and consultants. These "come together" meetings play a very important integrative role and can explain why "buzzwords" travel so fast to all corners of the world, surpassing the borders of the national subsystems. Actors learn and rhetorically internalize the same language and "symbolic orders" as they are socialized in the channel's routinized practices.

This system is maintained through the way in which system members express themselves as actors within the system and in relation to the wider world. Such rhetorical consensus can be understood as norms that also help to establish and maintain boundaries around the NGO channel, but, and this is crucial, a "consensus" to which a variety of and in reality competing value agendas and even manipulative attitudes have been attached. Some government organizations pose as NGOs to attract funds and legitimacy, some for-profit firms dress up as NGOs to earn money, some mission organizations act within the development-aid channel while using it as a shield for achieving their main aims, and some political parties and movements establish what have been called neutral humanitarian organizations to compete for funds. Although the character of the resource transfer has created the structural form of this system, one might say it is this rhetoric and the way it has been handled that have created the feeling of "systemness"—that has made it into, and reproduces it as, a social system. The rhetoric that has influenced the whole NGO scene can be analyzed as functional for the maintenance of the system as it has functioned in the past (this does not mean, however, that this language is necessary for its continued existence).

This has encouraged institutional isomorphism among a great number of NGOs all over the world—during an astonishingly short period of time (Tvedt 1998). Within a few years thousands of NGOs have been established in many European, American, Asian, African, and Latin American countries—in urban centers and in the remote countryside. These NGOs share the same development language that has been adopted by donors. Discussions and research on the role of NGOs that miss this aspect will underplay the aid channel's role as a transmission belt of a dominant discourse tied to Western notions of development and downplay the fact that this arena is actually a site of struggle between different development paradigms, ideologies, and NGOs.

By focusing on resource transfers and discursive domination within this system perspective, power mechanisms within the aid system can be highlighted. Aid in general and NGO assistance reflect inequality between "donor" and "receiver" at all levels within the system, the system's fundamental ethical justification aside. But because it is often the receiver, or the small NGO in a poor country, that bestows the system with its ethical and political legitimacy, power may be negotiated, and there are cases where rather small Southern NGOs—because they are seen by their donors as valuable organizations from a political or image-producing point of view—have made big Western donor governments dance to their tune (Tvedt 1998, 78–86). By analyzing NGOs as part of a broader system of power, accountability, image management, and organizational survival, one has to address ordinary system mechanisms that are at play here, from the maximization of organizational self-interest to the iron law of oligarchy, which also affects the most grassroots-oriented, progressive, and altruistic of organizations.

This system approach goes together with a non-normative definition of NGOs. The NGOs cannot be treated and understood as if they possess some shared values or capabilities. The idea, for example, that NGOs have a "comparative advantage" has been shown to be false (Tendler 1982). No study has so far substantiated a claim about either comparative advantages or "shared values" for this wide variety of organizations vis-à-vis another equally multifaceted group of states. The heterogeneity of the NGO scene makes it futile to ascribe to NGOs definite and similar political and ideological characteristics. The growth and role of NGOs cannot be explained by some essentialist characteristic or function(s), as is all too often the case. The point here is that these organizations basically share systemic and relational similarities rather than essentialist, ideological characteristics.

## Contra Global Civil Society

This system concept is radically different from conceptions of a global civil society (GCS). The term *global civil society* downplays a dominant empirical fact; namely, most influential organizations are financed by the state and are working in accordance with regulations issued by individual states or the international state system. On the one hand, the notion of GCS disregards the role of the state in funding and influencing NGOs. On the other hand, according to the underlying ideology, the civil society actors and the donor bureaucrats belong to opposing parts in a binary opposition—the state *vs.* civil society. In this conventional perspective the state is represented as "opponent," thus producing an image of the NGO world that places NGOs outside the influence and power of states.

The system concept makes it possible to analyze development NGOs individually and as a group, and how they articulate with donor communities, state administrations, and other and different types of nonprofit organizations, and not only with CSOs (which is a very recent label, and a label that fits very few organizations literally), or with only organizations defined as third-sector organizations, or with only voluntary organizations but with all types of organizations, including those who have no idea about what a "civil society" was—until very few years ago.

The development-aid system can, for lack of better words, be termed the DOSTANGO system. This is a global system, but it cannot be called a GCS, because the NGO system in aid is donor led, and many of the most influential NGOs are more influenced by states' donor policies than by what is going on locally or nationally, or at least, forced to be more accountable when it comes to resource management toward their donor state than toward what is called in system jargon the local constituency or beneficiaries. It is not a third-sector phenomenon, because it operates in countries where no third sector has been developed or has emerged, and it trespasses the boundaries of conventional sector definitions in all societies. It interacts with civil society and people all over the world and helps to transform the conceptual horizons of millions of people. The system concept as used here regards the empirical field as a pattern of relationships between actors and institutions, regarded as having emergent properties of its own, over and above the properties of the individual actors or institution.

The concept of social system has been criticized on the grounds that systems do not possess emergent properties over and above the social actors who compose them, but rather are produced and reproduced by structured and routine social practices, the systematic properties of social systems thus stem from the nature of social action rather than from the system itself. The DOSTANGO system and its properties cannot be reduced to properties produced and reproduced by structured and routine social practices, because of the historical importance of structures established by resource flows and language. The term does not imply that the system has an inherent tendency toward equilibrium, as much system theory argues, although it underlines the need to understand those mechanisms that maintain equilibrium, both internally and externally, in relation to other systems. It is a system that encourages and institutionalizes different forms of social integration, but despite the use of the word *integration* there is no assumption that the relationships so described are harmonious. The terms *social integration* and *system integration*, as used here, embrace both order and conflict.[6]

The DOSTANGO approach encourages a focus on the political and institutional environment, both externally and internally, and the particular types of linkages established in each society between these organizations and different types of states. It is therefore not only a question of addressing the obvious: bringing the state-society linkage back in. This approach advances a research strategy that transcends methodological nationalism and those theories—so popular after the fall of Eastern Europe—that argued that the organizational structure and landscape in a particular country should be seen as a reflection of that country's cultural and historical characteristics (see, e.g., Hood and Schuppert 1990; Salamon and Anheier 1992a; 1992b). There is no doubt that national organizational culture influences particular organizational landscape (DiMaggio and Anheier 1990, 137). But to give national tradition too much weight, or to claim that it is possible to "predict the legal form of most organizations if one knows the industry and nation-state in which they operate" (DiMaggio and Anheier 1990, 139) downplays the formative power of the international NGO system in aid. A national cultural perspective also tends to focus on factors that change slowly, that is, that what is required to understand an NGO scene is a "deep and holistic understanding of the individual political system within which these political decisions are made" (Hood and Schuppert 1990, 95). The analysis of the relationship between such organizations and the state or the position of the "third sector" tells, therefore, the way "in which societies choose to govern themselves" (Anheier and Seibel 1990). Much work on NGOs and the third sector in Western welfare states has been in a "national style vein" (Hood and Schuppert 1990, 95), and explanations of institutional patterns have been done on a country-by-country basis. It is, however, clearly insufficient if the aim is to explain the organizational landscape in developing countries and the development NGO landscape in donor countries.

A solely national focus cannot grasp the impact of the DOSTANGO system and diverts attention away from crucial questions of long-term development, namely, the relationship between the entire organizational landscape in the country and the role of this system, and the role and potentials it gives and has given to different types of national organizations and their relation to their own state. Present organizational landscapes are not organic outcomes of long-term, deep-seated traditions. In fact, they are rather superficial present-day products, often (but far from always) characterized by weak roots in the society they operate. For more than a decade there has been a rush among donors to find fundable national NGOs in developing countries. Such NGOs have usually mushroomed as a response to external funds and rapid political change, both concerning types of organizations, value orientations, and development rhetoric. A simplified chronology would be cooperatives in the 1970s, women's groups in the 1980s, environmental groups in late 1980s, and HIV/AIDS groups and CSOs in the 1990s. Simultaneously, their working style, nearness to the state, degree of integration with society and the public sector will reflect both cultural traditions, national institutional environments, and the dynamics between the organizational landscape and the international aid system.

In the literature it has been argued that the "existence of NGOs, their types, interests, activities etc., is an indication of the situation of civic society vis-à-vis the nation state" (Fowler 1988, 2). This not only is empirically wrong but also diverts attention away from the fact that many organizations are an outcome of primarily external influences, and in some cases, direct pressure. To argue that institutional designs tend to be deeply rooted in traditions, linked to fundamental constitutional rules and legal assumptions, which themselves change only very slowly, presupposes that strong state authority exists. Because many countries have weak states with often-feeble authority and power for efficient rule making and rule enforcement, the space for NGOs may be larger than fundamental legal assumptions and traditions assume.

What is crucial is the need to combine domestic and international structures in analysis. The domestic or national context affects the nature of the NGOs and of the NGO-government relationship and the institutions with which the NGOs interact. It is not a good guide to rely only on the "national past" in understanding this particular area of third-sector–government relations. Neither is it fruitful to introduce static, ahistorical terms such as *indigenous NGOs* as opposed to *not-indigenous NGOs*, because most organizations are an outcome of internal traditions and external influences. Structural, institutional history has to be combined with an analysis of the concrete historical process of how the system produces and reproduces particular relations and practices. By using this perspective the object of analysis can be constructed in a new and, it is to be hoped, more fruitful way. The DOSTANGO system should not be regarded as one unified whole, and it may well be that, for example, the American subsystem tends to affect and interact with the organizational landscape differently from the Scandinavian or Canadian subsystem. The fact that these questions have not been asked is an argument in favor of this perspective.

## Conclusion

The DOSTANGO approach addresses the research challenge of trying to objectify the research object by employing a language alien to the system and its actors. It addresses the problem of conceptual universalism, studying the NGO system as a universal system but establishing an empirical base for such an approach. It also addresses the question of power relations within the NGO community itself, among actors in the system, and between the system and the rest of the society. It allows all kinds of organizations into the picture—Islamic fundamentalists, the Moon sect, and Oxfam—but focuses only on one segment of the organizational landscape. Because the organizational field is defined in a nonnormative and relational way, it makes comparative analyses of historical developments possible (for a discussion of definitions and classifications of NGOs, see Tvedt 1998, 11–41). And the approach makes intelligible both Mandela's and Annan's viewpoints, both representing different state actors, who, because of different systemic relations, will tend to react differently to NGOs: the first state actors object to foreign-sponsored NGOs to legitimate and strengthen a national government; the latter actors need NGOs to legitimize world government. The aim must be to understand how national and GCSs have been influenced and shaped by different forces: corporate capital; local and global protest movements and authorities; and, not least, a new but powerful international social system, the aid system.

## Notes

[1] On March 11, 2002, the United States and Saudi Arabia acted jointly to block the funds of the Somalia and Bosnia-Herzegovina branches of the Al-Haramain Islamic foundation, because, as the two governments stated, these branches were diverting charitable funds to terrorism.

[2] The text of the WANGO Internet home page clearly embraces the global and dominant language of the NGOs.

[3] Congressional report 052–070–04729–1 suggested that the Moon organization had committed criminal acts such as tax evasion, money laundering, and evasion of currency controls. Subsequent media articles suggested that the Moon organization manufactures and trades weapons, promotes a view of women as inferior, and maintains close contacts with far-right movements.

[4] Social movements also transform, and may redefine themselves, and they do so as they also negotiate their role and position within the development-aid system. Cynical observers may argue that some NGOs will simply define their mission to agree with whatever a donor wants, but this is to simplify the issue and also to regard the power relationship as only a one-way affair. This relationship tends to be seen as a predominantly moral and political issue rather than as a social process that is important to understand. A typical example: "There is always the danger that NGOs administering funds are more accountable to their donors than to their beneficiaries" (Edwards 2000, 209). It is unclear why, by definition or in principle, it should be more "dangerous" to be accountable to a donor than to the beneficiaries.

[5] This, is of course, a general point as well. No organization can ever truly retain its independence. Organizations are both relatively autonomous and under the strong constraining influence of the environment.

[6] In literature on social integration and system integration it is often noted how conflict theorists emphasize the conflict between groups of actors as the motor of social change whereas normative functionalists downplay the role of actors and seek to emphasize the (functional or dysfunctional) relationships between the institutions of society. Neither approach is adequate, precisely because each deals with only one side of the agency *vs.* structure problem. The task should be to overcome this dualism, but the micro versus macro distinction cannot be overcome by regarding social integration as something which should only refer to situations where actors are physically co-present and system integration to where they are not. This is unsatisfactory because face-to-face interactions are not confined to micro-processes, and macro-processes may be organized as face-to-face interactions. The NGO system, if anything, demonstrates this in all its facets.

## References

Achieng, Judith. 1998. Ruling on Muslim charities averts a major strike. *International Press Service*, September 18. Available online.

Anheier, Helmut K., and Wolfgang Seibel, eds. 1990. *The Third Sector: Comparative Studies of Nonprofit Organizations*. New York: Walter de Gruyter.

Dhanapala, Jayantha. 2002. Keynote address, Session 6, the role of civil society in the implementation of the United Nations programme of action on small arms. Undersecretary-General for Disarmament Affairs United Nations African Conference on the Implementation of the UN Programme of Action on Small Arms: Needs and Partnerships, Pretoria, South Africa, March 18–21.

DiMaggio, Paul J., and Helmut K. Anheier. 1990. The sociology of nonprofit organizations and sectors. *Annual Review of Sociology* 16: 137–59.

Edwards, Michael. 2000. *NGO Rights and Responsibilities: A New Deal for Global Governance*. London: The Foreign Policy Centre.

Fowler, Alan. 1988. *Non-Governmental Organisations in Africa: Achieving Comparative Advantage in Relief and Micro-Development*. Brighton, England: Institute of Development Studies.

Hood, Christopher, and Gunnar Folke Schuppert. 1990. Para-government organizations in the provision of public services: Three explanations. In Anheier and Seibel, *The Third Sector*, 93–106.

Korten, David C. 1987. Third generation NGO strategies: A key to people-centered development. *World Development* 15 (Supplement): 145–60.

———. 1990. *Getting to the Twenty-first Century: Voluntary Action and the Global Agenda*. Bloomfield, Conn.: Kumarian Press.

———. 2000. Civilizing society: The unfolding cultural struggle. Paper presented at ISTR Conference, Trinity College, Dublin.

OECD (Organization for Economic Cooperation and Development). 1983. *The Role of Non-Governmental Organizations in Development Cooperation*. Bulletin no. 10, new series. Paris: OECD.

Paine, Harold, and Birgit Gratzer. 2001. Rev. Moon and the United Nations: A challenge for the NGO community. Available online.

Salamon, Lester M., and Helmut K. Anheier. 1992a. In search of the non-profit sector I: The problem of definition. *Voluntas* 3, no. 2: 125–53.

———. 1992b. In search of the non-profit sector II: The problem of classification. *Voluntas* 3, no. 3: 267–309.

Smith, Brian H. 1990. *More than Altruism: The Politics of Private Foreign Aid*. Princeton, N.J.: Princeton University Press.

Tendler, Judith. 1982. Turning private voluntary organizations into development agencies: Questions for evaluation. In "Program Evaluation Discussion Paper No. 12." Washington, D.C.: USAID.

Tvedt, Terje. 1998. *Angels of Mercy or Development Diplomats? NGOs and Foreign Aid*. Oxford: James Currey; Trenton, N.J.: Africa World Press.

# 9.

# Global Civil Society
# and the Lessons
# of European Environmentalism

## Christopher Rootes

## Introduction

The processes we have come to call globalization have made the world a smaller place. More than at any time in recorded history, the economies of states are integrated into a single global system. Unprecedentedly, effective means of transport and communication facilitate interaction among the world's people and erode the distance between and distinctiveness of national cultures. The governments of nation-states struggle to come to terms with these developments and, increasingly aware of their interdependence and of the transnational character of many of the issues that confront them, enter into international agreements and subscribe to new or existing international institutions.

At least for educated elites, national boundaries increasingly appear as little more than irritating impediments to their free movement across the globe. Increasingly aware of our common humanity and of the abuses of power in some of the more or less remote parts of the planet, we talk with increasing ease about universal human rights, and we support organizations that seek to promote or protect such rights. We have even begun to speak of global civil society (GCS) not as a noble aspiration but as an emergent reality.

If, however, we are to advance that aspiration, it is necessary that we should be clear-eyed about the obstacles that lie in its path. This requires critical analysis of some uncomfortable present realities.

There are, of course, a number of promising signs. We have, in the United Nations and its associated institutions and conventions and in other international agreements, an embryonic global political regime, the beginnings of a system of global governance, if not yet a global government. Nonetheless, the limitations of those developments are all too apparent. To state only the most obvious of them, the dominant superpower, the United States, honors only those agreements that it perceives to be in its interests and opposes the institution most fundamental to the establishment of GCS—a court of human rights with universal jurisdiction. Indeed, the administration of George W. Bush appears to be less respectful of international institutions and agreements than any of its predecessors. This hardly augurs well for the further development of the UN system.

## NGOs, Social Movements, Civil Society, and the State

In addition to—and partly as a consequence of—the continuing construction of transnational institutions and the increasing frequency of transnational agreements, we have seen the rise of new global actors in the shape of transnational NGOs. International agencies develop institution-building momentum of their own and seek to extend their remit beyond that envisaged by their patrons. Thus the United Nations has for some time sponsored or opened its councils to NGOs, recognizing that they deal with issues or reach constituencies that the United Nations itself and/or national governments do not or cannot, and encouraging NGOs to do what the United Nations or the member states cannot or will not do. The proliferation of NGOs and their increasingly accepted presence in the international consultative arena fill some of the gaps in the emerging global political system, and NGOs are sometimes regarded as representing a putative GCS. Nevertheless, NGOs do not themselves constitute civil society.[1] They are rarely democratic in their internal structures, and the extent to which they are representative of anybody beyond themselves is problematic (Yearley 1996, 91). Indeed, especially at the international level, given the frequency of their dependency upon national governments or international institutions, NGOs might often more accurately be portrayed as adjuncts to the sphere of the state rather than as phenomena of civil society.

Unlike NGOs, social movements have generally been regarded as unambiguously phenomena of civil society.[2] The terms *NGO* and *social movement* are sometimes used interchangeably, but *NGO*—in the official definition, "any non-state non-commercial organization"—is quite undiscriminating (Rootes 2001); social movements, as informal networks of actors linked by a shared identity and engaged in collective action (Diani 1992), are rarer and more complex. They may include NGOs, but they cannot be reduced to the organizations that constitute (part of) their networks, let alone to any one such organization. Although it is at least implicit that social movements are critical of existing arrangements, there is less agreement about the extent to which, by definition, social movements are required to be oppositional, much less about whether they should be deliberately working for the structural transformation of societies, national or global.

It is, however, generally agreed that social movements are phenomena of civil society. Yet sometimes they are seen as the vehicles by which civil society is introduced, as democratic practices and politically relevant skills may be learned and trust built up in the course of mobilization in circumstances in which civil society is at best embryonic. Thus accounts of democratization in Spain (Castells 1983) and Central and Eastern Europe (Pickvance 1998) privilege the role of social movements in the building of civil society. Even in established liberal democratic states, social movements are seen as having the capacity to re-create civil society eroded by the intrusions of the market and the state (Brulle 2000, 101). However, in the postmodern account of politics, social movements are not merely phenomena of civil society but their increasing importance, together with the progress of globalization, is claimed to be making the nation-state increasingly irrelevant (see, e.g., Nash 2000).

Such claims are at variance with the accumulated evidence of a generation of studies of social movements, the great majority of which have addressed demands to the state and very often have advanced their demands by means of alliances, explicit or tacit, with formal political actors (see, e.g., Kriesi et al. 1995; Tarrow 1998a). Social movements are indeed phenomena of civil society, but the development of both is dependent upon the state. Their increasing prominence in democratic states is better interpreted as evidence of the extension of repertoires of democratic political contention and as an adjunct rather than as a threat to, much a less a replacement for, formal politics (Dalton 2002).

The idea of a GCS has developed by analogy with, and is an extension of, the idea of civil societies that have developed in a relatively small, if growing, number of nation-states. For that reason, if we are to assess properly the prospects of soon realizing a GCS, we need to consider the conditions under which those national civil societies have developed.

Political scientists have long observed the relationship between the forms of the state and the development of social movements. Broadly, the relationship is curvilinear: social movements flourish neither in states where the apparatus of repression is highly developed nor in those where it is scarcely developed at all; it is in, broadly speaking, liberal democratic states where the apparatus of repression is sufficiently developed but where its use is relatively restrained that the conditions for the development of civil society are optimal and the incidence of social movements is greatest (Rootes 1997a). In such circumstances, opportunities for access to the decision-making arena exist, but they are not completely open and unconstrained (Eisinger 1973; Tarrow 1998a).

The experience of third-world states demonstrates clearly that the development of civil society is dependent upon that of the state—more precisely upon the development of a liberal democratic state with institutionalized avenues of political participation and legal protection for human rights (Haynes 1999; Mittelman 1998). Only under such conditions does the ensemble of relationships that constitute civil society become fully developed. As Michael Walzer puts it, "Only a democratic state can create a democratic civil society" (Walzer 1998, 305; cf. Kumar 1993, 191).

It is often claimed that the increased numbers of NGOs and social movement organizations (SMOs) operating on a transnational basis are a sign of the emergence or, at least, a step in the building of a GCS. Perhaps it is, but political action is shaped by the opportunities offered and constraints imposed by political institutions. The international institutions that have so far been constructed are almost always just that—international, or even simply intergovernmental; there is as yet no global polity analogous to that of a nation-state. The pattern of action adopted by transnational NGOs and SMOs is an adaptation of an international political milieu dominated by intergovernmental negotiations and agreements. As Sidney Tarrow has observed, "The main fulcrum around which transnational groups organize are international institutions, which serve as sources of group claims, as targets for their protests, and as sites that can bring parallel groups together internationally" (Tarrow 2001, 246–47). The problem is that those international institutions lack both the autonomy and the openness of democratic institutions within nation-states.

Despite assertions that social movements are phenomena of civil society and that their prevalence makes the institutions and politics of nation-states less and less relevant, it is clear from empirical examination of the experience of actual social movements that they are much more oriented toward the state than such claims allow. The development of social movements is a drama played out in an arena well peopled by conventional political actors. Indeed, in many respects it is an arena structured by the state itself. Not the least obstacle to the development of global social movements—and to the development of GCS itself—is the absence of a global state. Indeed, establishing a truly global social movement or even the more limited ambition of establishing a truly global social movement *organization* is almost impossibly difficult in the absence of the supporting infrastructure of democratic global political institutions.

But would the establishment of formal political institutions on a truly global scale remove all the obstacles to the development of a GCS? Differences of language, culture, and history would, at the very least, present impediments to the full development of a GCS capable of maintaining effective democratic control of a global executive. In order better to understand the nature of such obstacles, it is instructive to consider the experience of the most globally conscious social movement—the environmental movement.

## An Environmental Movement?

There has undoubtedly been an increase in awareness of global environmental issues and an increase in the number of organizations, including environmental movement organizations (EMOs) that address those issues, as well as increased linkage between environmental organizations of North and South. Yet it is only if we use the term *social movement* rather loosely that we can speak in the present tense about the existence of a global environmental movement. Even in the most favorable circumstances, in the most highly developed supranational polity that yet exists—the European Union (EU)—the obstacles are apparent. The EU still bears strong institutional legacies of its origins in agreements between the governments of nation-states. Nevertheless, it is the best laboratory we have in which to observe a natural experiment concerning the likely impact of a supranational global political system upon environmental movement activity and, hence, upon the development of a truly *global* civil society. However, as we shall see, despite the development and increasing powers of EU institutions, especially with regard to environmental policy, it is at best questionable whether there is yet a truly European environmental movement. The underdevelopment of such a movement suggests some of the constraints upon the development of civil society beyond the nation-state.

Adapting the concept of social movement proposed by Mario Diani (1992), an environmental movement may be defined as a loose non-institutionalized network that includes, as well as individuals and groups who have no organizational affiliation, organizations of varying degrees of formality, that is engaged in collective action, and that is motivated by shared identity or, at least, shared environmental concern (Rootes 1997b, 326). In respect of each of these three elements—network, engagement in collective action, and shared concern—the existence of a European, let alone a global, environmental movement is problematic.

## Networks?

There are a number of signs of the Europeanization of environmental movements in the formation of new pan-European or, at least, pan-EU organizations. One stimulus to the formation of these new organizations was the recognition of the limitations of what could be achieved without them. It is increasingly acknowledged that environmental problems cannot simply be solved within the boundaries of nation-states, but so long as it was ad hoc, effective cross-national collaboration between environmental campaigners was rare. In most cases, "cooperation was sporadic, limited and informal" (Rucht 1993, 80).

In recognition of the need for more effective transnational cooperation, the EU has developed incentives and opportunities. As awareness spread of the interest and increasing power of EU institutions, especially in matters concerning the environment, new European EMOs were established to address those institutions. These new EMOs were not, however, simply clones of their counterparts at the national level.

Most European-level EMOs take the form of more or less stable transnational alliances consisting of loose networks of *national* organizations. Some are not strictly European organizations but the European branches of more extensive international organizations attracted to Brussels by the efficiency of concentrating their European lobbying activities in one place and, increasingly, by the recognition that in matters of environmental policy the EU is now considerably more important than any of the member states.[3] Thus the European coordination of Friends of the Earth (FoE) established a Brussels office in 1985, followed by the Climate Action Network in 1989, not least to prepare policy advice for the European Parliament (Rucht 1993, 81). In some cases the connection with the European Commission (EC) was more direct; the European Environmental Bureau (EEB) was formed in 1974, with financial assistance from the EC Environment Directorate General, as a direct response to the EC's first Environmental Action Programme and the EC's desire to encourage a broadly representative forum bringing together environmentalists from across Europe. By 1999 the EEB encompassed 130 member organizations in twenty-four countries. However, alongside it other, more specialized networks established representation in Brussels. To mitigate the fragmentation that might otherwise result, an umbrella network, initially comprising the EEB, FoE, Greenpeace, and WWF, but now expanded to the G8, was formed to coordinate activities (Rootes 2002).

Although the growth of transnational SMOs such as Greenpeace and FoE was dramatic during the two decades following their establishment in the 1970s, in most countries the numbers of their supporters and/or members has stagnated or declined in recent years.[4] Greenpeace, in particular, has closed national offices and consolidated branches in response to a decline in its global income. Moreover, in all but a few European countries, such avowedly internationalist EMOs remain relatively small by comparison with the established national nature-and-wildlife protection organizations. Although the latter organizations are increasingly linked, albeit loosely, by international umbrella organizations to similar organizations in other countries, they remain primarily national as well as relatively specialized in their scope and orientation. Thus, although in most of the advanced industrialized world the environmental movement has grown in organizational complexity as well as popular support, the most globally conscious part of that movement remains in a minority. It is a moot point to what extent this has been offset by the increasing recognition of transnational issues by national EMOs.[5]

Within the EU, the transnational networking of environmental groups is more limited than might be supposed. Stephen Ward and Philip Lowe found that many of the thirty British environmental organizations they surveyed in 1998 reported that they were heavily reliant on one another when dealing with EU matters, the smaller organizations especially so (Ward and Lowe 1998). But if this encouraged networking among environmental organizations *within* Britain, it does not appear to have produced dense or overlapping networks at the European level, or to have stimulated any very extensive collaboration with European organizations. Although four-fifths of the thirty groups surveyed claimed membership of a European network, twenty different networks were mentioned. Although one-third claimed membership of the EEB (the most frequently named network), most saw its function as limited to the exchange of information.

A more extensive survey of environmental groups undertaken as part of the Transformation of Environmental Activism project produced similar results.[6] Of eighty-six British environmental groups surveyed in 1999, only twenty-two even so much as claimed to have exchanged information with the EEB, and only seven claimed ever to have collaborated in a campaign with the EEB. Figures for the Climate Action Network were similar. The results of similar surveys in six other EU states (France, Germany, Greece, Italy, Spain, and Sweden) do not suggest that EMOs elsewhere in the EU were any more likely to be actively involved in EU level networks.

Transnational environmental movement networks within the EU are, then, neither very dense nor very active. Most are highly specialized, and most EMOs remain primarily oriented toward the national rather than the European stage. Among British EMOs, transnational collaborative *action* tends to be confined to the larger multinational organizations, such as FoE (Ward and Lowe 1998, 162). For the most part British EMOs appear to prefer their habit to their advantage by dealing with the familiar milieu of British politics rather than focusing their energies upon EU institutions that they perceive as being "greener" than national institutions, but to which they feel outsiders. Again, it does not appear that the British experience is in this respect dissimilar from that of other EU member states (Long 1998, 117).

A lack of resources is a major constraint upon collaboration among European EMOs. Despite the proliferation of EMOs represented in Brussels, they simply have had too few personnel for them to be very effective (Long 1998, 115; Ruzza 1996, 217). Because their resource bases are mostly at the national level, they tend to be more concerned with strengthening their national organizations than with providing the substantial resources required by disproportionately expensive organization at the European level. The lack of transparency of EU institutions does not encourage them to do otherwise. Access is informal rather than institutionalized; it generally appears that it is the EC that sets the agenda; and it is usually difficult to evaluate the effectiveness of investment in European activities (Rucht 1993; 1997).

Another major obstacle to the success of European-level EMOs is the persistence of national differences that affect the relationship between EMOs and the EC as well as EMOs themselves. The EC is insulated from public opinion because the political debate about environmental issues occurs mainly within nation-states and has only limited direct impact upon EC policymaking. EMOs, however, are not so insulated. They depend for their legitimacy and their resources upon their ability to command public support, and, in the absence of a genuinely European public opinion, it is public opinion at the national level to which EMOs must be responsive.

Relations among EMOs at the European level may be more cooperative than at the national level, not least because they are not, at the EU level, competing for public support and visibility (Rucht 1993, 91), but cooperation is impeded by the very diversity of the groups and their national backgrounds. They differ in their organizational forms and styles, in their policy styles, in their perceptions of the relative importance of various environmental issues, and in the magnitude of their expectations. In all these respects the imprint of national experience lies heavily upon EMOs in Europe.

## Collective Action

Environmentalists have staged a few, mostly small and symbolic transnational demonstrations in Brussels and Strasbourg and at recent EC summits. For the most part these demonstrations have been mounted in order to attract the attention of national media. Apart from the lobbying undertaken in Brussels and Strasbourg, the collective action of environmentalists occurs overwhelmingly *within* nation-states in the form of mobilizations confined to the local or national level.[7] It is, moreover, mainly focused upon local or national issues and aimed at local or national targets. Examination of environmental protests reported in one leading national newspaper in each of Britain, France, Germany, Greece, Italy, Spain, and Sweden over the years 1988 to 1997 disclosed only very small numbers of environmental protests that were European in their level of mobilization, the scope of the underlying issues, or their targets (Rootes 2003b).[8]

Protests mobilized at the EU level ranged from 0.4 percent of all reported environmental protests in Britain to 4 percent of the much smaller number of protests reported in France. Only in three states (Germany 8.1 percent, Britain 6.4 percent, and France 5.7 percent) was the EU identifiable as the scope of the underlying issue behind the protest in more than a handful of cases. Even the small number of cases in which the EU was the level of the target (ranging from 0.7 percent in Italy to 4.0 percent in Germany and 5.1 percent in Spain) included protests whose targets were companies, associations, and governments of other EU states.[9] Of the 52 British protests whose target was at the level of the EU, only 12 (less than 1 percent of the protests for which a target could be identified) were targeted at the EU itself. Moreover, there was no evidence from any of the seven countries of any trend toward increasing Europeanism, let alone internationalism, over the decade (Rootes 2003b).[10]

Thus it appears that, except at the most elite levels, environmental politics in the EU is still very much *national* politics. Mass environmental movement activity, in particular, occurs almost exclusively at the local, regional, or national level *within* nation-states.

The existence of the EU and the increasing breadth of its environmental remit have created new opportunities, and these opportunities have encouraged actors who are prepared to use them (Marks and McAdam 1999). Nevertheless, even if environmental policy is increasingly made at the European level, policy *implementation* is still national and local. A great deal of environmental movement action is not addressed to the grand scheme of policymaking but to battling over the particular ways in which and the sites at which policy is implemented. Because even semi-institutionalized national EMOs are well aware of the extent to which their vitality depends upon their ability to keep faith with those engaged in local campaigns (Rootes 1999a), the objects of contention that are most important to the environmental movement remain largely local and national.

Even to the extent that real power lies in Brussels and national governments appear increasingly as mere agents of the EC, environmental activists will tend to mobilize against those local tokens of European power rather than against the EC itself, and they will do so not least because the logistics of doing otherwise are so intimidating (cf. Imig and Tarrow 2001a). The resources of EMOs—principally the money and the presence of their supporters—are local and national and are not easily transportable to Brussels or Strasbourg.[11] Moreover, by comparison with the political institutions of the nation-state, those of the EU are remote and inaccessible. For resource-poor EMOs, national institutions are therefore much more attractive targets for collective action than are those of the EU.

It might nevertheless be expected that, as a consequence of the embedding of common institutions and policies at the EU level and the increasing frequency of transnational communication within the EU, there should by now be some evidence of convergence upon a shared repertoire of political action, or at least of some diffusion of tactics.

Casual empiricism suggests that some diffusion of repertoires of collective action is occurring, and that the number of instances of cross-border emulation of protest tactics has increased. In 1999, inspired by their French counterparts, Welsh farmers blocked the passage of trucks carrying Irish lamb, and British truckers blockaded motorways around London. In 2000, truckers blockaded fuel depots to protest high prices of road fuel, first in France and then in Britain, Germany, and Spain. More often, however, even when Europeans have mobilized on the same issue, as in 2000, they have done so in different ways. Thus in 1995, the British, French, and German publics reacted quite differently to Shell's attempts to dump the Brent Spar oil storage buoy at sea (Jordan 2001) and the French nuclear tests in the South Pacific. Indeed, in Britain both these issues were overshadowed by more protracted protests against the export of live animals, an issue that was met with incomprehension in many other EU countries.

Systematic investigation confirms the impression of diversity. In reported protests in the years 1988–97, moderate actions predominated everywhere. Only in Germany and Britain were as many as one-third of reported protests more disruptive than demonstrations. Large demonstrations became less common everywhere, but otherwise there was little evidence of convergence of repertoire. In Britain, confrontational action became markedly more common during the mid-1990s as the number of protests increased, whereas in Greece, where confrontational tactics were also relatively common, they declined. Confrontation was relatively uncommon—and declined—in Sweden and Italy. Germany was the only other country where the relative incidence of confrontation increased, but this was principally associated with protests against the transport and processing of nuclear waste, an issue that rarely arose elsewhere.

The national peculiarities of environmental movements reflect the persistent impact of national cultures and political structures that remain significantly distinct (Faucher 1999; Imig and Tarrow 1999; 2001a; Rootes 1997c). If, however, national cultures and political institutions are relatively stable, opportunities for political action are not; they change in the course of dynamic relationships whose structure and timing vary from state to state. There is no evidence that the trajectories of environmental protest within EU member states are converging; rather, they appear to respond chiefly to political timetables, events, and opportunities that are nationally idiosyncratic (Rootes 2003b).[12]

Although there has everywhere been a trend toward the institutionalization of EMOs, the extent to which it has occurred and the forms it has taken have varied significantly from one European country to another. Comparing France, Germany, the Netherlands, and Switzerland, Hein-Anton van der Heijden found the last three to be highly institutionalized but the first scarcely institutionalized at all (van der Heijden 1997). There are important differences in the specific features of institutionalization in each of these countries, as there are in the other European countries that have recently been studied systematically (see, on France, Hayes 2002; on Germany, Brand 1999; Rucht and Roose 1999; and on Spain, Jiménez 1999). The imprint of nationally specific institutional structures, prevailing constellations of political power and competition, and of political culture is evident everywhere (Tarrow 1995). It is likely that whether and how EMOs lobby or mobilize in Brussels will be influenced by the way they are used to behaving at the national level, and it appears that there remain significant, albeit temporally variable, differences among the patterns of action employed by EMOs in the several EU states (Koopmans 1996; Kriesi et al. 1995).

## Shared Concerns?

Even if effective transnational movement organizations and mass mobilization at the European level are rare, it is nevertheless possible that Europeanization may occur in the form of the development of common conceptions of environmental politics and of common issues among the various national movements. Certainly this is something that the EC itself has been concerned to encourage, not only for its own administrative convenience but also as part of the process of building a common European political culture.

Previous research has shown that there are considerable north-south and east-west differences in the conception of environmental problems among European populations, and that these are reflected in the policies and actions of national EMOs (Dalton 1994). Surveys in the 1980s concluded that whereas southern European environmentalism was disproportionately one of "personal complaint," in northern Europe "postmaterialist" concerns were more evident (Hofrichter and Reif 1990).

If we consider the issues associated with nationally reported environmental protests during the decade 1988–97 in the seven EU states covered by the Transformation of Environmental Activism project, the pattern is broadly consistent with that revealed by those earlier surveys. Issues of pollution and the effects of environmental degradation upon human health were more frequently raised in the southern European countries (Greece, Italy, and Spain).[13] More surprising was the diversity among the kinds of issues raised in the four northern European countries (Britain, France, Germany, and Sweden). In Britain and Sweden there was a relatively even spread among nature conservation, pollution and urban/industrial issues, transport, and animal rights, but in France protests concerning nature protection and especially animal welfare were relatively rarely reported. Most strikingly, in Germany over half of all protests involved nuclear energy, an issue that was only relatively infrequently raised elsewhere, particularly in more recent years. Not only was there no common pattern, but also, apart from a modest decline in the distinctiveness of environmental protests in southern Europe, there was no apparent trend toward convergence (Rootes 2003b). If there is shared environmental concern among the citizens and environmental activists of EU states, it is concern shared only at the most general and abstract level. It is the particular concerns of the citizens of particular nation-states that predominate.

A similarly diverse pattern is evident if one considers the issues that have been raised contemporaneously in several EU states. There is evidence of increased global environmental consciousness among the better educated in the more affluent countries, but that consciousness is largely limited to those better-educated citizens (Witherspoon 1994), and there remain considerable differences from one country to another in the predominant forms of environmental consciousness of mass publics. It is not, however, simply that people are more concerned about environmental issues in the north and west than in the east and south. Environmental concern is nearly universal and at very high levels. Where Europeans differ is in the *kinds* of concern they voice, the *priority* they attach to environmental issues, the *forms of action* they are prepared to take in the expression of their environmental concerns, and the *knowledge* they have of the processes of environmental change.

If consciousness of environmental deterioration is a necessary condition of collective action of an environmentalist or ecological kind and/or support for environmental movements and Green parties, it is by no means a sufficient one. Wolfgang Rüdig reports cross-nationally comparative data for knowledge and concern about global warming (Rüdig 1995). At first glance, the pattern of the results is paradoxical. In 1993 about one-third of southern Europeans had not even heard of global warming; nonetheless their overall levels of concern were all above the EU average. In Denmark and the Netherlands the pattern was reversed: levels of knowledge were high but concern was relatively low.

Clearly, more than thirty years of broadening and deepening the EU have not produced a common European environmental consciousness. Perhaps it does not matter too much that mass publics do not share global environmental consciousness if the educated elites who are mobilized by EMOs do. It appears, however, that, despite their best intentions, the thinking and values of even environmental activists are heavily imprinted with the peculiarities of the national cultures from which they come.

## Prospects for a Global Environmental Movement

If such obstacles exist to the development of a truly transnational environmental movement within the EU, they are writ large when we consider the prospects for a *global* environmental movement. Environmentalists may be enjoined to "think globally, act locally" but, because political thinking, no less than political action, is contextualized by the peculiarities of national cultures and institutions, citizens of different states tend to think differently even when attempting to think globally. It is apparent that when would-be global movement actors do attempt to think globally, they tend to do so in terms shaped by the assumptions of the cultures from which they originate (Bramble and Porter 1992; Yearley 1996, 92, 137). "Global" environmental issues do not have the same significance, nor are they constructed in the same ways, in all parts of the globe (Cudworth 2003, chap. 5).

As a result of increasing contacts with activists from Africa, Asia, and Latin America, especially since Rio, activists in transnational EMOs based in the more affluent industrialized countries have become more sensitive than they were to differences of perspective and balances of interest. Yet the agenda of even so avowedly internationalist an EMO as Greenpeace has generally reflected the views and assumptions of an ecological elite in those countries where it is strongest (Kellow 2000). Moreover, the various national branches of Greenpeace reflect national peculiarities and not simply a global agenda (Dalton 1994; Shaiko 1993). Recent contacts and initiatives may have tempered these differences, but they have not obliterated them.

Easier communication and more frequent interaction can be expected to erode the distinctiveness of national cultures, to aid the diffusion of political repertoires, and to diminish the obstacles to their universal adoption, but this is likely to be part of a long, and no doubt contested, process of cultural globalization. In the meantime, even determinedly internationalist environmental activists will struggle to think in terms uncolored by their national cultures and experiences.

In his gloomy prognosis for an effective democratic global environmental movement, Leslie Sklair cites Robert Michels in support of his contention that revolutionary goals will likely be subordinated to bureaucratic means (Sklair 1995, 498). However, this reading of Michels is unduly pessimistic, for although Michels believed that the inescapable price of the organization of democratic mass parties was an unequal distribution of power within them, he did not suppose that the *degree* of that inequality was immutable. On the contrary, he suggested that, with increased levels of education, an increasing proportion of citizens would be capable of effective political participation (Michels 1959, 406–7). Optimism is encouraged by the surge of aspirations to democratic participation, often by unconventional means, which has been the general experience of advanced Western societies since the late 1960s (Dalton 2002). Levels of education are generally increasing, and the highly educated are everywhere an increasing proportion of the population. This, the foundation of the participatory surge in Western liberal democracies, gives grounds for optimism that a more educated population may be better able both to understand global issues and to sustain democratic organizations capable of addressing them.

## Conclusion

The last two decades of the twentieth century were remarkable for the speed with which new transnational agreements on environmental protection were forged and new institutions to implement them were developed. Informed by considerations of economic and environmental justice as well as concern for environmental protection, new institutions—such as the Global Environmental Facility—become arena for interaction between environmental NGOs and the economically dominant powers.

The opening of new arena has consequences, however. Groups that enter negotiations with the powerful become domesticated both in order to do so and as a result of so doing. Yet those who remain outside do so at the expense of limiting their influence. The dilemmas that confront SMOs at the national level are thus reflected at the transnational level. Indeed, they are magnified, because the resources needed to play on a global stage are so much greater than those required at the national level. To a much greater extent than is true at the national level, SMOs that seek to be international players are dependent upon international and often intergovernmental organizations, even for the funding required to participate in international meetings.

Whether we consider organizations such as Greenpeace or any of the plethora of smaller and more specialized groups that address global forums, action on global issues is almost always elite action; seldom is it mass direct action of the kind we have conventionally associated with social movements. Social movements and SMOs have often been regarded as prefigurative of a participatory democratic society, but the organizations that act at the transnational level are not democracies, or even bureaucracies; rather, as young organizations in a new institutional environment, they are "ad-hocracies" (Young 1999, 252). The possibilities for genuine democratic accountability of any kind are limited, and especially so if the public to whom they might be held accountable is a global one. There is no democratic global state and, if there is a GCS, it is one in which the possibilities of effective communication remain infinitely greater among elites than among the masses.

It is difficult to see this lack of democratic accountability as a merely temporary stage in the development of a GCS. Yet, given the accumulated evidence of the limited effectiveness of purely local or even national attempts to secure redress of environmental grievances (see, e.g., Rootes 1999c), there is no alternative for committed actors but to attempt to play on the global stage. This is especially so for activists in economically and politically dependent states whose destinies are, rather more obviously than are those of the advanced industrialized states of the North, determined by events and processes originating beyond their borders. Yet for many who do attempt to enter the global arena, the experience is discouraging.

Environmentalists in the post-Communist states of Central and Eastern Europe have complained that the intervention of Western EMOs and charitable foundations has tended to promote Western agenda at the expense of local concerns, made local environmentalists increasingly dependent upon increasingly fickle Western benefactors, and removed incentives to local mobilization (Fagan and Jehlicka 2003; Yanitsky 1999). For those from the global South, things are often no better.

Because international organizations themselves are so lacking in democratic procedures and accountability, it can be argued that the efforts of transnational EMOs make an important contribution to the democratization of global politics. Consider, for example, EarthAction, a transnational organization that works to help its affiliates participate in the global arena and that, rather than mounting its own campaigns, identifies campaigns consonant with its goals, and provides affiliates with "action kits" to encourage them to mobilize around those campaigns. EarthAction's affiliates in the global South testify that they derive sustenance from their transnational ties and, confident that they are part of a transnational movement, are better able to resist repression locally and to acquire the skills necessary to participate effectively in global arena (Smith 1997; 2002). Yet there remains the risk that, in encouraging EMOs to recognize the global dimensions of their particular struggles, such organizations may disproportionately broadcast the perspectives of environmentalists in the industrialized North. EarthAction supports only campaigns "consonant with its goals," and this criterion inevitably conceals the extent to which those goals may be ethnocentric rather than genuinely universal.

The experience of environmentalism in western Europe suggests the magnitude of the obstacles to the development of an effective global social movement. If it has been difficult to achieve common purpose even in western European states that have a broadly shared heritage in the culture and institutions of Western Christendom and that are increasingly closely connected by transnational movements of people and commerce, and in a policy domain in which the transnational character of the issues is so clear, how much more difficult will it be to achieve political integration on a global level, especially with respect to issues where the necessity of a transnational approach is less apparent?

It may be thought that this pessimistic conclusion is a consequence of our adopting an unduly restrictive definition. Surely, if we were only to relax the requirements of the definition, we would see that there is already a global environmental movement and, by implication, a GCS? As Tarrow has observed, it is always possible, by relaxing the strictures of definition, to find more evidence of a phenomenon (Tarrow 1998b, 234). But there are in these case very good reasons for not doing so. "Shared environmental concern" may not require identity of consciousness or values, but the demonstrable differences in consciousness and values that exist both within and among countries are clearly obstacles to effective concerted action. "Collective action" may take many forms but the forms conventionally associated with social movements are un- or semi-institutionalized actions characterized by mass participation; even in those countries where environmentalism has been relatively institutionalized, as it has in western Europe as well as in most other advanced industrialized countries, mass direct action remains a part of the armory of environmental activists. "Networks" may be more or less loose but they are generally effective in proportion to their density and activity, and the evidence is that, even under relatively favorable circumstances, transnational environmental movement networks are neither very dense nor very active. To be sure, even weak links are better than none, but strong links would be more effective.

It is, of course, possible that, as Sklair suggests, global organizations may, for a relatively ill-resourced constituency, require more energy and resources to construct and to maintain than could be justified by the results (Sklair 1995). If so, then the present form of environmental movement networks in the EU may, given existing resources, be optimal and may provide a model of loose transnational association that deserves emulation in other policy domains and on a global scale. It may even be that the facilitation of exchanges of information is sufficient to maintain the transnational coordination of activists' efforts while action is limited to bringing pressure to bear where it may be most effective—at the national level and on national governments. Perhaps, but it is nevertheless the case that even the coordination of separate national actions would be more effective if transnational movement networks were more dense and more active.

It might be thought that the argument developed here is contradicted by the advent of campaigns such as Peoples' Global Action and the succession of Global Action Days, the attempted disruptions of the WTO summit in Seattle in 1999 and the IMF/World Bank meeting in Prague in 2000, and the demonstrations against neoliberal globalization at more recent EC and global economic summits. But neither protests nor erratically maintained websites themselves constitute a social movement. Indeed, the frustrations of many of the Prague demonstrators and the users of such websites would seem to emphasize the difficulties of constructing a genuine and effective global movement.

Jubilee 2000, the transnational campaign for third-world debt relief, is more difficult to discount because it clearly involved a network, collective action, and shared concern. It was, however, a campaign mounted by a coalition of diverse groups, in which aid charities and church groups were especially prominent, assembled to campaign on a single, important but circumscribed issue.[14] It is not in any way to disparage the achievement of Jubilee 2000 to describe it as a campaign rather than a social movement or, more precisely, as a network of campaigns each operating on the terrain of the civil society of a particular nation-state (Collins, Gariyo, and Burdon 2001). Jubilee 2000 was an impressive and practical demonstration of solidarity across national boundaries, it demonstrated the potential of new communications technologies to facilitate transnational campaigns, and it may even prefigure a genuinely global social movement (Pettifor 2001), but it was not itself a social movement, and it is too soon to declare that it has inaugurated a GCS.

Some interpret the spread of universal conceptions of human rights as evidence of the development of civil society beyond the confines of the nation-state, and the development of a post-national citizenship based on "deterritorialized notions of persons' rights" (Soysal 1994, 3). "Universal personhood replaces nationhood; and universal human rights replace national rights" (ibid., 142). In view of the fact that Soysal develops her argument in the context of a discussion of the treatment of immigrants in the EU, it is especially ironic that there is so much evidence of the weakness of any tendencies to the transcendence of nationality in the EU (cf. Koopmans 2003). Indeed, as another writer by no means ill disposed to ideas of the postmodern transcendence of the nation-state observes, "the link between nationality and citizenship is reproduced rather than undermined in the current conception of European citizenship" (Nash 2000, 209).

International and supranational institutions clearly find it difficult to transcend the categories of inclusion and exclusion that have been institutionalized by nation-states. As the history of even so deliberately transnational a social movement as the environmental movement suggests, it seems improbable that they can simply be bypassed by "world civic politics" (Wapner 1996). A great deal of honest and laudable effort has been invested in building transnational NGOs and movement organizations, but thus far such organizations have neither convincingly escaped the constraints of national politics and cultures nor become truly global in their reach. A GCS remains a noble aspiration rather than an accomplished fact.

## Notes

[1] On the limitations of NGOs and their relationship with the United Nations, see McCormick 1999.

[2] There is now a considerable and growing literature on transnational NGOs and social movements that recognizes these classificatory distinctions (see especially Smith, Chatfield, and Pagnucco 1997; and della Porta, Kriesi, and Rucht 1999; McCarthy 1997 and Rucht 1999 are particularly useful in their application of social movement theory to transnational activism).

[3] Former British Environment Secretary John Gummer's 1994 estimate that 80 percent of UK environmental legislation originated in Brussels (Lowe and Ward 1998, 25) may be an overestimate but, for smaller EU member states such as Spain, Portugal, Greece, and Ireland, 80 percent would be an underestimate.

[4] The decline has been most marked not in Europe but in the United States. Greenpeace, which in 1990 was much the most widely supported US EMO with 2.35 million members, was by 1998 reduced to 350,000 members. It appears to have been the principal casualty of the increasing localization of environmentalism in the United States (Bosso 2000).

[5] On such developments in British EMOs, see Rootes 2003a.

[6] The project was coordinated by Christopher Rootes and funded by the EC Directorate General for Research (contract no. ENV4–CT97–0514).

[7] This observation is based on perusal of the British press over recent years and the activities of Greenpeace. Rucht makes a similar remark on the basis of German media (Rucht 1999, 210). Of course, in a media-saturated age, token, symbolic action designed to attract the attention of press and television cameras is not necessarily any less effective than larger-scale mobilization.

[8] I am indebted to my collaborators in the Transformation of Environmental Activism project—Olivier Fillieule and Fabrice Ferrier, Dieter Rucht and Jochen Roose, Maria Kousis and Katerina Lenaki, Mario Diani and Francesca Forno, Manuel Jiménez, Andrew Jamison and Magnus Ring, Sandy Miller, Ben Seel and

Debbie Adams—who were responsible for the data on which this discussion is based.

[9] On the basis of data drawn from different newspapers, Rucht reports that in Germany less than 1 percent of pro-environmental protests reported during 1970–94 were EU related (2001).

[10] Similarly, Imig and Tarrow found that 95 percent of all the protest they identified in EU countries from Reuters reports was domestic rather than European in character (Imig and Tarrow 2001b, 33–34). However, they also found that the proportion of EU-related protests rose significantly between 1983 and 1997 (Imig and Tarrow 1999; 2001b). In fact, their data appears to show a pattern of trendless fluctuation until about 1995, with only 1997 showing a very marked increase. In any case, their data and ours are not strictly comparable: their data covered all protests whereas ours were restricted to protests about environmental issues (well under 20 percent of the protests examined by Imig and Tarrow); their data, aggregated for ten or twelve EU states, was derived from Reuters reports, probably selected for their national/international importance and their interest to the business community, whereas ours were drawn from all environmental protests reported in one national newspaper in each country. On Imig and Tarrow's own account, it is likely that the Reuters data was biased toward the "more important" and higher-level protests. Moreover, it is likely that as the business community has become increasingly persuaded of the importance of the EU, so Reuters, as a news service selling its services primarily to business, will have become more assiduous in its coverage of EU-related protests. However, if Imig and Tarrow's data probably exaggerates the relative incidence of EU-related protest, particularly in more recent years, our own, because it is limited to protests occurring on the territory of just seven states, might tend to underestimate it. Unfortunately, we have no systematic evidence for the incidence of EU-related environmental protests in Brussels, but since there was no increase in overall EU-related protest in Belgium from 1980 to 1995 (Rucht 2001, 141 n. 20), it does not appear likely that such evidence would contradict our conclusions.

[11] Rucht suggests that the environmental movement's influence at EC level is limited by the formidable obstacles to transnational mass mobilization (Rucht 1997). This may be too pessimistic; even mobilizations restricted to the national—or even the local—level have the power to disrupt EC-favored projects and, by putting pressure on national governments, may tip the balance within the Council of Ministers.

[12] Thus, in Britain the incidence of environmental protest was relatively stable before rising significantly following the reelection of an environmentally unresponsive Conservative government in 1992 to a peak in 1995 before falling sharply in 1997, the year in which a Labour government pledged to "put the environment at the heart of government" came to power (Rootes 2000), only to rise sharply in 1998 as new issues emerged and EMOs sought to hold Labour to its promises. In Germany, protest peaked in 1990 and fell sharply thereafter before rising again from the mid-1990s, the twilight years of the CDU/CSU government, to sustained high levels from 1995 through 1997.

[13] To label concern with pollution and health as an environmentalism of personal complaint is not, however, to suggest that they were any less capable of

sustaining collective action, albeit such action was more concentrated at the local level than was environmental protest in the northern countries.

[14] On the importance of the distinction among coalitions, campaigns, and social movements, see Diani 1995, 5–6.

## References

Bosso, Christopher J. 2000. Environmental groups and the new political landscape. In *Environmental Policy*, 4th ed., ed. Norman J. Vig and Michael E. Kraft, 55–76. Washington, D.C.: CQ Press.

Bramble, Barbara, and Gareth Porter. 1992. Non-governmental organizations and the making of US international environmental policy. In *The International Politics of the Environment*, ed. Andrew Hurrell and Benedict Kingsbury, 313–53. Oxford: Clarendon Press.

Brand, Karl-Werner. 1999. Dialectics of institutionalisation: The transformation of the environmental movement in Germany. *Environmental Politics* 8, no. 1: 35–58; reproduced in Rootes 1999b.

Brulle, Robert J. 2000. *Agency, Democracy and Nature: The U.S. Environmental Movement from a Critical Theory Perspective.* Cambridge, Mass.: MIT Press.

Castells, Manuel. 1983. *The City and the Grassroots.* London: Edward Arnold.

Collins, Carole, Zie Gariyo, and Tony Burdon. 2001. Jubilee 2000: Citizen action across the North–South divide. In *Global Citizen Action*, ed. Michael Edwards and John Gaventa, 135–48. Boulder, Colo.: Lynne Rienner.

Cudworth, Erika. 2003. *Environment and Society.* London: Routledge.

Dalton, Russell J. 1994. *The Green Rainbow: Environmental Groups in Western Europe.* New Haven, Conn.: Yale University Press.

———. 2002. *Citizen Politics: Public Opinion and Political Parties in Advanced Industrial Democracies.* 3rd ed. New York: Chatham House.

Della Porta, Donatella, Hanspeter Kriesi, and Dieter Rucht, eds. 1999. *Social Movements in a Globalizing World.* London: Macmillan.

Diani, Mario. 1992. The concept of social movement. *Sociological Review* 40, no. 1: 1–25.

———. 1995. *Green Networks: A Structural Analysis of the Italian Environmental Movement*, Edinburgh University Press, Edinburgh.

Eisinger, Peter K. 1973. The conditions of protest behavior in American cities. *American Political Science Review* 67, no. 1: 11–28.

Fagan, Adam, and Petr Jehlicka. 2003. Contours of the Czech Environmental Movement. *Environmental Politics* 12, no. 2: 49–70.

Faucher, Florence. 1999. *Les habits verts de la politique.* Paris: Presses de Sciences Po.

Hayes, Graeme. 2002. *Environmental Protest and Policymaking in France.* Basingstoke: Palgrave Macmillan.

Haynes, Jeff. 1999. Power, politics, and environmental movements in the Third World. *Environmental Politics* 8, no. 1: 222–42; reproduced in Rootes 1999b.

Hofrichter, Jürgen, and Karlheinz Reif. 1990. Evolution of environmental attitudes in the European Community. *Scandinavian Political Studies* 13, no. 2: 119–46.

Imig, Doug, and Sidney Tarrow. 1999. The Europeanization of movements? In della Porta, Kriesi, and Rucht 1999, 112–33.

———, eds. 2001a. *Contentious Europeans: Protest and Politics in an Emerging Polity*. Lanham, Md.: Rowman and Littlefield.

———. 2001b. Mapping the Europeanization of contention. In Imig and Tarrow 2001a, 27–49.

Jiménez, Manuel. 1999. Consolidation through institutionalisation? Dilemmas of the Spanish environmental movement in the 1990s. *Environmental Politics* 8, no. 1: 149–71; reproduced in Rootes 1999b.

Jordan, Grant. 2001. *Shell, Greenpeace and Brent Spar*. Basingstoke: Palgrave.

Kellow, Aynsley. 2000. Norms, interests, and environment NGOs: The limits of cosmopolitanism. *Environmental Politics* 9, no. 3: 1–22.

Koopmans, Ruud. 1996. New social movements and changes in political participation in western Europe. *West European Politics* 19, no. 1: 28–50.

———. 2003. Beyond the nation-state? Multi-level patterns of claims-making on immigration and ethnic relations in five European countries. Paper presented at the conference on transnational processes and social movements, Villa Serbelloni, Bellagio, Italy, July 22–26.

Kriesi, Hanspeter, Ruud Koopmans, Jan Willem Duyvendak, and Marco G. Giugni. 1995. *New Social Movements in Western Europe*. Minneapolis: University of Minnesota Press.

Kumar, Krishan. 1993. Civil society: An inquiry into the usefulness of an historical term. *British Journal of Sociology* 44, no. 3: 375–95.

Long, Tony. 1998. The environmental lobby. In *British Environmental Policy and Europe: Politics and Policy in Transition*, ed. Philip Lowe and Stephen Ward, 105–18. London: Routledge.

Lowe, Philip, and Stephen Ward. 1998. Britain in Europe: Themes and issues in national environmental policy. In *British Environmental Policy and Europe: Politics and Policy in Transition*, ed. Philip Lowe and Stephen Ward, 3–30. London: Routledge.

McCarthy, John D. 1997. The globalization of social movement theory. In Smith, Chatfield, and Pagnucco 1997, 243–59.

McCormick, John. 1999. The role of environmental NGOs in international regimes. In *The Global Environment: Institutions, Law, and Policy*, ed. Norman J. Vig and Regina S. Axelrod, 52–71. Washington, D.C.: CQ Press.

Marks, Gary, and Doug McAdam. 1999. On the relationship of political opportunities to the form of collective action: The case of the European Union. In della Porta, Kriesi, and Rucht 1999, 97–111.

Michels, Robert. 1959. *Political Parties: A Sociological Study of the Oligarchical Tendencies of Modern Democracy*. New York: Dover. The original work was published in 1911.

Mittelman, James H. 1998. Globalisation and environmental resistance politics. *Third World Quarterly* 19, no. 5: 847–72.

Nash, Kate. 2000. *Contemporary Political Sociology*. Oxford: Blackwell.

Pettifor, Ann. 2001. Why Jubilee 2000 made an impact. In *Global Civil Society 2001*, ed. Helmut Anheier, Marlies Glasius, and Mary Kaldor, 62 (box). Oxford: Oxford University Press.

Pickvance, Katy. 1998. *Democracy and Environmental Movements in Eastern Europe: A Comparative Study of Hungary and Russia.* Boulder, Colo.: Westview.

Rootes, Christopher A. 1997a. Social movements and politics. *African Studies* 56, no. 1: 67–95.

———. 1997b. Environmental movements and Green parties in western and eastern Europe. In *International Handbook of Environmental Sociology*, ed. Michael Redclift and Graham Woodgate, 319–48. Cheltenham, England: Edward Elgar.

———. 1997c. Shaping collective action: Structure, contingency and knowledge. In *The Political Context of Collective Action*, ed. Ricca Edmondson, 81–104. London: Routledge.

———. 1999a. The transformation of environmental activism: Activists, organisations and policy-making. *Innovation: The European Journal of Social Sciences* 12, no. 2: 155–73.

———, ed. 1999b. *Environmental Movements: Local, National and Global.* London: Frank Cass.

———. 1999c. Acting globally, thinking locally? Prospects for a global environmental movement. *Environmental Politics* 8, no. 1: 290–310; reproduced in Rootes 1999b.

———. 2000. Environmental protest in Britain 1988–1997. In *Direct Action in British Environmentalism*, ed. Benjamin Seel, Matthew Paterson, and Brian Doherty, 25–61. London: Routledge.

———. 2001. Non-governmental organizations (NGOs). In *Encyclopaedia of Democratic Thought*, ed. Paul Berry Clarke and Joe Foweraker, 465–68. London: Routledge.

———. 2002. The Europeanisation of environmentalism. In *L'action collective en Europe* [Collective action in Europe], ed. Richard Balme, Didier Chabanet, and Vincent Wright, 377–404. Paris: Presses de Science Po.

———. 2003a. The transnationalization of environmentalism. Paper presented at the conference on transnational processes and social movements, Villa Serbelloni, Bellagio, Italy, July 22–26.

———, ed. 2003b. *Environmental Protest in Western Europe.* Oxford: Oxford University Press.

Rucht, Dieter. 1993. "Think globally, act locally": Needs, forms and problems of cross-national environmental groups. In *European Integration and Environmental Policy*, ed. J. Duncan Liefferink, Philip D. Lowe, and Arthur P. J. Mol, 75–95. London: Belhaven.

———. 1997. Limits to mobilization: Environmental policy for the European Union. In Smith, Chatfield, and Pagnucco 1997, 195–213.

———. 1999. The transnationalization of social movements: Trends, causes and problems. In della Porta, Kriesi, and Rucht 1999, 206–22.

———. 2001. Lobbying or protest? Strategies to influence EU environmental policies. In Imig and Tarrow 2001a, 125–42.

Rucht, Dieter, and Jochen Roose. 1999. The German environmental movement at a crossroads? *Environmental Politics* 8, no. 1: 59–80; reproduced in Rootes 1999b.

Rüdig, Wolfgang. 1995. Public opinion and global warming: A comparative analysis. *Strathclyde Papers on Government and Politics*, no. 101. Glasgow: Department of Government, University of Strathclyde.

Ruzza, Carlo. 1996. Inter-organisational negotiations in political decision-making: Brussels' EC bureaucrats and the environment. In *The Social Construction of Social Policy*, ed. Colin Samson and Nigel South, 210–23. London: Macmillan.

Shaiko, Ronald G. 1993. Greenpeace USA: Something old, new, borrowed. *Annals of the American Academy of Political and Social Science* 528: 88–100.

Sklair, Leslie. 1995. Social movements and global capitalism. *Sociology* 29, no. 3: 495–512.

Smith, Jackie. 1997. Building political will after UNCED: EarthAction International. In Smith, Chatfield, and Pagnucco 1997, 175–91.

———. 2002. Bridging global divides? Strategic framing and solidarity in transnational social movement organizations. *International Sociology* 17, no. 4: 505–28.

Smith, Jackie, Charles Chatfield, and Ron Pagnucco, eds. 1997. *Transnational Social Movements and Global Politics*. Syracuse, N.Y.: Syracuse University Press.

Soysal, Yasemin Nuhoglu. 1994. *Limits of Citizenship: Migrants and Post-National Membership in Europe*. Chicago: University of Chicago Press.

Tarrow, Sidney. 1995. The Europeanisation of conflict: Reflections from a social movement perspective. *West European Politics* 18, no. 2: 223–51.

———. 1998a. *Power in Movement: Social Movements and Contentious Politics*. 2nd ed. Cambridge: Cambridge University Press.

———. 1998b. Fishnets, Internets, and catnets: Globalization and transnational collective action. In *Challenging Authority: The Historical Study of Contentious Politics*, ed. Michael P. Hanaghan, Leslie Page Moch, and Wayne te Brake, 228–44. Minneapolis: University of Minnesota Press.

———. 2001. Contentious politics in a composite polity. In Imig and Tarrow 2001a, 233–51.

van der Heijden, Hein-Anton. 1997. Political opportunity structure and the institutionalisation of the environmental movement. *Environmental Politics* 6, no. 4: 25–50.

Walzer, Michael. 1998. The civil society argument. In *The Citizenship Debates*, ed. Gershon Shafir, 291–308. Minneapolis: University of Minnesota Press.

Wapner, Paul. 1996. *Environmental Activism and World Civic Politics*. Albany, N.Y.: State University of New York Press.

Ward, Stephen, and Philip Lowe. 1998. National environmental groups and Europeanisation. *Environmental Politics* 7, no. 4: 155–65.

Witherspoon, Sharon. 1994. The greening of Britain: Romance and rationality. In *British Social Attitudes: The 11th Report*, ed. Roger Jowell, John Curtice, Lindsay Brook, and Daphne Ahrendt, 107–39. Aldershot, England: Dartmouth.

Yanitsky, Oleg. 1999. The environmental movement in a hostile context: The case of Russia. *International Sociology* 14, no. 2: 157–72.

Yearley, Steven. 1996. *Sociology, Environmentalism, Globalization*. London: Sage.

Young, Zoe. 1999. NGOs and the Global Environmental Facility: Friendly foes? *Environmental Politics* 8, no. 1: 243–67; reproduced in Rootes 1999b.

# 10.
# The World Social Forum and New Forms of Social Activism

## Jacklyn Cock

## Introduction

One of the most exciting spaces in global civil society is the World Social Forum (WSF). It is unique in several ways, being the only global event organized by and for civil society. Located in the South, the WSF has an organizational novelty in its rejection of leaders and hierarchies. Its significance as an open, inclusive, non-directed space of free exchange is difficult to overemphasize at a time when a closure of political space is taking place in much of the world. As Jai Sen observed, it permits "a scale of talking across boundaries that has rarely been dreamed of before, and . . . is thereby powerfully contributing to building a culture of open debate across conventional walls and boundaries" (Sen 2003, 14; also see Hardt 2002). In this sense "the World Social Forum is one of the most promising civil society processes that may both contribute significantly to global democracy initiatives and constitute possibly such an initiative in itself" (Teivainen 2002, 627). The slogan of the World Social Forum is "Another world is possible."

This chapter suggests that the WSF is an event characterized by an extraordinary level of "solidarity in diversity" and that its significance lies in its capacity to transform itself, as the core of an emerging global justice movement, from an annual event into a process with an increasingly global reach—particularly into Africa and Asia—that involves new forms of social activism. These forms of activism are new in that they involve new targets, connections, and types of organizing. Some of these new forms of social activism are emerging on the local scene, and in this

The Centre for Civil Society at the University of KwaZulu-Natal, Durban, South Africa, sponsored the primary research on which this chapter is based.

regard, the strength of the global justice movement largely depends on its capacity to connect the local and the global.

## The Nature of the World Social Forum

The WSF was born in 2001 as an alternative to the World Economic Forum, which meets annually in Davos to celebrate the world of power and privilege. The WSF is a unique meeting place for civil society organizations (CSOs) to develop networks, build alliances, and develop social and economic alternatives to corporate globalization. It emphasizes participation, diversity, and pluralism, describing itself online as,

> an open meeting place for reflecting thinking, democratic debate of ideas, formulation of proposals, free exchange of experiences and interlinking for effective action, by groups and movements of civil society that are opposed to neoliberalism and to domination of the world by capital and any form of imperialism, and are committed to building a planetary society centred on the human person.

According to one of its founders, Cândido Grzybowski,

> The WSF must be seen as an initiative designed to overcome neoliberal globalization and bring about a globalization based on solidarity, democracy and sustainability. [It] draws its inspiration from the ethical principles set out in the Charter of the WSF which rejects the principles of the market as the foundation of society, denounces violence as a form of political action, and says no to a single way of thinking and yes to equality and diversity.[1]

"Solidarity in diversity" is the most striking characteristic of the WSF. The numbers and social diversity of the 100,000 participants at the third meeting of the WSF at Porto Alegre in January 2003 illustrate how popular resistance to corporate globalization is growing and slicing through differences of party, class, gender, race, ethnicity, nationality, and age. Participation was extremely broad and varied. There were constituencies brought together that have rarely connected in the past—faith-based organizations, unions, youth organizations, HIV/AIDS and other health activists, environmentalists, representatives of indigenous people, landless peasants, homeless people, and community-based formations of all kinds.

This social diversity was most dramatically expressed in a document issued at the end of WSF2 in 2002, the "Call of Social Movements," which reads:

We are diverse—women and men, adults and youth, indigenous peoples, rural and urban, workers and unemployed, homeless, the elderly, students, migrants, professionals, peoples of every creed, color and sexual orientation. The expression of this diversity is our strength and the basis of our unity. We are a global solidarity movement, united in our determination to fight against the concentration of wealth, the proliferation of poverty and inequalities, and the destruction of our earth. We are living and constructing alternative systems, and using creative ways to promote them. We are building a large alliance from our struggles and resistance against a system based on sexism, racism and violence, which privileges the interests of capital and patriarchy over the needs and aspirations of people.[2]

A key characteristic of the WSF is its diversity not only of social composition but also of constituent ideas. It is a meeting place of diverse people with inchoate ideologies of varying shades. It involves a respect for difference among networks of individuals with a shared commitment to a very loose political agenda frequently comprised of extremely broad and inclusive values such as social justice, human rights, and sustainable development expressed in universalist imagery. But critical debate and disputes are highly valued. As Grzybowski writes, "In the WSF disagreements are a virtue, not a problem" (Grzybowski 2003, 13). The WSF is new in its celebration of social and ideological diversity.

In many meetings at WSF3 there was a strong repudiation of a corporate globalization that is concentrating wealth and power in the hands of a global elite and deepening poverty, inequality, and social exclusion around the world. There was agreement that deeper and more responsive democracies were required, but many differences emerged over tactical questions.[3]

The ideological and social diversity of the WSF means that one of its key features is an emphasis on openness and inclusivity. Anyone could attend WSF3. Any group (excluding political parties) could run a workshop; it simply had to get a title to the organizing committee. In comparison to earlier meetings there was a strong American presence, with up to one thousand mostly community-based activists, including many at the youth camp. The number of registered participants has grown from 20,000 at the first meeting of the Forum in 2000, to some 60,000 officially registered in 2002, to 100,000 in 2003. In January 2003 alone, some 1.5 million people from more than 120 countries visited the WSF website.

The size of WSF3 was overwhelming not only in terms of the number of participants, but also in terms of the intellectual range and number of organized events. Overall the Forum comprised 1,286 workshops, 114 seminars, 36 panel debates, 22 testimonies, 10 conferences, and 4 roundtables. The discussions covered five broad thematic areas, each of which was conceived as a catalyst of concerns, proposals, and strategies that were already being pursued by the organizations participating in the WSF process. Through the WSF the organizers aim was to give them visibility and, if possible, have them adopted as widely as possible by the various actors of "planetary civil society" struggling against neoliberal globalization. The five themes were democratic sustainable development; principles and values—human rights, diversity, and equality; media, culture, and counter-hegemony; political power, civil society, and democracy; and democratic world order—combating militarization and promoting peace.

It is difficult to generalize, but three interrelated concerns surface strongly in the ambit of the WSF:

*Resistance to the "commodification" of public goods.* Emphasis is placed on how corporate globalization now reaches into every aspect of life and transforms every activity and natural resource into a commodity. Corporate globalization is widely understood to involve a mass transfer of wealth and knowledge from public to private—through measures such as the patenting of life and seeds, the privatization of water, and the concentrated ownership of agricultural land. As one of the WSF founders expressed it, "In the name of the market all human relations are commercialized—even life itself, the biodiversity of nature, water, knowledge, faith. . . . The term 'free market' is a deceptive euphemism for a market for the strongest, namely the major financial-economic corporations. The world and all it contains seem to be up for sale" (Grzybowski 2003). Similarly, as Maude Barlow from Canada's largest NGO, the Council of Canadians, stated at WSF3: "The global water giants have been busy transforming this life-giving resource into a commodity to be sold on a for-profit-basis to those who have the ability to pay. In short, everything is now for sale to the highest bidder, including seeds, genes, and water."

*Resistance to the concentration of power.* A central concern in many discussions is power: Who holds it? Who is exercising it? How can we make our political leaders accountable for the power they have? How can we change the power of the United Nations to make it part of the solution rather than part of the problem? How can we limit the power of corporations? How can we empower citizens and make their political participation meaningful? Particular focus is on the threats embodied in the concentration of power in the multinational corporations and in the United States—now seen by many to be the most powerful empire in world history. It is stressed that we need new ways to think about power, resistance, and globalization—and new ways of imagining power. The WSF itself does not constitute a locus of power to be disputed by the participants in its meetings. As Peter Waterman has pointed out, the Charter of Principles "will provoke participants to work out ways that will minimize the power disputes that have weakened and destroyed previous internationals" (Waterman 2002).

*The threats of war and neoliberalism.* At WSF3, Mario Soares, European MP and former president of Portugal, warned, "The world sits on the edge of the abyss for two reasons: the war Washington is threatening against Iraq and the economic recession that is a symptom of the crisis of capitalism." A person who has articulated that the coming world might be worse than the present is the Paris-based author and activist Susan George, who warns of the increasing misery of millions as famine, aids, and unemployment increase. In George's analysis, capitalism cannot be maintained in 2020, when there will be eight billion people on earth. So war and famine and disease will be allowed to take their toll, "The rich and powerful seem to have concluded that hundreds of millions of people are surplus and redundant. . . . There will not be an Auschwitz model of exterminism but a postmodern twenty first century model in which no one can be blamed and nothing can be done." In similar terms Noam Chomksy has warned, "It is not clear that the species can survive very long under the present conditions of world capitalism" and the US "grand strategy of global rule by force." This is why, it is argued, the struggle against neoliberal corporate globalization must not fail.

Overall, the major achievements of the WSF have been to consolidate and strengthen the global solidarity of networks—on every issue on the global justice agenda from labor and human rights, to militarism and environmental issues—and to puncture the basic conceit of the Davos agenda, that there is no alternative to neoliberalism.

It has been claimed that "one of the intellectual problems of the WSF has been the lack of open debate between different visions of how the world should be concretely reorganized if, as the main slogan of the WSF says, another world is to be possible" (Teivainen 2002, 629). However, since its inception the WSF has posed an alternative perspective on globalization rooted in the principles of social justice, democracy, and sustainability—and many activists at WSF3 were engaged in working not only for concrete alternatives but for ways in which the alternatives can be achieved, what Eric Olin Wright has termed "rooted utopianism." Beverly Bell has observed that,

> the alternatives being advocated transcend general principles for more participatory, rights-based and autonomously controlled local and national economies. Many of the coalitions, networks and movements articulate specific, detailed policy positions regarding new forms of international economic organization. These range from taxing speculative flows of capital, to supplanting debt service payments from impoverished countries with payment of reparations for failed development projects. (Bell 2002, 6)

In the variety of alternative systems of energy, transport, agriculture, manufacturing, governance, and so forth, the common thread is an emphasis on participatory democracy—on alternatives including neighborhood councils, participatory budgets, cooperative farming, and so on.

Beyond this, however, there are strategic tensions between mainstream statist NGOs and more militant grassroots social movements with respect to a reformist or radical positioning on three analytically distinct but related issues: (1) whether the "enemy" is capitalism, neoliberalism, or globalization; (2) whether intergovernmental institutions like the World Bank, International Monetary Fund (IMF), and World Trade Organization (WTO) are reformable; and, (3) whether working to strengthen state power—including working with and through political parties—is a viable strategy for social transformation. Also, according to Peter Waterman, WSF3 was "marked by a questioning of the extent to which the Forum itself embodies what it is preaching to others." This kind of questioning and introspection has led to the formulation of a number of criticisms of the WSF itself.

One of the leading figures in the struggle against corporate globalization, Naomi Klein, is of the view that "participatory democracy is being usurped at the WSF by big men and swooning crowds" (Klein 2003, 2)—and it can be argued that too many of these "big men" are white and middle aged. Few Africans, Asians, Arabs, or Afro-Brazilians have been present. Jai Sen has also pointed to the problem of "giganticism," "The most obvious success of the WSF is its size and growth and its most obvious problem is this too and the breakdowns that come with this, the increasing need of an efficient management culture" (Sen 2003, 6). Certainly, it is difficult to determine just how decisions are made in the WSF organizational structure, and the fact that for WSF3 there was no timely published program for events spread over four different locations, and that a large number of events were rescheduled, relocated, or canceled, were sources of frustration. But as Grzybowski himself asked at one meeting, "How can you organize a tide? The fundamental issue is how to strengthen the WSF without imploding it" (Grzybowski 2003, 14).

The WSF is not just an annual meeting. It is not an event but rather an ongoing process of forming networks, coalitions, campaigns, alliances, and movements. The charter of the WSF makes it clear that the construction of a new world order is as much a matter of process as of program: "The WSF has become a process, one of the forms in which a great citizen's movement is spreading throughout the world" (Grzybowski 2003, 14). Since 2001 activists have been organizing smaller or regional or country specific social forums to complement the global event. For instance, prior to WSF2 in Porto Alegre a regional social forum was held in Genoa, Italy, and an African Social Forum in Bamako, Mali. In January 2003 the African Social Forum met in Addis Ababa, Ethiopia, and attracted 210 participants from forty countries who reaffirmed a strong conviction that "another Africa is possible." According to Mondli Hlatswayo, there was agreement on a number of issues—particularly "a total rejection of all forms of privatization of social services in Africa" (Hlatswayo 2003, 38).

The WSF is expanding rapidly across the world, it is in other words, globalizing; in fact it forms part of a wider globalizing process—the transformation of various progressive initiatives and struggles around the world into a new movement. The real significance of the WSF is its centrality in an emerging global justice movement marked by new forms of social activism. The "anti-globalization" label is not appropriate for understanding this movement and is rejected by the WSF (George 2002). Rather, the WSF is best defined as part of the global justice movement, a movement conceptualized by Lisa Jordan as the "sum of many vibrant, disparate civil society parts which allow multiple local, national and global initiatives around different issues to co-exist, connect and understand themselves as belonging together in a global community oriented toward social change" (Jordan 2002, 6).

Until very recently we had what Klein has termed " two activists solitudes"—"international globalization activists who seem to be fighting faraway issues, unconnected to people's day-to-day struggles" and "thousands of community-based organizations fighting daily struggles for survival" (Klein 2002, 245). These two forces are converging in a global justice movement—supported and hastened by new forms of social activism that presage an alternative world.

As Victor Munnik and Jessica Wilson (2003) assert, the WSF is a "centre of gravity for civil society" involving a multiplicity of social movements. The decentered multiplicity and interconnectivity (through new technologies) of these movements signifies new forms of collective action. And this multi-agency character of social movements points toward the need to abandon the rigid prescriptions of the mainstream (and Northern) social movement literature on collective action (Taylor and Naidoo, Chapter 11 herein). The contemporary world of social movements is to be found in the combination of both different sorts of organizations and different forms of social action (Castells 1996; 1997).

## New Forms of Social Activism

New forms of social activism, centered on the WSF have emerged in the last few years—new in the sense that they involve new terrain, targets, connections, and forms of organizing, as well as being premised on new forms of power.

The fact that WSF3 attracted participants from 156 different countries illustrates how the resistance to corporate globalization is increasingly global in scope. It is a struggle being waged on its own terrain—the whole world. Action is increasingly mobilized around issues of global concern—whether human rights, the environment, or labor standards.

The state is no longer the sole focus of political struggles; increasingly targeting is directed to the corporations and the global agencies, particularly the World Bank, the IMF, and especially the WTO, which is fast becoming the most powerful multilateral organization in the world. This is in contrast to the pattern throughout the sixties, seventies, and eighties when we witnessed the ascendance of national liberation movements throughout Africa, Latin America, and the Caribbean that focused on the nation-state as the target of their struggle. The fact that the primary target for change has changed from national governments to trade and financial institutions and multinational corporations has important implications. Beverly Bell writes:

> Since domestic matters are no longer the primary unit of analysis, national social movements have, in their majority, become too weak to stand alone. As a result, the last 5 years or so have witnessed a tremendous growth in cross-border organizing. (Bell 2002, 4)

This "cross-border organizing" has involved forging new connections between issues. Social movements have traditionally organized around geography, sector, or identity (for example, indigenous peoples) or focus area (for example, land rights). Today these movements are finding common ground in what they perceive as fundamental to their concern with poverty and social exclusion: unjust trade policies in global and regional trade agreements and an unjust model of development imposed by international institutions such as the World Bank and IMF.

As a result a more diverse range of people are joining together, a diversity dramatically illustrated at the WSF. Activists are forming new allegiances in ways never before seen. Positioned at the heart of the global justice movement, the WSF promotes a unique mode of talking across boundaries—boundaries between disciplines, issues, and countries. Many social issues are now defined as interconnected, such as the ecological impact of military activity that unites both peace and environmental activists. There is a new energy that is connecting different issues and citizens around the globe (Shepard and Hayduk 2002). The members or components are interconnected in a variety of ways, drawing on the new organizational and strategic possibilities that are emerging through new technologies, which facilitate communication across the boundaries of space and time.

Overall, the global justice movement has assumed a decentralized, diversified network of nodes of different sizes that form strategic alliances of different kinds: tight and loose, direct and virtual, permanent and temporary. As the International Forum on Globalization (IFG) writes:

> Unified by a deep commitment to universal values of democracy, justice and respect for life, this alliance functions with growing effectiveness without a central organization, leadership, or defining ideology. It also takes different forms in different settings. (IFG 2002, 12)

The different organizational form of this new kind of social activism is illustrated by the Brazilian landless-rural-workers movement, MST (Movimento dos Trabalhadores Rurais Sem Terra), which at WSF3 Chomksy described as "the most exciting popular movement in the world." The MST is

> a mass social movement whose principal objective is to gather people for the struggle. How do you join? There is no membership, no cards and it's not enough just to declare that one wants to be in the MST. The only way to join is to take part in one of the land occupations on the ground. (Stedile 2002, 54)

The MST has been at the forefront in organizing the WSF.

With respect to the question of power, the WSF dramatically illustrates a de-centered conception of power, which involves a rejection of all blueprints for change. There is no attempt to bring about agreement on declarations, agendas, or manifestos. Nobody speaks in the name of the WSF. The IFG writes of the WSF: "Its emphasis on pluralism and diversity manifests the spirit of a movement that seeks a future based on open global dialogue, not decisions imposed by a new elite" (IFG 2002, 64). Here, Chico Whitaker and Patrick Viveret argue, power involves "a sense of creation with the other, rather than domination over the other" (Whitaker and Viveret 2003, 19). Networking is the dominant relational form, and in a decentralized social network there is no center of power. More broadly, within the global justice movement there is much concern with the transformation of the nature and application of power:

> Political and social organizing among grassroots movements today strives to redefine power between people, place, state, class, and social groups—what it is, how it is shared and how it is used. New modes of organizing incorporate the belief that money and real-politik power are not the only units of analyses; morality and dignity must be integrated into the new paradigm. Leadership must be decentralized and based on the idea of direct—as opposed to

representative—democracy. . . . The models of organizing have evolved in keeping with the comment that . . . "how we organize reflects our goal." (Bell 2002, 9)

Beyond this, many of the new networks and alliances promote alternative political identities that emphasize human rights, tolerance of difference, and reconciliation. This involves challenging or loosening the notion of racial and ethnic identities as fixed, essentialist, and antagonistic—and this changes and advances the quality of social interactions. Social diversity is distinctively different to that found among the predominantly middle-class supporters of the so-called new social movements of an earlier period (Williams 1983). Indeed, Richard Falk has argued that what we are witnessing is the rise of powerful new social identities and new images of solidarity and connectedness "on behalf of an invisible community or polity that lacks spatial boundaries" (Falk 1992, 224). Clearly, this is very different from notions of citizenship that assert obligations of military service to the nation-state.

For many activists in the networks that constitute the global justice movement, social interactions have a depth and density that provides for new forms of solidarity and connectedness, new social bonds that contrast with the "thin," atomized identities of citizen and consumer. They provide something of a counter to the social dislocations and displacements of globalization. At a time when in the North there is a withdrawal from conventional political struggle and dissolution of many traditional political identities, the global justice movement offers a collective identity that is not linked to state structures or the market; it reconnects rights and responsibilities (Barber 1995). Eric Hobsbawm has written that "the decline of the organized mass parties, class-based, ideological or both, eliminated the major social engine for turning men and women into politically active citizens" (Hobsbawm 1994, 581). The intensity of the social interactions within the global justice movement now provides such an engine for many.

All this raises interesting questions about an emerging global or "planetary" citizenry and of the extent to which the WSF is advancing the emergence of a "new political actor, planetary civil society" (Whitaker 2003, 23). Oded Grajew, founder of the WSF, certainly sees it as the concrete expression of a new political culture and "an emerging global citizenry."[4] Thus, at this level the actors in the global justice movement are involved in the construction of a political community.

In fact, "the WSF, and the movement it both represents and shapes, already has the power to transform the thinking and acting of the Old Left" (Waterman 2002). In this regard, it is important to emphasize that international trade unionists have increasingly been part of the WSF; there are a dozen international unions on the International Council of the WSF. An important development that should facilitate a closer relationship is the emergence of what Robert Lambert and Edward Webster (Chapter 6 herein) term "global social movement unionism" that could create a "borderless solidarity" and provide an important new form of resistance to corporate globalization. New forms of social activism do build on earlier traditions of proletarian, peace, and feminist internationalism. *Internationalism*, however,

> as the name implies, was a relationship between nation-states, nationalities, nationalisms and nationalists. Despite heroic efforts and achievements, it became increasingly attenuated and hollow during the C20th, until it no longer moved anyone or anything. (Waterman 2002)

A further important set of questions concerns the process whereby global struggles recognize and empower local struggles. John Gray maintains that behind all the various meanings of globalization is "a single, underlying idea, which can be called de-localization: the uprooting of activities and relationships from local origins and cultures" (Gray 1998, 57). Consequently, within the global justice movement—and voiced loudly at the WSF—there is a strong emphasis on subsidiarity, favoring the local over the global, reinvigorating the conditions by which local communities regain power. Indeed, activists are forging global alliances that seek to shift power to democratic, locally rooted, human-scale institutions. Whereas "the history of the World Bank has been to take power away from communities, give it to a central government, then give it to the corporations through privatization" (Shiva, cited in Klein 2002, 36), the global justice movement is a fight for local democracy.

In this regard the rise of neoliberalism has, in many countries, provoked the rise of new grassroots movements concerned with social citizenship and survival issues. In South Africa, for example, a range of new social movements have emerged (Desai 2002; Gentle 2002; Munnik and Wilson 2003), such as the Anti-Privatization Forum, Environmental Justice Networking Forum, and Landless People's Movement—all of whom have been inspired by the earlier protests in Seattle and Genoa, and all of whom attended WSF3. One of the key South Africans active in these new social movements, Trevor Ngwane, has emphasized the importance of linking up with the WSF as "the movement of the millennium" (Ngwane 2003, 55). Such developments are sowing "the seeds of a South African Social Forum" (Bond 2002, 360).

In addition to the WSF, global events, such as the World Summit on Sustainable Development conference in Johannesburg in 2002, can become focal points for galvanizing local interests and activism. For example, being the hosts of the Global NGO Forum, the South African environmental NGOs became reanimated in their efforts to promote diverse agendas that linked environmental issues to questions of health, development, and social justice. One activist at WSF3 maintained that at Porto Alegre the WSF "succeeded in making that elusive local–global connection. The discussions were rooted around local problems but causes and solutions were framed in a global context."[5] Much, however, needs to be done to connect such initiatives with global civil society, and a crucial question is whether these linkages and alliances are sustainable.

## Conclusion

Overall there is much debate about the WSF, its transformative capacity, its sustainability and transferability in the future. To some there is a danger that it will be limited to a forum for debate, a colorful expression of democratic pluralism for the privileged elite—Pico Iyer's "global souls" (Iyer 2001)—who have access to the resources to travel. However, as Jai Sen has suggested, the WSF "has the seeds of being one of the most significant initiatives of the past many decades—and perhaps even over the past 100 years" (Sen 2002).

The major achievement of the WSF as a key component of the global justice movement is the consolidation and advancement of networks opposing neoliberal globalization. It is possible that these networks are, as Raymond Williams wrote of the new social movements that emerged in the 1970s, a "major positive resource" (Williams 1983, 173). The future challenge will be to combine greater organizational impetus while maintaining the inspirational spirit of WSF meetings. As James Petras pointed out of WSF2, "Probably as important as the physical presence of large numbers of people and movements was the spirit of the forum: the rousing hope and optimism" (Petras 2003, 11). At this level, the tangible sense of mass solidarity at WSF is providing a social and intellectual impetus to the huge citizens movement that is challenging corporate globalization and the path it is taking: "The mobilization has recreated an enormous movement of hope. It has given new wind to the idea that another world is possible" (Massiah 2003).

Much further work needs to be done to develop an empirical and theoretical understanding of the social dynamics behind the development of the WSF, the rise of the global justice movement, and the new forms of social activism it encompasses. To what extent is a new global solidarity, a new collective identity, being advanced? What is its transformative capacity? And do the new forms of social activism reflect a new logic based in a new political moment? Altogether, though, it is clear that the WSF is a beacon of a new kind of politics from which we have much to learn.

## Notes

1. Cândido Grzybowski, Presentation, New York, July 2002, personal notes.
2. "Call of Social Movements" is available online.
3. The following draws upon the author's own participant-observation at WSF3; in those cases where no specific source is cited the information is based on personal notes and observations.
4. Oded Grajew, interview, New York, July 2002.
5. Interview with the author.

## References

Bond, Patrick. 2002. *Unsustainable South Africa: Environment, Development and Social Protest*. Pietermaritzburg: University of Natal Press.

Bell, Beverly. 2002. Social movements and economic integration in the Americas. Albuquerque, N.Mex.: Center for Economic Justice.

Barber, Benjamin. 1995. *Jihad vs McWorld*. New York: Random House.

Castells, Manuel. 1996. *The Rise of the Network Society*. London: Blackwell.

———. 1997. *The Power of Identity*. London: Blackwell.

Desai, Ashwin. 2002. *We are the Poors*. New York: Monthly Review Press.

Falk, Richard. 1992. *Explorations on the Edge of Time*. Princeton, N.J.: Princeton University Press.

Gentle, Leonard. 2002. Social movements in South Africa. *South African Labour Bulletin* 26, no. 5: 16–19.

George, Susan. 2002. The global citizens movement. *New Agenda* (second quarter), 108–121.

Gray, John. 1998. *False Dawn: The Delusions of Global Capitalism*. London: Granta.

Grzybowski, Cândido. 2003. Why reflect on the World Social Forum? *Democracia Viva* 6, 3–4.

Hardt, Michael. 2002. Today's Bandung. *New Left Review* 14, 112–18.

Hlatswayo, Mondli. 2003. Report of the African Social Forum. *Khanya* 3, 37–39.

Hobsbawm, Eric. 1994. *The Age of Extremes*. Harmondsworth: Penguin.

IFG (International Forum on Globalization). 2002. *Alternatives to Economic Globalization*. San Francisco: Berrett-Koehler Publishers.

Iyer, Pico. 2001. *The Global Soul*. New York: Vintage.

Jordan, Lisa. 2002. Report on the World Social Forum. Paper. April.

Klein, Naomi. 2002. *Fences and Windows: Dispatches from the Front Lines of the Globalization Debate*. London: Flamingo.

———. 2003. The hijacking of the WSF. Available online.

Massiah, Gustave. 2003. The worldwide citizen's movement. *The Aisling Magazine* 31. Online magazine.

Munnik, Victor, and Jessica Wilson. 2003. *The World Comes to One Country: An Insider History of the World Summit on Sustainable Development*. Johannesburg: Heinrich Böll Foundation.

Ngwane, Trevor. 2003. Sparks in the township. *New Left Review* 22, 37–58.

Petras, James. 2003. Porto Alegre 2002: A tale of two forums. *Khanya* 1, 11–13.

Sen, Jai. 2002. On building another world: or: Are other globalizations possible? The World Social Forum as an instrument of global democratization. Available online.

———. 2003. The WSF as logo, the WSF as commons. Available online.

Shepard, Benjamin, and Ronald Hayduk. 2002. *From Act Up to the WTO*. London: Verso.

Stedile, Joao Pedro. 2002. Landless battalions. *New Left Review* 15, 77–104.

Teivainen, Teivo. 2002. The World Social Forum and global democratization: Learning from Porto Alegre. *Third World Quarterly* 23, no. 4: 621–32.

Waterman, Peter. 2002. Reflections on the second WSF in Porto Alegre: What's left internationally? Working paper series no. 362. The Hague: Institute of Social Studies.

Williams, Raymond. 1983. *Towards 2000*. Harmondsworth: Penguin.

Whitaker, Chico. 2003. The World Social Forum. *Democracia Viva* 6, 16–20.

Whitaker, Chico, and Patrick Viveret. 2003. The Third World Social Forum. *Democracia Viva* 6, 21–24.

# 11.

# Taking Global Civil Society Seriously

## Rupert Taylor and Kumi Naidoo

## Introduction

To comprehend the sociological meaning and significance of global civil society (GCS) is a challenging task. This is due to one straightforward reason: we lack agreement on a definition of *global civil society*—indeed, some social scientists (and media commentators) go so far as to reject the very term (Johnston and Laxer 2003; Keck and Sikkink 1998; Tarrow 1998; 2001). To move the debate forward—beyond circumscribed theoretical or disciplinary concerns—it is imperative to reflect upon how GCS has been, and should be, defined and related to what constitutes both politics and society.

What is problematic is that within mainstream social science, any normative conception of politics is generally read in conventional liberal pluralist terms in which the state assumes central focus, and society, in turn, is reduced to descriptive analysis in relation to the state (Nash 2000; Ricci 1984). Consequently, to pursue the study of GCS from within this state-centric frame of reference—as in fact those schooled in mainstream political sociology do—will inevitably result in a displacement of, and skepticism toward, the idea of GCS itself. This works to mask how GCS seeks to radicalize society as a critical category and intends a new *polis*—a new definition of politics.

## Global Civil Society Revealed

Beyond the negative media hype and the unilateral designs of American politicians, the purposive impulse of GCS is not hard to detect—it is one of reclaiming and advancing, at a global level, the social and political space for human freedom. The political actions recently witnessed on the streets of Seattle and Genoa, and at Porto Alegre, have emerged in direct response to a perception that important decisions affecting people's lives are being made in nontransparent ways in supranational institutions that are neither accountable nor accessible to citizen engagement and are fundamentally unjust. There is a widely held view of a failure of global government (Monbiot 2001), a sense reinforced through growing levels of public alienation from national political order (Hertz 2002), and a feeling that the world is ever more interconnected as "One World." Reinforced by a shift from materialist to postmaterialist values (Inglehart 1997), it is increasingly the case that, for more and more people, "the extension of democracy now seems to be the central issue in public life" (Touraine 2001, 87–88). Here, democracy is no longer seen to be bounded by the nation-state; rather, it is seen to extend to, and to relate to, a global space of sociopolitical concern within which "we begin to consider ourselves as members of an imagined community of the world" (Singer 2002, 171; see also Korten et al. 2002).

The "Big Three" multilateral economic institutions—the World Trade Organization (WTO), the International Monetary Fund (IMF), and the World Bank—have attracted prime criticism. In a world in which "the interstate system is increasingly embedded within an evolving system of multilayered regional and global governance" (Held and McGrew 2002, 130), these institutions assume ever-increasing import. The charges against these bodies are many, but the main ones are that subject to the dictates of neoliberalism—as pursued by hegemonic nation-states and transnational corporations—they prioritize economic considerations and market relations, and that they are unjust and undemocratic (e.g., Stiglitz 2002). The IMF and the World Bank are demonstrably under the sway of the United States Treasury Department, and within the WTO there is "no way that unofficial, non-corporate, voices can make themselves heard" (Mandle 2003, 33).

It is in the context of such concerns that a number of international nongovernmental organizations (INGOs) and global social movements have been involved in an institutionalized form of complex multilateralism with the Big Three so as to gain incremental reforms (O'Brien et al. 2000), and beyond this that a series of major highly spectacular protests to seek more radical reforms have occurred. The most notable protests were those in Seattle (N30, 1999) and Genoa (J19, 2001), but also including Washington, D.C. (A16, 2000), Prague (S26, 2000), Québec City (A20, 2001), and Gothenburg (J14, 2001). Here, along with the Big Three, the targets of attack have been the Organization of American States (OAS), the European Union, and the G8.

In each of these demonstrations, protestors represented a wide range of actors, from unionized labor to local grassroots groups. A significant number of global NGOs were present at more than one of these events, notably, 50 Years Is Enough, ATTAC, Direct Action Network, Friends of the Earth, Global Exchange, Greenpeace, International Forum on Globalization, Ruckus Society, and Third World Network. To enhance overall mobilization, such organizations have readily and strategically linked up with nationally and locally based groups (see, e.g., Smith 2001). The number of protestors involved in the above protest events well exceeded a quarter of a million, with "unity in diversity" much in evidence—among a rainbow of protest blocs (red, pink, yellow, blue, green), direct actions, teach-ins, cross-continental caravans, global witnessing, and street theater with giant puppets ("puppet-ganda"), dancers, and cuddly toys. While in Seattle, Teamsters and turtles were "together at last"; in Prague, activists from Greece and Turkey took joint command of a protest column.

Collectively—and particularly within mainstream media portrayals (such as those featured in *Time* and *Newsweek*)—these protests have been negatively framed in terms of constituting an anti-globalization movement. The term *anti-globalization* is, however, a misnomer. The problem as the protestors understand it is not globalization per se; what is at issue is that neoliberal globalization, contrary to its stated claims, is fueling poverty and intensifying inequality within and across societies. Hence, more accurate terms are "anti-neoliberal globalization movement" (e.g., Seoane and Taddei 2002) or that preferred here, the "global justice movement" (e.g., Bond 2002).

In light of all this, the boundaries of GCS extend wide, encompassing a multitude of INGOs and global social movements involved in complex multilateralism *and* protests for global justice. There is a complex network of networks that tie organizations, individuals, and resources together around myriad campaign strategies and tactics—combining behind-the-scenes facilitation, policymaking, advocacy work, and direct action. Within this field there is much internal differentiation. For example, INGOs have chosen to interrelate with key multilateral economic institutions in terms of either complete-, operational-, or non-engagement, or as with the Third World Network selective engagement through case-by-case assessment. Nonetheless, all actors are concerned to advance issues of global concern, to promote and build greater global democratic governance—especially with regard to human rights, and socioeconomic, and environmental hazards. At a formal level this has also been advanced through participation at various world conferences—notably with respect to UN world summits, from the 1992 Earth Summit in Rio de Janeiro through to the 2002 World Summit on Sustainable Development in Johannesburg.

From this standpoint, many groups—in addition to those listed above—fall within the ambit of GCS: Amnesty International, Earth First!, Human Rights Watch, Jubilee 2000, Movimento dos Trabalhadores Rurais Sem Terra, Rainforest Action Network, Reclaim the Streets, The

Sierra Club, United Students Against Sweatshops (USA and Canada), and Via Campesina—among others. There are a number of multi-issue networks of networks—such as CIVICUS and the Catalan-backed World Forum of Civil Society Networks.

However, it is at the World Social Forum (WSF) that GCS has come to project its most visible and readily acknowledged face. The WSF is motivated, in the words of Samir Amin, "to move beyond the fragmentation of all kinds of protest and to build an alternative to neo-liberal globalization" (Amin et al. 2002). The 2003 WSF in Porto Alegre, Brazil, attracted some twenty thousand delegates from civil society organizations—a fourfold increase on the first WSF in 2001. Undoubtedly, the WSF has drawn particular sustenance from the rise of social protest in Latin America, the solidarity of Brazilian trade unions, and the support of ATTAC–France, but the WSF is primarily a forum in which North American and European movements globally connect. Many of the aforementioned INGOs and global social movements—as well as the American Federation of Labor-Congress of Industrial Organizations—have attended the WSF.

Acknowledging a transformative democratic purpose and pulling the various levels of the above discussion together—the WSF, the global justice movement, the global protest events, and their targets, the multilateral economic and political institutions—enables us to present the basic context and outlines of a multi-organizational field *of* GCS. Our representation of this multi-organizational field is presented in Figure 11–1, which should not be read to include the multilateral economic and political institutions *within* GCS, or in terms of a hierarchical ordering. Figure 11–1 presents a cartography that both reflects the geometric imagination that is integral to the very structuring of GCS and conveys the point that the power of this movement is best grasped in terms of its totality.

This representation goes beyond previous attempts to develop a typology of GCS (Starr 2000; Kaldor 2003) in that it views GCS in terms of a progressive politics that is dialectically evolving in the context of new organizational structures and forms of activism, and through which individuals are transformed into being part of a global civil "society." For, GCS is marked by a change in how individuals and groups behave toward one another, both in the purpose and the structure of those relationships. In other words, the politics projected by GCS is prefigured in its own practice. Writing over thirty years ago, critical theorist Herbert Marcuse, argued that "our goals, our values, our *own* and new morality, must be visible already in our actions. The new human beings who we want to help to create—we must already strive to be these human beings right here and now" (Marcuse 1970). And it is precisely this that can be seen in these new organizational structures and forms of activism of GCS.

FIGURE 11-1. THE MULTI-ORGANIZATIONAL FIELD
OF GLOBAL CIVIL SOCIETY

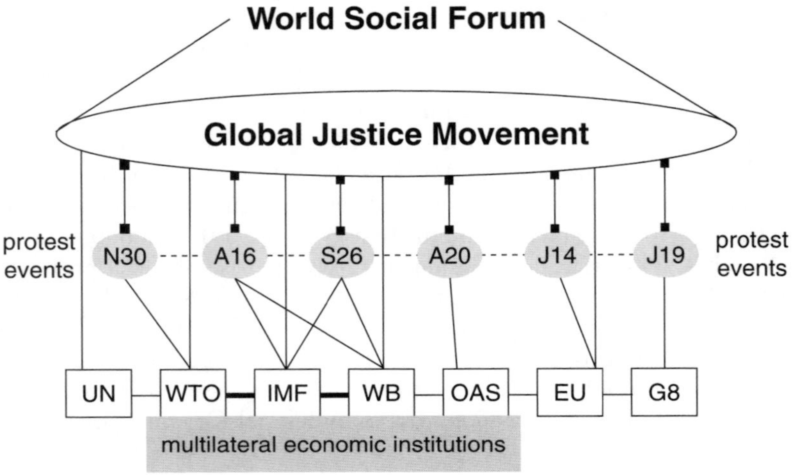

## World Social Forum

## Global Justice Movement

protest events | N30 ---- A16 ---- S26 ---- A20 ---- J14 ---- J19 | protest events

UN — WTO — IMF — WB — OAS — EU — G8

multilateral economic institutions

Taken together there is a dense multi-organizational field of inter-locked networks made up of different types and clusters of organizations, marked by a powerful synergistic dynamic, pursuing multiple ends within a bounded—but ever increasing—space. The large-scale network structure is, as Naomi Klein has described it, comprised of "thousands of movements" that are "intricately linked to one another, much as 'hotlinks' connect their websites on the Internet" (Klein 2001a, 4). And within this multi-organizational field not only are varying contradictions creatively contained but a high rate of network replication is evident. Notably, what have emerged are innovative and alternative supra-statal organizational forms tied to more open, autonomous, non-hierarchical, and above all, democratic structures.

Breaking with orthodox coalition or united front styles, a core defining feature of this field is the way in which it includes principles of "dis/organization," as in following a commitment to flat hierarchies: "Flat hierarchies for co-ordination mean allowing all who want to participate to do so" (Jordan 2002, 69). The development of horizontal and autonomous forms of social organization has been influenced by the ideas of the European autonomia movement (Katsiaficas 1997) and the work of Gilles Deleuze and Felix Guattari (1987); such forms have proved themselves to be effective in de-centering power relations and in promoting wide-scale and fluid mobilization. A defining feature of much protest for global justice has been how it has been planned and organized without any conspicuous exercise of top-down central authority or control. The main movements have—as with the interdependency and complexity that constituted the Seattle protest coalition and Genoa Social Forum—been decentralized and loose, consisting of clusters, spokescouncils, and affinity groups.

At a technological level this has been driven by the acceleration of computing power and connectivity—as it flows through the Internet, cell phones, and the independent digital media. As Lance Bennett notes, new digital network configurations facilitate "permanent campaigns, the growth of broad networks despite (or because of) relatively weak social identity and ideology ties, the transformation of both individual member organizations and the growth patterns of whole networks, and the capacity to communicate messages from desktops to television screens" (Bennett 2003, 33). Not surprisingly, the centrality of embedded identities has been significantly challenged, for there is much strength to the kind of thin ties formed through digital communication; this is so because they provide for more personal and fluid forms of association, and for more adaptive and resistant protest repertoires. In fact, new technology can render the need for direct face-to-face interaction redundant and can, in itself, be used to launch protest actions in cyberspace, with mass online protests, "hacktivist" disruption of information flows, and culture jamming (Jordan 2002; Klein 2001b).

Moreover, within this general context, new experimental, symbolic, and creative forms of direct activism have arisen. In particular, the Black Bloc and White Overalls have sought to develop militant nonviolent action, "combining elements of street theatre, festival and what can only be called non-violent warfare," nonviolent "in that it eschews any direct physical harm to human beings" (Graeber 2002, 66). This is a new spectrum of protest, in black and white. The protest tactic of the Black Bloc is to engage in public property destruction and sabotage while masked in black—complete with black motorcycle helmets, ski masks, and uniform black clothing—so as to better resist police attack and victimization. The White Overalls' tactic "involves attaching all manner of protection to an activist's body: foam rubber, inner tubes, helmets, padded gloves" and then donning white overalls to symbolize the invisible victims of neoliberal globalization (Jordan 2002, 75). Thus dressed, the White Overalls (now renamed The Disobedients) have occupied places of exploitation and concealment, and in demonstrations have acted as a buffer in confronting police lines—adopting tortoise-style formation with Plexiglas shields.

Taken together, these developments signify the need for new intellectual engagement and theorizing on GCS. These developments particularly challenge the central arguments of American social movement theory, which has underpinned the position of many mainstream political sociologists who question, and are skeptical of, GCS (e.g., Johnston and Laxer 2003; Keck and Sikkink 1998; Tarrow 2001). Contrary to key presuppositions (see Mayer 1995; Nash 2000; Piven and Cloward 1995), collective action is primarily driven by substantive moral purpose; collective action has eclipsed nationally framed repertoires of protest; movement organizations are not all marked by formal and professionalized hierarchical structures; primary interaction and embedded ties are not of such central import; and network overlap and density cannot be readily correlated to levels of mobilization. Additionally, as it is increasingly evident that "individuals can involve themselves coherently in different associations or collectivities at different levels and for different purposes" (Held and McGrew 2002, 92), strong nationally based social networks do not preclude the possibility of making global social networks.

The problem is that although mainstream social movement theory can be used to present a number of important insights, many leading practitioners do not embrace a sufficiently broad field of vision to stand outside their *own* restrictive historical and nationally determined understanding of politics and society (Mayer 1995). As a result here—as also in most mass media coverage—the full meaning and significance of GCS is not apprehended seriously enough and therefore insufficiently comprehended. Taking GCS seriously requires recognizing both its critical purpose and radical social form.

## Possibilities

In addition to the above interpretative limitations, GCS faces a number of practical challenges that restrict its possibilities. In particular, among skeptics it has become common to argue that the prospects for GCS have been put even further into question with the impact of 9/11, and the resurgence of a "state-centric" view of the world in which the United States has placed the national interests of its own citizens above all others (Ayres 2003). Certainly, with the Orwellian sounding "war against terrorism" there has been a criminalization of anti-globalization protest (Panitch 2002)—with heightened police repression and stricter border controls. Furthermore, INGOs such as Friends of the Earth and Human Rights Watch have been subjected to right-wing propaganda attacks by the American Enterprise Institute and Federalist Society.[1] Writing in the *New Statesman*, Johann Hari has gone so far as to argue that "the fuzzy anti-globalisation movement as we saw it in Seattle and Genoa is passing into history" (Hari 2002, 22).

The negative effect of 9/11 on GCS should not, however, be so simplistically read. On the one hand, even before 9/11, America constituted a major stumbling block to building a global community—having rejected the Ottawa Convention banning landmines, the Kyoto Protocol on global warming, and the International Criminal Court. In contradistinction, recent events have witnessed the strengthening of the peace movement, with worldwide antiwar demonstrations, and a sharpening of arguments around US global unilateralism, underscoring the demand for rigorous international humanitarian law enforcement (CIVICUS Statement 2001).

Beyond this juxtapositioning, GCS does face a number of internal challenges—most notably with respect to issues of inclusiveness and representation. At times GCS strongly mirrors the unequal power and resource structures of the world. Without question, GCS is overly Northern dominated; few global NGOs are headquartered in the Southern hemisphere, in fact "60 per cent of the secretariats of INGOs are based in the European Union" (Anheier, Glasius, and Kaldor 2001, 7). Levels of participation within GCS vary significantly across countries, with the citizens of France being most active, those of Middle Eastern countries least active (Wiest, Smith, and Eterovi 2002). The 1999 Seattle protest was almost exclusively white in complexion, and the 2003 WSF had less than 1 percent African representation. It can also be argued that to be part of GCS you have to be rich enough to travel and attend various events and protests (Neale 2002). And while many also speed off on the information superhighway, more than one-third of the world's population has no access to telephones, let alone other information technologies. There are, for example, more telephone line connections in Manhattan than in sub-Saharan Africa (Naidoo 2003).

A further internal challenge for GCS is to improve its level of connectedness. Where is the network of networks not connecting? "Disconnections" do exist with regard to levels of engagement (micro, meso, and macro) and questions of strategy and tactics. For example, it has been argued that more could be done to globally connect those working along sectoral lines (Desai 2002) and to strengthen horizontal local, regional, and global networks (Naidoo 2003). To such ends, it has to be recognized that the well-known slogan "think globally, but act locally" has to be reformulated—to push too hard for delinking and relocalization to escape the forces of globalization is to remain captive to the existing balance of power in the contemporary world system. If the real locus of power is global, then there is a need to "think locally and act globally" (Naidoo 2000).

Nonetheless, despite these external and internal challenges, GCS has to be taken as a power of increasing global weight. Indeed, former UN High Commissioner for Human Rights Mary Robinson has maintained that the next superpower is global public opinion (Toh 2003). Precisely because it seeks to transcend nationally driven self-interest, GCS presents a serious challenge to the national and international governmental systems currently in place. Moreover, the purpose and form of GCS potentially enables it to move faster and to be intellectually and strategically ahead of its opponents.

Noreena Hertz has observed with respect to conventional liberal pluralist politics that "never since the development of the mass franchise has there been such disengagement" (Hertz 2002, 136; also see Dalton and Wattenberg 2000). Yet, while affiliation with traditional political parties and institutions is on the decline, the number of progressive INGOs and their network density is growing (Sikkink and Smith 2002), and rising identification with GCS represents engagement with a new transformative project. Back in the mid-1960s, in his book *One-Dimensional Man*, Herbert Marcuse was of the view that the "liberation of inherent possibilities" was no longer seriously on the historical agenda (Marcuse 1964, 254–55). The advent of GCS has changed this. Now another world is possible.

### Note

[1] "Holding Civic Groups Accountable," *The New York Times*, July 21, 2003.

### References

Amin, Samir, Michael Hardt, Camilla A. Lundberg, and Magnus Wennerhag. 2002. How capitalism went senile. Available online.

Anheier, Helmut, Marlies Glasius, and Mary Kaldor. 2001. Introducing global civil society. In *Global Civil Society 2001*, ed. Helmut Anheier, Marlies Glasius, and Mary Kaldor, 3–22. Oxford: Oxford University Press.

Ayres, Jeffrey M. 2003. Global civil society and international protest: No swan song yet for the state. In *Global Civil Society and Its Limits*, ed. G. Laxer and S. Halperin, 25–42. Basingstoke: Macmillan.

Bennett, W. Lance. 2003. Communicating global activism: Strengths and vulnerabilities of networked politics. Available online.

Bond, Patrick. 2002. *Against Global Apartheid*. London: Pluto Press.

CIVICUS Statement. 2001. A Joint Civil Society Statement on the Tragedy in the United States. September 21. Available online.

Dalton, Russell J., and Martin P. Wattenberg, eds. 2000. *Parties Without Partisans: Political Change in Advanced Industrial Democracies*. Oxford: Oxford University Press.

Deleuze, Gilles, and Felix Guattari. 1987. Rhizome. In *A Thousand Plateaus: Capitalism and Schizophrenia*, 3–25. Minneapolis: University of Minnesota Press.

Desai, Nitin. 2002. WSSD: Opening address by Mr Nitin Desai, UN Assistant Secretary General, Johannesburg, August 26. Available online.

Graeber, David. 2002. The new anarchists. *New Left Review* 13 (January/February), 61–73.

Hari, Johann. 2002. Whatever happened to No Logo? *New Statesman*, November 11, 20–22.

Held, David, and Anthony McGrew. 2002. *Globalization/Anti-Globalization*. Cambridge: Polity Press.

Hertz, Noreen. 2002. *The Silent Takeover: Global Capitalism and the Death of Democracy*. London: Arrow Books.

Inglehart, Ronald. 1997. *Modernization and Postmodernization: Cultural, Economic, and Political Change in 43 Societies*. Princeton, N.J.: Princeton University Press.

Johnston, Josée, and Gordon Laxer. 2003. Solidarity in the age of globalization: Lessons from the anti-MAI and Zapatista struggles. *Theory and Society* 32, 39–91.

Jordan, Tim. 2002. *Activism! Direct Action, Hacktivism and the Future of Society*. London: Reaktion Books.

Kaldor, Mary. 2003. *Global Civil Society: An Answer to War*. Cambridge: Polity Press.

Katsiaficas, George N. 1997. *The Subversion of Politics: European Autonomous Social Movements and the Decolonization of Everyday Life*. Atlantic Highlands, N.J.: Humanities Press.

Keck, Margaret E., and Kathryn Sikkink. 1998. *Activists Beyond Borders: Advocacy Networks in International Politics*. Ithaca, N.Y.: Cornell University Press.

Klein, Naomi. 2001a. Farewell to "The End of History": Organization and vision in anti-corporate movements. In *Socialist Register 2002*, ed. Leo Panitch and Colin Leys, 1–14. London: Merlin Press.

———. 2001b. *No Logo*. London: Flamingo.

Korten, David C., Nicanor Perlas, and Vandana Shiva. 2002. Global civil society: The path ahead. Available online.

Mandle, Jay R. 2003. *Globalization and the Poor*. Cambridge: Cambridge University Press.

Marcuse, Herbert. 1964. *One-Dimensional Man*. Boston: Beacon Press.

———. 1970. Nothing is forever in History. *Countdown 2*. April.

Mayer, Margit. 1995. Social movement research in the United States: A European perspective. In *Social Movements: Critiques and Concepts*, ed. Stanford M. Lyman, 168–95. London: Macmillan.

Monbiot, George. 2001. Let the people rule the world. *The Guardian*, July 17. Available online.

Naidoo, Kumi. 2000. The new civic globalism. *The Nation*, May 8.

———. 2003. Civil society, governance, and globalization. World Bank Presidential Fellows Lecture, World Bank, Washington, D.C., February 10. Available online.

Nash, Kate. 2000. *Contemporary Political Sociology: Globalization, Politics, and Power*. Oxford: Blackwell.

Neale, Jonathan. 2002. *You are G8: We are 6 Billion: The Truth Behind the Genoa Protests*. London: Vision Paperbacks.

O'Brien, Robert, Anne Marie Goetz, Jan Aart Scholte, and Marc Williams. 2000. *Contesting Global Governance: Multilateral Economic Institutions and Global Social Movements*. Cambridge: Cambridge University Press.

Panitch, Leo. 2002. Violence as a tool of order and change: The war on terrorism and the antiglobalization movement. *Monthly Review* 54, no. 2: 12–23.

Piven, Francis Fox, and Richard A. Cloward. 1995. Collective protest: A critique of resource mobilization theory. In *Social Movements: Critiques and Concepts*, ed. Stanford M. Lyman, 137–67. London: Macmillan.

Ricci, David M. 1984. *The Tragedy of Political Science: Politics, Scholarship, and De-mocracy.* New Haven, Conn.: Yale University Press.

Seoane, José, and Emilio Taddei. 2002. From Seattle to Porto Alegre: The anti-neoliberal globalization movement. *Current Sociology* 50, no. 1: 99–122.

Sikkink, Kathryn, and Jackie Smith. 2002. Infrastructures for change: Transnational organizations, 1953–93. In *Restructuring World Politics: Transnational Social Movements, Networks, and Norms,* ed. Sanjeev Khagram, James V. Riker, and Kathryn Sikkink, 24–44. Minneapolis: University of Minnesota Press.

Singer, Peter. 2002. *One World: The Ethics of Globalization.* New Haven, Conn.: Yale University Press.

Smith, Jackie 2001. Globalizing resistance: The Battle of Seattle and the future of social movements. *Mobilization* 6, no. 1: 1–19.

Starr, Amory. 2000. *Naming the Enemy: Anti-Corporate Movements Confront Globalization.* London: Zed Books.

Stiglitz, Joseph. 2002. *Globalization and Its Discontents.* London: Penguin.

Tarrow, Sidney. 1998. Fishnets, Internets, and catnets: Globalization and transnational collective action. In *Challenging Authority: The Historical Study of Contentious Politics,* ed. Michael P. Hanagan, Leslie Page Moch, and Wayne te Brake, 228–44. Minneapolis: University of Minnesota Press, Minneapolis.

———. 2001. Beyond globalization: Why creating transnational social movements is so hard and when is it most likely to happen. Available online.

Toh, Hsien Min. 2003. On the control of information. *Quarterly Literary Review Singapore* 2, no. 3.

Touraine, Alain. 2001. *Beyond Neoliberalism.* Cambridge: Polity Press.

Wiest, Dawn, Jackie Smith, and Ivana Eterovi. 2002. Uneven globalization? Understanding variable participation in transnational social movement organizations. Paper presented to American Sociological Association meeting, Chicago, August 17.

# About the Contributors

MASSIMILIANO ANDRETTA is in the Department of Political Science and Sociology, University of Florence, Italy. He is co-author, with Donatella della Porta, Lorenzo Mosca, and Herbert Reiter, of *Global, Noglobal, New Global: La protesta contro il G8 a Genova* (Rome: Laterza, 2002). He is a member of the Group of Research on Collective Action in Europe, directed by Donatella della Porta.

SRILATHA BATLIWALA is a practitioner-scholar with long experience in bridging those two worlds. She has worked as a grassroots activist for over twenty-five years in both rural and urban communities in India; she has also researched and written extensively on a range of issues related to gender, poverty, development, and civil society. She is currently based at the Hauser Center for Nonprofit Organizations, Harvard University.

JACKLYN COCK is Professor of Sociology at the University of the Witwatersrand, Johannesburg. She is the author of *Maids and Madams: A Study in the Politics of Exploitation* (Johannesburg: Ravan Press, 1980), and her most recent book, co-written with Alison Bernstein, is *Melting Pots and Rainbow Nations: Conversations About Difference in the United States and South Africa* (Urbana, Ill.: University of Illinois Press, 2002).

ROBERT LAMBERT is Associate Professor at the University of Western Australia in Perth, where he co-chairs the International Studies Program. He is editor of *State and Labour in New Order Indonesia* (Perth: University of Western Australia Press, 1997) and is on the editorial board of the *South African Labour Bulletin*. He has organized a number of international conferences that have focused on the impact of global change on work organizations.

LORENZO MOSCA is in the Department of Political Science and Sociology, University of Florence, Italy. He is co-author, with Massimiliano Andretta, Donatella della Porta, and Herbert Reiter, of *Global, Noglobal, New Global: La protesta contro il G8 a Genova* (Rome: Laterza, 2002), and with Donatella della Porta co-editor of *Globalizzazione e movimenti sociali* (Rome: Manifestolibri, 2003).

RONALDO MUNCK is at Dublin City University, where he leads the internationalization and interculturalism agenda, having previously been Professor of Political Sociology at the University of Liverpool. His works include *Labour and Globalisation: The New "Great Transformation"* (London: Zed Books, 2002), and *Globalization and Social Exclusion: Toward a Transformationalist Perspective* (Bloomfield, Conn.: Kumarian Press, forthcoming).

195

GILLIAN HUGHES MURPHY is in the Department of Sociology, University of Washington, Seattle. She is the project coordinator for the WTO History Project housed at the University of Washington Libraries. She was a participant-observer in the Seattle protests and has written several papers about the central protest organizations.

KUMI NAIDOO is Secretary General and CEO of CIVICUS: World Alliance for Citizen Participation. He has previously been a visiting fellow at the University of Warwick and Yale University. He edited, for CIVICUS, *Civil Society at the Millennium* (Bloomfield, Conn.: Kumarian Press, 1999). He currently serves as a board member for the Association for Women's Rights in Development and is the chairperson of the Partnership for Transparency Fund.

PAUL NELSON is Assistant Professor in the Graduate School of Public and International Affairs, University of Pittsburgh. He is author of *The World Bank and NGOs: The Limits of Apolitical Development* (London: Macmillan, 1995). Other publications include articles in *Development in Practice, Global Governance, Millennium, Public Administration and Development*, and *World Development*.

CHRISTOPHER ROOTES is Reader in Political Sociology and Environmental Politics, and Director of the Centre for the Study of Social and Political Movements at the University of Kent at Canterbury. He is co-editor with Dick Richardson of *The Green Challenge* (London: Routledge, 1995), and editor of *Environmental Movements: Local, National and Global* (London: Frank Cass, 1999) and *Environmental Protest in Western Europe* (Oxford: Oxford University Press, 2003).

RUPERT TAYLOR is Associate Professor of Political Studies at the University of the Witwatersrand, Johannesburg. He has written widely in the areas of South African politics and the Northern Ireland conflict. His publications include articles in *African Affairs, Ethnic and Racial Studies, Peace and Change, Race and Class, The Round Table*, and *Telos*. He is currently editor of *Voluntas: International Journal of Voluntary and Nonprofit Organizations*.

TERJE TVEDT is Professor and Research Director at the Centre for Development Studies, University of Bergen, Norway. He is author of *Angels of Mercy or Development Diplomats? NGOs and Foreign Aid* (London: James Currey, 1998) and *The River Nile in the Age of the British: Political Ecology and the Quest for Economic Power* (London: IB Tauris, 2004). He is currently co-editing a book on the "DOSTANGO–system" (the donor–state–NGO relationship within the international development aid system).

EDWARD WEBSTER is Professor of Sociology and Director of the Sociology of Work Unit at the University of the Witwatersrand, Johannesburg. He was a senior Fulbright Scholar at the University of Wisconsin–Madison in 1995. He is currently president of the Research Committee on Labor Movements for the International Sociological Association. He is co-editor, with Glenn Adler, of *Trade Unions and Democratization in South Africa, 1985-1997* (New York: St. Martin's Press, 2000).

# Index

# Also from Kumarian Press...

## *International Development and Civil Society*

**Buddhism at Work**
Community Development, Social Empowerment and the Sarvodaya Movement
George D. Bond

**Civil Society at the Millennium**
CIVICUS, edited by Kumi Naidoo

**Global Civil Society:** Dimensions of the Nonprofit Sector, Volume One
Lester M. Salamon, Helmut K. Anheier, Regina List, Stefan Toepler, S. Wojciech Sokolowski and Associates

**Global Civil Society:** Dimensions of the Nonprofit Sector, Volume Two
Lester M. Salamon, S. Wojciech Sokolowski, and Associates

**Going Global:** Transforming Relief and Development NGOs
Marc Lindenberg and Coralie Bryant

**Nongovernments:** NGOs and the Political Development of the Third World
Julie Fisher

**When Corporations Rule the World,** Second Edition
David C. Korten

**Worlds Apart:** Civil Society and the Battle for Ethical Globalization
John Clark

## *International Development, Humanitarianism, Conflict Resolution*

**Ethics and Global Politics:** The Active Learning Sourcebook
Edited by April L. Morgan, Lucinda Joy Peach, and Colette Mazzucelli

**Human Rights and Development**
Peter Uvin

**Nation-Building Unraveled?** Aid, Peace and Justice in Afghanistan
Edited by Antonio Donini, Norah Niland and Karin Wermester

**Southern Exposure**
International Development and the Global South in the Twenty-First Century
Barbara P. Thomas-Slayter

**War and Intervention:** Issues for Contemporary Peace Operations
Michael V. Bhatia

Visit Kumarian Press at **www.kpbooks.com** or
call **toll-free 800.289.2664** for a complete catalog.